The Shields of the Empire:
Eastern Roman Military Elites during the Reigns of the Emperors Theodosius II, Marcian and Leo I

Łukasz Pigoński

BYZANTINA LODZIENSIA

seria wydawnicza Katedry Historii Bizancjum UŁ

założona przez

Profesora Waldemara Cerana

w

1997 r.

№ XLVII

BYZANTINA LODZIENSIA
XLVII

The Shields of the Empire: Eastern Roman Military Elites during the Reigns of the Emperors Theodosius II, Marcian and Leo I

Łukasz Pigoński

WYDAWNICTWO
UNIWERSYTETU
ŁÓDZKIEGO

Łódź–Kraków 2023

Łukasz Pigoński
Centrum Badań nad Historią i Kulturą Basenu Morza Śródziemnego
i Europy Południowo-Wschodniej im. Prof. Waldemara Cerana, Ceraneum
ul. J. Matejki 32/38
90-237 Łódź, Polska
ceraneum@uni.lodz.pl
pigonski@zoho.com

Published by Łódź University Press & Jagiellonian University Press
First edition, Łódź–Kraków 2023
W.10797.22.0.M

ISBN 978-83-8331-094-7 – paperback Łódź University Press
ISBN 978-83-233-5230-3 – paperback Jagiellonian University Press
ISBN 978-83-8331-095-4 – electronic version Łódź University Press
ISBN 978-83-233-7432-9 – electronic version Jagiellonian University Press (epub, mobi)
ISBN 978-83-233-7431-2 – electronic version Jagiellonian University Press (pdf)

Łódź University Press
34A Matejki St., 90-237 Łódź
www.wydawnictwo.uni.lodz.pl
e-mail: ksiegarnia@uni.lodz.pl
phone: 42 635 55 77

Distribution outside Poland

Jagiellonian University Press
9/2 Michałowskiego St., 31-126 Kraków
phone: +48 (12) 631 01 97, +48 (12) 663 23 81, fax +48 (12) 663 23 83
cell phone: +48 506 006 674, e-mail: sprzedaz@wuj.pl, www.wuj.pl

Contents

Chapter III
The Military Elite during the Reign of Marcian

Introduction

The military history of the Roman Empire in the fifth century is perceived to have some interesting peculiarities. Recent decades have seen much growth in the interest in late antiquity, and thanks to this development, the earlier misconception of the late Roman Empire as a declining state on a trajectory towards inevitable fall has largely been done away with. However, while the focus has been on rehabilitating late Roman culture, it has not quite been the case for the political and military aspects. After all, the 'soft power' of the Roman civilization contributed to the survival of its legacy, even after the dissolution of its political institutions in the West. If there have been attempts to defend the leadership under which the Empire crumbled, they generally focused on select, extraordinary individuals among whom one can name Stilicho, Majorianus or, the famous 'last Roman', Flavius Aetius. There are two notable points which all of these examples have in common. Firstly, they all faced adversity from a corrupt establishment or lesser, power-hungry opponents, who ultimately brought about their downfall. Secondly, they were all from the Western part of the Roman Empire.

It is interesting that the leadership in the East is so rarely lauded for the accomplishment of preserving its own part of the Empire. However, its survival cannot be simply attributed to external factors. While it may be true, albeit difficult to quantify, that the East had a superior economic base, it was also dealing with a society far more fractured by religious conflicts. The pressure from the barbarians was no less of a challenge and sharing a border with a peer superpower of late antiquity, Sassanid Persia, stretched the limited defensive capabilities of the Eastern military. The fact that the Eastern Roman Empire managed to weather the storm of the tumultuous migration period has to be, at least to an extent, credited to those responsible for its protection: the emperors who decided on the foreign policy and the military commanders who took action when diplomacy failed.

The object of the present work is that second group, the military elite, however, with an emphasis on the variety of ways in which its representatives affected the functioning of the Eastern Roman state. This means that just as much of the focus has been placed on the relationships between the generals themselves on one hand and the generals and the emperors on the other. One of the observations which I made at the very early stages of the research was that many of the military leaders were not satisfied with simply being the executors of the Imperial will and rather wanted to be involved in the process of decision-making. The throne, however, was not always responsive to their wishes; having to consider many more factors, the emperors often disagreed with the priorities set by the military. This was not, however, because one side was motivated by selfish reasons or acting in otherwise underhanded ways, while the other was clearly in the right. The resulting political conflicts were complex and originated from the difference of perspectives. Analysis of how they played out will constitute a major portion of the following chapters.

One cannot, however, approach the impact of the military elite on the political landscape of the Empire without the broader context of its duty: the protection of the state and its citizens from external threats. Unfortunately, the wars which the Eastern Roman Empire fought during the discussed period rarely get the attention they deserve. Because of this unsatisfactory state of affairs, I have seen the need to re-analyse and synthesize the events which form the background to the main problems outlined in the present work. For this reason, the following proposes a new outlook on the underappreciated military conduct of the Eastern Roman army in the years 408–471.

This book is the result of my long-lasting interest in the history of the Mediterranean in the fifth century, the migration period, and the struggle of the Roman Empire to survive this difficult epoch. My previous research was concerned with the diplomatic and military responses of the Eastern Roman Empire under the rule of emperors Marcian and Leo I to the crisis in the West and the two main barbarian threats, the Vandals and the Huns[1]. The present work, which

---

[1] Ł. P i g o ń s k i, *Polityka zachodnia cesarzy Marcjana (450–457) i Leona I (457–474)*, Łódź 2019.

is based on the Ph.D. thesis entitled *Military Elites and their Influence on the Eastern Roman Empire during the Reigns of Theodosius II, Marcian, and Leo I* which I defended in 2021 at the University of Łódź, expands and elaborates on the ideas developed throughout my earlier academic career.

In the following pages I intend to collate and re-evaluate existing sources and interpretations related to the topic of the military elites in the fifth-century Eastern Roman Empire. Even though there is no shortage of contributions, they often present conflicting views, while certain problems remain untouched. I shall try, to the best of my ability, to fill the gaps where possible and provide a coherent historical narrative. It is, however, important to note that my views often stand in contrast to those which predominate in the scholarship. The present work is thus less of a synthesis of up-to-date findings and more of an interpretative proposition, a novel look at the problems it tackles. I have paid special attention to basing my arguments on as strong research as possible and always to present a detailed overview of established theses whenever I disagree with them, so that the reader may judge my views himself. Nevertheless, I am aware of the contentious nature of such an approach, and if the presented ideas do not gain recognition in the scholarly world, I do at least hope that they will serve as a subject for discussion which is interesting and worthy of consideration.

The book consists of four main chapters. The first one serves as an introduction to the problems outlined in the present work, providing a cursory overview of the primary sources, the structure of the late antique military and its command, the prerogatives of the generals, and the ways in which they secured power and influence. The following three chapters, dedicated to the reigns of the respective emperors, recount political and military events, focusing on the areas of activity of the members of the military elites. The book also includes two appendices which contain additional arguments elaborating on some of the views expressed in the main text which did not fit well in the structure of the narrative.

***

I would like to extend sincere thanks to those who have reviewed the present work: professors Rafał Kosiński and Marek Wilczyński for their valuable and constructive critical remarks which certainly helped iron out many mistakes and gave me directions on how to improve it.

I would also like to express my deep gratitude to Professor Mirosław J. Leszka, the supervisor of the thesis whose guidance was invaluable in helping me navigate through the intricacies of the topic of the fifth-century military elites. His patience and unfaltering support were essential in my enduring through the highs and lows of writing a doctoral thesis.

I would like to thank Professor Teresa Wolińska who guided me in the earliest stages of my academic research. In addition, I would like to express gratitude to all of the members of the Department of Byzantine Studies and the 'Ceraneum' Center of the University of Łódź, Professor Kokoszko, Professor Bralewski, Professor Marinow, Professor Brzozowska, Dr. Filipczak, Dr. Kompa, Dr. Wolski, and the others whom I had the honour to meet over the years.

I would also like to extend sincere thanks to Professor Hans Boemelburg and the University of Giessen for their hospitality and the opportunity to gather many scholarly resources which were instrumental in the writing of the present work.

Finally, I would like to thank my friends and family on whom I always knew I could count. Without you and your support this work would never have come to be.

***

This book was written as part of a research project financed by the National Research Centre (Poland). Decision number DEC-2018/31/B/HS3/03038 (*Wschodniorzymskie elity wojskowe od Teodozjusza II do Anastazjusza I (408–518). Studium społeczno-polityczne*).

The Military in the Fifth Century

When one studies the political and military history of the fifth-century Eastern Roman Empire, one thing becomes apparent: the presence and influence of those holding the highest ranks in the army can be widely observed in the sources. The immense impact that the powerful generals had on the various affairs and the ways in which they interacted with the state, society, and each other is thus the starting point for this work.

Who Constitutes 'Military Elites'?

For the lack of a better alternative, I decided to classify the people mentioned above as 'military elites'. Those who could be defined under that term usually served the Empire in the highest rank of *magister militum*, the master of arms. However, the choice of a vague term 'elite' over selecting a specific military office was my conscious decision. First of all, it was done to indicate that the aim of the present work is not to put forward an administrative survey or prosopography of all known persons holding certain rank. Due to the nature of the sources, such approach would create a woefully incomplete and inconsistent image of the group. It is important to note that it is more common that we do not know who served in the rank of *magister militum* than we do. Even when the sources speak of military commanders, it is largely only the interpretation of the scholars attributing various offices to vague passing mentions in ancient texts. Legal documents, which are the only truly reliable sources for determining the exact ranks at exact points in time, are few and far in-between.

In addition to the uncertainty mentioned above, there were instances when military officers of lower ranks played just as important role in the events shaping the political landscape of the fifth century. Thus the extraordinary impact that the military elites had on the events, which are the subject of analysis in the following work, is not necessarily resulting from their serving in specific military offices. Naturally, it was a factor, but as there were many prominent *magistri militum* of great power and influence, some barely appear in the sources while others are completely unknown. In addition, some commanders of lower ranks had a much greater impact on the fate of the Empire than their place in the military hierarchy would indicate.

Furthermore, it is a safe assumption that every known powerful member of the military elite was not just an important individual. He had numerous clients and supporters, a network of associates, and various connections in the army. The sources at our disposal only rarely allow for such a unique glimpse into the people who were in the background, but arguably constituted a foundation of their superiors' power. Sadly, oftentimes that background is unreachable through the data at our disposal, however, it would be, in my opinion, misrepresenting the complexity of the group that constituted the military elite, if the title of the present work mentioned only one particular rank of commanders. This holds true, even if the reality of the situation is that its focus had to be placed on select *magistri militum*, both due to their disproportionate impact on the analysed events, and the selective nature of the sources.

This study is, thus, dedicated to the military elites, both as a group and individual persons that constituted it, and how they affected the Eastern Roman Empire under the rule of the three emperors, Theodosius II, Marcian, and Leo. I decided to select those specific reigns, because the period they cover almost exactly coincide with the emergence of the new military elite, its rise to power and prominence, which was eventually successfully challenged by the emperor what resulted in the fall of the established elite, and the birth of a new one. While the genesis of those events can be traced back to the reign of Arcadius, and the story of the new elites that emerged under Leo continues throughout the reigns of Zeno and Anastasius, I decided to narrow the scope of the present work to the events of the years 408–474. Such approach allowed for an in-depth analysis of that important period which does not always feature prominently in the literature that generally tends to concentrate on the events in the Western part of the Empire instead.

An Overview of the Sources

Unfortunately, research on the topic in question is limited by the availability of the sources. Even when establishing basic facts about Eastern Roman generals, the researcher needs to realize that there are only singular documental sources for the military elite in the period between 408 and 474 in the Eastern Roman Empire. The most important one is *Notitia Dignitatum*[1], a list of offices of the Roman Empire; it is indispensable for any research into the military and administration in late antiquity. This document contains detailed lists of high military offices, including all the posts of *magistri militum* alongside the units under their command. However, there are multiple problems with it, most of which have already been discussed in previous parts of the chapter. In addition to *Notitia*, there are collections of laws, the codes of Theodosius and Justinian, which contain legislation pertaining to military matters, sometimes addressed to field commanders. That being said, compilations of laws provide only fragmentary information, only in regard to specific circumstances in which these laws were issued. They are far from representative as far as the development of the military elite and its influence on the Eastern Roman Empire is concerned. Documentary sources in this case are invaluable, but woefully insufficient for nearly any topic concerning the main part of the narrative. Thus, for the most part, they serve as credible but complementary sources.

Most of the information regarding the military elites has to be discerned from various narrative sources. Since the interests of ancient authors usually concerned political and military events and the period in question was a turbulent one, the members of the military elite are often recorded in the pages of histories and chronicles.

Probably the most important one for this period is the *History* of Priscus of Panium[2], an Eastern Roman historian and diplomat. This classicizing work concentrated mainly on the foreign policy of the Eastern Roman Empire. Its

---

[1] M. K u l i k o w s k i, *Notitia Dignitatum as a Historical Source,* Hi 49, 2000, p. 358–377; A. S z o p a, *Notitia Dignitatum – „najbardziej rzymski z dokumentów"?*, ReG 8, 2015, p. 183–191.

[2] In the sources there are three different versions of the title and it is impossible to say what it was in reality. Thus, from now on I will continue to refer to it by this title for consistency's sake. Cf. R.C. B l o c k l e y, *Fragmentary Classicising Historians of the Later Roman Empire*, t. I, Liverpool 1981, p. 49.

author was a state official involved in politics and diplomacy of the time, thus he likely had a very good understanding of the events the present work concerns[3]. Unfortunately, Priscus' *History* did not survive in full, but only in fragments collected in *Excerpta de legationibus* of Constantine Porphyrogennetos and some references by other historians who used it. Thankfully, almost all authors who later wrote about the events of the fifth century utilized his work in some capacity.

One of those was the famous Procopius of Caesarea, the author of the *History of the Wars*[4]. Even though it concentrates on the conflicts fought by the emperor Justinian, the extensive digressions and references provide quite detailed information on the earlier periods, especially on the campaigns against the Vandals. Be that as it may, the historian did likely modify the original account by Priscus to suit the needs of his narrative[5]. Priscus' *History* was also used by Antiochene authors: John Malalas and John of Antioch. The former was the author of *Chronographia* which describes the events from the creation of the world to ca. 563–574[6]. It was a po-

---

[3] On Priscus and his work, cf. *PLRE*, vol. II, p. 906 (s.v. *Priscus 1*); R.C. B l o c k l e y, *Fragmentary...*, p. 49–70; R.C. B l o c k l e y, *The Developement of Greek Historiography. Priscus, Malchus and Candidus*, [in:] *Greek and Roman Historiography in Late Antiquity. Fourth to Sixth Century A.D.*, ed. G. M a r a s c o, Boston 2003, p. 289–312; D. R o h r b a c h e r, *Historians of Late Antiquity*, London 2002, p. 82–92; B. B a l d w i n, *Priscus of Panium*, B 50, 1980, p. 18–61. There are also several important works, focusing on specific problems: B. C r o k e, *The Context and Date of Priscus Fragment 6*, CP 78, 1983, p. 297–308; D. B r o d k a, *Priskos und der Feldzug des Basiliskos gegen Geiserich (468)*, [in:] *Griechische Profanhistoriker des fünften nachristlichen Jahrhundert*, ed. T. S t i c k l e r, B. B l e c k m a n n, Stuttgart 2014, p. 103–120; D. B r o d k a, *Priskos von Panion und Kaiser Marcian. Eine Quellenuntersuchung zu Procop. 3,4,1–11, Evagr. HE 2,1, Theoph. AM 5943 und Nic. Kall. HE 15,1*, Mil 9, 2012, p. 145–162.

[4] A. C a m e r o n, *Procopius and the Sixth Century*, London 1996; A. K a l d e l l i s, *Procopius of Caesarea: Tyranny, History and Philosophy at the End of Antiquity*, Philadelphia 2004; D. B r o d k a, *Die Geschichtsphilosophie in der spätantiken Historiographie. Studien zu Prokopios von Kaisareia, Agathias von Myrina und Theophylaktos Simokattes*, Frankfurt am Main 2004, p. 14–151; For a more thorough and recent (2003–2014) bibliography on this essential Byzantine historian alongside with a commentary, cf. G. G r e a t r e x, *Perceptions of Procopius in Recent Scholarship*, HOJ 8, 2014, p. 76–121.

[5] A. C a m e r o n, *Procopius...*, p. 211.

[6] Elisabeth J e f f r e y s (*Malalas' Sources*, [in:] *Studies in John Malalas*, ed. E. J e f f r e y s, B. C r o k e, R. S c o t t, Sydney 1990, p. 1–91) suggests that Malalas could have used Priscus' work, even if indirectly. On Malalas and his work, cf. *Studies in John Malalas*, ed. E. J e f f r e y s, B. C r o k e, R. S c o t t, Sydney 1990; B. C r o k e, *Introduction*, [in:] *The Chronicle of John Malalas*, ed. E. J e f f r e y s, M. J e f f r e y s, R. S c o t t, Sydney 1986, p. XXI–XLI; M. M e i e r, C. D r o h i s n, S. P r i w i t z e r, *Einleitung*, [in:] J o h a n n e s M a l a l a s, *Weltchronik*, ed. J. T h u r n, M. M e i e r, Stuttgart 2009, p. 1–37; E. J e f f r e y s, *The Beginning of Byzantine Chronography: John Malalas*, [in:] *Greek and Roman Historiography...*, p. 497–527; M. K o k o s z k o, *Descriptions of personal appearance in John Malalas' Chronicle*, Łódź 1998, p. 6–11.

pular work concentrating primarily on the history of his native town, sometimes confused about more distant events, however, it can still provide valuable and often unique information. The work of John of Antioch unfortunately survived only in fragments, but because of his extensive usage of Priscus' work it is being used to reconstruct the latter parts of the *History*[7].

Priscus was also likely used by Theophanes the Confessor in his *Chronographia*[8] when describing the events of the fifth century. He was a monk living at the turn of the eighth and ninth centuries, who continued the work of his friend, George Synkellos, of writing a history from the creation of the world[9]. Due to his having been so distant from the events he described, his account is prone to misunderstandings and inaccuracies; however, he seems to have related the narrative of his sources relatively directly and with little conscious alterations of his own.

Another historian that needs to be mentioned is Jordanes, the sixth-century Gothic monk and author of *Getica* and *Romana*[10]. The former source is especially valuable as it focuses on the history of the Gothic peoples. Thus, it provides many unique information, however, its veracity may at times be questionable due to a pro-Gothic bias. It is also likely that Jordanes used Priscus as a source.

Unfortunately, another source that certainly would have been very helpful in researching this topic, the *History* of Candidus[11], has not been used as extensively as that of Priscus. Only a short synopsis written by Photius remains; despite its brevity, it is still invaluable for understanding the reign of Leo.

Some information regarding the later periods of Leo's reign can be found in the partially surviving *Byzantine History* of Malchus of Philadelphia; however, this historian focused primarily on periods beyond the scope of the present work[12].

---

[7] R.C. B l o c k l e y, *Fragmentary...*, p. 114.

[8] A. K a z h d a n, *A History of Byzantine Literature (650–850)*, Athens 1998, p. 205–234.

[9] Cf. A. K o m p a, *In search of Syncellus' and Theophanes' own words: the authorship of the Chronographia revisited*, TM 19, 2015, p. 73–92.

[10] W. G o f f a r t, *The Narrators of Barbarian History (A.D. 550–800). Jordanes, Gregory of Tours, Bede, and Paul the Deacon*, New Jersey 1988, p. 20–111; B. C r o k e, *Latin Historiography and the Barbarian Kingdoms*, [in:] *Greek and Roman Historiography...*, p. 367–375; R. K a s p e r s k i, *Teodoryk Wielki i Kasjodor. Studia nad tworzeniem „tradycji dynastycznej Amalów"*, Kraków 2013.

[11] H. B r a n d t, *Zur historiographischen konzeption des Izaurers Candidus*, [in:] *Griechische Profanhistoriker des fünften nachristlichen Jahrhundert*, ed. T. S t i c k l e r, B. B l e c k-m a n n, Stuttgart 2014, p. 162–167; M. M e i e r, *Candidus: um die Geschichte der Isauriers*, [in:] *Griechische Profanhistoriker...*, p. 171–193; R.C. B l o c k l e y, *The development...*, p. 312–314.

[12] R.C. B l o c k l e y, *Fragmentary...*, p. 71–74; H.U. W i e m e r, *Malchos von Philadelphia. Die Vandalen und das Ende des Kaisertums im Westen*, [in:] *Griechische Profanhistoriker...*, p. 121–126.

Even though they appear unrelated to the events at hand, Western chronicles also provide some important information, especially pertaining to Eastern military involvement in the West. Out of those the primary ones are the works of a Spanish bishop, Hydatius[13], and a secretary to the Pope, Prosper of Aquitaine[14]. Those accounts are supplemented by panegyrics of the poet Sidonius[15], especially important is the one on the emperor Anthemius, who was, before his accession in Rome, an Eastern Roman general. Around the same time Marcellinus Comes wrote his *Chronicle*[16]. It is another important account, especially since its author used otherwise unknown Byzantine chronicles which did not survive to our times.

One more important group of sources are the various Christian texts, Church histories, and hagiographies, all of which focus mostly on religious developments, however, against the background of socio-political history. Thus, they still provide valuable information regarding the military elite, and not only in the areas of the generals' relationships with the Church and their religious convictions. For example, the primary source for Theodosius' first war against Persia is the *Church History* of Socrates Scholasticus[17]; however, his narrative ends in 439. Contemporary to Socrates' work was the *Church History* of Sozomen[18], which reaches until about 425. Another, much later *Church History* that bears mentioning was written by Evagrius Scholasticus, which comprises of six books,

---

[13] On Hydatius and his work, cf. C. Cardelle de Hartman, *Philologische Studien zur Chronik des Hydatius von Chaves*, Stuttgart 1994; R.W. Burgess, *The Chronicle of Hydatius and Consularia Constantinopolitana*, Oxford 1993, p. 3–68; H. Börm, *Hydatius von Aquae Flaviae und die Einheit des Römiches Reiches im 5. Jahrhundert*, [in:] *Griechische Profanhistoriker...*, p. 195–214; G. Zecchini, *Latin Historiography: Jerome, Orosius and the Western Chroniclers*, [in:] *Greek and Roman Historiography...*, p. 342–344; A. Gillett, *Envoys and Political Communication in Late Antique West 411–533*, Cambridge 2003, p. 36–83.

[14] J.M. Kotter, M. Becker, *Einleitung*, [in:] Prosper Tiro, *Chronik. Laterculus Regnum Vandalorum et Alanorum*, ed. J.M. Kotter, M. Becker, Paderborn 2016, p. 3–60; *PLRE*, vol. II, p. 926–927, (s.v. *Prosper Tiro*); G. Zecchini, *Latin...*, p. 338–340.

[15] J. Harries, *Sidonius Apollinaris and the Fall of Rome AD 407–485*, Oxford 1994; D. Alvarez Jimenez, *Sidonius Apollinaris and the Fourth Punic War*, [in:] *New Perspectives on Late Antiquity*, ed. D.H. de la Fuente, Cambridge 2011, p. 158–172; J. Styka, *Sydoniusz Apollinaris i kultura literacka w Galii V wieku*, Kraków 2008; A. Horvath, *The Education of Sidonius Apollinaris in the Light of his Citations*, ACUSD 36, 2000, p. 151–162.

[16] B. Croke, *Count Marcellinus and his Chronicle*, New York 2001; M.J. Leszka, Sz. Wierzbiński, *Komes Marcellin vir clarissimus. Historyk i jego dzieło*, Łódź 2022, p. 11–101.

[17] Th. Urbainczyk, *Socrates of Constantinople. Historian of Church and State*, Ann Arbor 1997; G. Chesnut, *The First Christian Histories. Eusebius, Socrates, Sozomen, Theodoret and Evagrius*, Paris 1986, p. 167–189.

[18] G. Chesnut, *The First...*, p. 192–200.

covering the period from 431 to 593[19]. What makes this work valuable is the fact that its author was among those dependent on Priscus.

In addition to these works, one should mention a very important and informative hagiographical text, the *Life of St. Daniel the Stylite*[20]. Even though it is an overtly religious source, due to the involvement of the saint in political matters as an advisor to the emperor Leo and the interests of the author, it records many political events, especially those relating to the conflict between Leo and Aspar and the rise of Tarasikodissa-Zeno.

This list does not exhaust all the sources that have been used in the present work. Some singular remarks regarding issues of interest to the present work can also be found in *Chronicon Paschale*, *Church Histories* of Philostorgius and Theodoret, the works of John Zonaras, *De Magistratibus* of John the Lydian, the *History* of Zosimus, and the Armenian histories of Yeghishe, Moses of Khoren, and Ghazar of Parp'i. The letters of Theodoret of Cyrrhus, primarily those addressed to generals, are also helpful in painting the whole picture.

The above overview is meant not only to present the *corpus* of the sources that has been used as a basis of this dissertation, but also to illustrate a major problem facing the research into the subject matter. There is not one source that could provide a comprehensive support for the narrative; instead, there is a variety of texts, often surviving only in fragments, written from different perspectives, focusing on different things, and conceived in different time periods and places. It would appear that this could allow for extensive cross-referencing and facilitate views from different angles, but, unfortunately, that is rarely the case. Many events are only reported in single sources and the narratives tend to overlap only when the most famous events are described. Considering that the focus of the present work is a very specific aspect of late antique history, there is rarely a satisfactory amount of information at our disposal.

In addition, it needs to be realized that none of the sources specialize in the topic of the military of the fifth century[21]. The only author who was a member

---

[19] P. A l l e n, *Evagrius Scholasticus the Church Historian*, Leuven 1981, p. 1–20; O. J u r e - w i c z, *Historia literatury bizantyńskiej*, Wrocław 1984, p. 46; M. W h i t b y, *Introduction*, [in:] *The Ecclesiastical History of Evagrius Scholasticus*, ed. M. W h i t b y, Liverpool 2000, p. XIII–XLIII; K. G i n t e r, *Wizerunek władców bizantyńskich w Historii Kościelnej Ewagriusza Scholastyka*, Łódź 2018, p. 19–79.

[20] R. K o s i ń s k i, *Holiness and Power. Constantinopolitan Holy Men and Authority in the 5th Century*, Berlin 2016, p. 119–129.

[21] There is one source in that period which vaguely fits such a description, a dissertation on military matters written by Vegetius. It is a very important source on the late Roman army, armaments, training regime, etc.; however, the author was not a military professional, so his analysis is not without faults. Unfortunately, it is of very limited use for this dissertation on account of having been written in

of the military (and even then only in a loose sense) was Procopius, who wrote from the perspective of almost a century after the events he is described. Priscus, due to his involvement in the structures of the state and diplomatic experience probably had a good idea of the chain of command, but the military is not the focus of his work. The other authors were only further detached from military knowledge and usually also more distant chronologically.

This causes numerous problems when trying to establish the information base for the subject. For example, most of the sources do not use technical terms. The most common term denoting a military commander is στρατηγός (*strate-gos*)[22]. Many modern scholars seem to assume that whenever it is used, it specifically signifies the *magister militum*; however, it is most likely a misinterpretation. To give an analogy, when a modern news outlet, or even a scholar, uses the word 'general', unless it is of utmost importance to his narrative, he would not specify whether he means 'brigadier general', 'lieutenant general', 'general major', 'general', or the 'general of the army'[23]. Thus, unless the author of the source in question was being very specific, which would be a rare occurrence, or unless the source is a legal text displaying a clear application of technical terms, the usual assumption should be that the sources are vague when referring to military ranks.

This is one of the primary reasons why this dissertation does not aim to offer a prosopography of *magistri militum*, but instead focuses on presenting the military elites and their influence, as well as their impact on the politics of the time, against the background of the events of the fifth century during the reigns of Theodosius II, Marcian, and Leo.

The Roman Army

Naturally, the primary and most obvious reason for the importance of the members of the military elite was their role in serving as the commanders of the army. Roman Army of the late antiquity barely resembled the iconic legions

---

the West, being filled with anachronisms, and taking little interest in the topic of the chain of command. For more information on Vegetius and his work, cf. N.P. M i l n e r, *Introduction*, [in:] *Vegetius: Epitome of Military Science*, ed. N.P. M i l n e r, Liverpool 1996, p. XIII–XLIII; F.L. M ü l l e r, *Einleitung*, [in:] *Publii Flavii Vegetii Renati, Epitoma rei militaris*, ed. F.L. M ü l l e r, Stuttgart 1997, p. 11–26.

[22] Which simply means 'commander'. The other commonly used term was στρατηλάτες (*stratelates*) which appears in Z o s i m u s (II, 33) when he is referring to the establishing of the office of *magister militum*. Cf. A.E.R. B o a k, *The Roman Magistri in the Civil and Military Service of the Empire*, CP 26, 1915, p. 119–120.

[23] As per the officer ranks in the United States Army.

which had originally carved out the Empire through their glamorous victories and conquests[24]. As time went on, however, and changing circumstances demanded, it was undergoing transformations that culminated in the reforms attributed to Diocletian and Constantine which gave it the form which it generally retained through the fifth century[25]. Nevertheless, those changes have been lamented both by their contemporaries[26] and modern scholars[27]. It is therefore important to establish how effective the late Roman army was at protecting the Empire and projecting its power in the tumultuous fifth century, so as further to understand how these matters affected the generals who stood at its helm.

The late Roman army was divided into two primary categories: the *limitanei* and the *comitatenses*. The former were border troops, garrisoning the forts of the *limes* and they were responsible for various tasks, which included fighting against banditry or repelling minor raids. To facilitate these tasks, a greater portion of their force was mounted[28]. The units of *limitanei* were generally of lower quality, but they were not meant to take up the fight against any major foes. That task was reserved for the *comitatenses*, the mobile field army. Those units were better trained and equipped and situated in strategic locations so as to be able to respond to any threat too serious for the border troops to tackle. In theory, the organization of the late Roman army was intended to provide enough numbers to cover the full extent of the borders and reduce their porousness, and still to make it possible to muster high quality troops to react to sudden hot-spots or

---

[24] On the topic of Late Roman Army, cf. A.H.M. J o n e s, *The Later Roman Empire 284–602. A Social, Economic and Administrative Survey*, vol. I–III, Oxford 1964, p. 607–686; W. T r e a d g o l d, *Byzantium and its Army 284–1081*, Stanford 1995; Y. B o h e c, *L'Armee Romaine sous le Bas-Empire*, Paris 2006; M. W h i t b y, *Army and Society in the Late Roman World: A Context for Decline?*, [in:] *A Companion to the Roman Army*, ed. P. E r d k a m p, Oxford 2007, p. 515–531; M. W h i t b y, *The Army c. 420–602*, [in:] *CAH*, vol. XIV, *Late Antiquity: Empire and Successors, AD 425–600*, ed. A. C a m e r o n, B. W a r d-P e r k i n s, M. W h i t b y, Cambridge 2008, p. 288–314; H. E l t o n, *Military Forces*, [in:] *The Cambridge History of Greek and Roman Warfare*, vol. II, ed. P. S a b i n, H. v a n W e e s, M. W h i t b y, Cambridge 2008, p. 270–309; P. S o u t h e r n, K. D i x o n, *Late Roman Army*, London 2014; H. E l t o n, *Military Developments in the Fifth Century*, [in:] *Companion to the Age of Attila*, ed. M. M a a s, Cambridge 2015, p. 125–139.

[25] On the formation of the late Roman army, cf. W. S e s t o n, *Dioclétien et la Tétrarchie*, Paris 1946, p. 295–320; W. K u h o f f, *Diokletian und die Epoche die Tetrarchie. Das römische Reich zwischen Krisenbewältigung und Neuaufbau (284–313 n. Chr.)*, Frankfurt am Main 2001, p. 411–483; P. S o u t h e r n, K. D i x o n, *Late...*, p. 4–38.

[26] V e g e t i u s, I, 28. He does, however, recognize improvements in certain spheres, especially in the cavalry, cf. Ve g e t i u s, III, 26.

[27] See for example: P. S o u t h e r n, K. D i x o n, *Late...*, p. 52–55.

[28] W. T r e a d g o l d, *Byzantium...*, p. 50–52.

to project force outside the borders of the Empire. Nominally, the whole army of the Eastern Roman Empire numbered between 300,000 and 350,000 soldiers[29] of whom 104,000 were *comitatenses*[30].

The evolution of the Roman military affected not only the army as a whole, but also the individual soldiers and their equipment. The Roman infantry started to make more common use of spears, which in conjunction with large round or oval shields facilitated fighting in tight formation and were also better suited to dealing with mounted enemies, who were very commonly encountered in this time-period. These innovations were probably also better suited to keeping cohesion among less disciplined and not always well-trained troops. The short sword, while still in use, was generally replaced with the much longer *spatha*[31]. In fact, this emphasis on range can be widely observed, since the use of various missile weapons, such as javelins, bows, and arrows, was very common, especially of darts weighted with lead called *plumbata*, which could be thrown up to seventy metres[32]. Even though the infantry still constituted the bulk of the forces, there was a much greater focus on high quality cavalry, some of which was fully clad in armour in order to act as shock troops[33].

All this equipment was provided to the Roman soldiers by *fabricae*, which were state-controlled workshops specialized in producing armaments in large numbers and to a uniform, high-quality standard[34]. Soldiers were supplied food and other necessary produce (*annona*) as well as fodder for the horses (*capitum*), which were taxed of Imperial subjects[35]. Recruits for the army were mostly acquired through conscription[36]. Despite various privileges which the soldiers enjoyed, military service in late antiquity was not popular among citizens and

---

[29] A.H.M. J o n e s, *The Later...*, p. 683; W. T r e a d g o l d, *Byzantium...*, p. 50–51.

[30] A.H.M. J o n e s, *The Later...*, p. 679; W. T r e a d g o l d, *Byzantium...*, p. 50. It is, however, likely that these numbers diminished quickly, or are otherwise unreliable, cf. J.H.W.G. L i e b e s c h u e t z, *Barbarians and Bishops. Army, Church, and State in the Age of Arcadius and Chrysostom*, Oxford 1991, p. 40–42.

[31] P. S o u t h e r n, K. D i x o n, *Late...*, p. 103–111.

[32] *Ibidem*, p. 113–115.

[33] M. M i e l c z a r e k, *Cataphracti and Clibanarii: Studies on the Heavy Armoured Cavalry of the Ancient World*, Łódź 1993, especially p. 73–85; V. N i k o r o n o v, *Cataphracti, Catafractarii and Clibanarii: Another Look at the Old Problem of their Identifications*, [in:] *Military Archeology. Weaponry and Warfare in the Historical and Social Perspective*, ed. G.V. V i l i n b a k h o v, V.M. M a s s o n, St. Petersburg 1998, p. 131–138.

[34] P. S o u t h e r n, K. D i x o n, *Late...*, p. 89–91; P. L e t k i, *The state factories (fabricae) during the time of tetrarchy*, SKA 5, 2009, p. 49–64.

[35] A.H.M. J o n e s, *The Later...*, p. 626–630; P. S o u t h e r n, K. D i x o n, *Late...*, p. 79–82.

[36] A.H.M. J o n e s, *The Later...*, p. 615–616.

the practice of avoiding enrollment was quite common[37]. Thus, very often soldiers had to be sourced from various barbarian peoples. To them, the standards of living provided to a Roman soldier must have appeared much more appealing. Despite the criticisms of the 'Germanization' of the army, there is no evidence whatsoever of barbarian troops having been less reliable than their Roman counterparts, and they often easily assimilated into the Roman society[38].

It cannot be stressed enough how massive an undertaking the managing of late Roman army and keeping it in a combat-ready shape was. In fact, the complexity involved is to where much of its weakness can be traced. In peace-time, it was certainly tempting for the administrators of an already stretched budget to cut funding, slack on recruitment standards, or limit enlistment numbers. Similarly, any cases of corruption were extremely damaging to the capabilities of the army. For example, there was a sadly not uncommon practice among corrupt commanders to keep 'ghost troops' on the roster and pocket the money intended to pay their wages.

But even if it was difficult to keep the military ready and able in peace-time, it was even more difficult to make up for any set-backs, losses, not to mention major defeats in the field. To recover from those, the state had to undertake the massive expense of producing new equipment, finding new recruits, and training them. A common practice quickly to make up for losses in the field army was to supplement it with units of former border troops as *pseudocomitatenses*; unfortunately, to the detriment of the over-all quality of the force.

The *Foederati*[39]

One of the solutions to the dangers facing the Roman Empire was the practice of using allied barbarian tribes in the defence system. This was done under an agreement, called *foedus*, which obliged an allied tribe to fight against the enemies of the Empire, for which it received land and tribute. The primary

---

[37] *Ibidem*, p. 617–619; P. S o u t h e r n, K. D i x o n, *Late...*, p. 68–69.

[38] A.H.M. J o n e s, *The Later...*, p. 621–622.

[39] T. S t i c k l e r, *Foederati*, [in:] *A Companion to the Roman...*, p. 495–514; J.H.W.G. L i-e b e s c h u e t z, *Barbarians...*, p. 32–43; M. W i l c z y ń s k i, *Germanie w służbie zachodnio-rzymskiej w V w. n.e.*, Oświęcim 2018, p. 483–494. Ralph S c h a r f (*Foederati. Von der völker-rechtlichen Kategorie zur byzantinischen Truppengattung*, Wien 2001, p. 52–55) claims this formation existed in the East only since the reign of emperor Zeno; however, there are sources which contradict this claim, cf. M a l a l a s, XIV, 40.

difference between relying on such tribes and the recruitment of barbarians into the Roman army is that in cases of the former, the warriors remained under the command of their tribal leaders and were not incorporated directly into the Roman military structure. It was a much more common practice to employ *foederati* in the military forces in the West due to the fact that maintaining a regular Roman army was much more of a problem there than in the East[40]. However, the conclusion of a *foedus* was also a means to normalize the relationship between the Empire and a barbarian people. Most often *foederati* tribes were settled on the frontier to serve as a buffer against foreign incursions. Be that as it may, there were instances in which the interests of the leaders of *foederati* tribes and those of the Romans collided, sometimes resulting in open conflicts.

In contrast, the enemies of the Empire did not suffer from such problems. This was especially the case with the bellicose 'barbarian' tribes of the North, who cultivated a warrior culture in which every able-bodied man was expected to take up arms and fight. This meant that they were able to pose a considerable, and disproportionate to their over-all numbers, threat to the defences of the Empire. Furthermore, they could take military defeats and recover from them much more easily.

Considering the above, it is no wonder that the Eastern Roman Empire developed a military theory which recommended avoiding of inherently uncertain resolutions of conflicts in the field of battle, instead and seeking other means, either diplomatic or of the nature of subterfuge. It seems that the experiences from late antiquity echoed through the later Byzantine military manuals, where such concepts were explicitly formulated[41].

Commanding the Roman Army

The whole Roman security system was divided into several territorial commands. Units of *limitanei* were led by local *duces*, while the field army was subordinate to commanders in the rank of *comes rei militaris* and *magister militum*. The latter were the highest-ranking military officers of the Roman army, and, arguably, the people most responsible for keeping the Empire safe from external

---

[40] On this phenomenon and the disintegration of the regular army of the Western Roman Empire, cf. J. W i j n e n d a l e, *'Warlordism' and the Disintegration of the Western Roman Army*, [in:] *Circum Mare: Themes in Ancient Warfare*, ed. J. A r m s t r o n g, Leiden 2016, p. 185–203.

[41] M a u r i c i u s, *Strategikon*, VIII, 2, 4; *Peri strategias*, 33. See also: W. K a e g i, *Some Thoughts on Byzantine Military Strategy*, Brookline 1983.

threats. The title itself was created by the emperor Constantine. The field army accompanying the emperor, the *comitatus*, was greatly expanded by permanently attaching frontier units to it. To lead the new force, the emperor created two new offices, *magister equitum* commanding the cavalry units and *magister peditum* in charge of the infantry. This system slowly went through changes over the course time, a process which eventually led to the stationing of field armies in different regions of the Empire and the permanent creation of territorial offices of the *magistri militum*.

The distribution of those commands was recorded by a document called *Notitia Dignitatum*, which is one of the main sources of information on the late Roman military. According to it, there were five such offices in the Eastern Roman Empire. *Magister militum per Orientem* was stationed in the Levantine provinces, likely in Antioch. Two *magistri militum* were located in the Balkans, one in Thrace, in Marcianopolis, and one in Illyria. Other two commanders accompanied the emperor, having their units stationed by the capital city. They were the *magistri militum praesentales*, those 'in the presence' of the emperor, and theirs were considered the most prestigious of all the senior commanding posts.

Each *magister militum* headed a considerable military force, numbering around 20,000 troops[42]. It appears that such a force was sufficient to conduct independent military operations. Soldiers of the highest quality were found in the most prestigious units subordinate to the *magistri militum praesentales*, and those armies were usually the ones used in offensive campaigns. It seems that the reason why there were two was so that if one of them was engaged in some distant military campaign, the capital would not be left unprotected.

The system outlined above was not entirely static throughout the discussed period, even if it may appear so from a cursory glance at the literature concerning the late Roman army. The previously mentioned document, *Notitia Dignitatum*, depicted the state of affairs at the very specific moment of its writing. The part of the document concerning the East was not updated after ca. 395[43], and any changes to the Eastern Roman military system would not have been recorded in it. The state and composition of the Roman army and its command in the fourth century[44] were completely different from those in the sixth century[45]. Thus, it would

---

[42] W. T r e a d g o l d, *Byzantium...*, p. 63.

[43] M. K u l i k o w s k i, *Notitia Dignitatum as a Historical Source*, Hi 49, 2000, p. 372.

[44] Cf. p. 21, n. 25.

[45] On the Byzantine forces in the sixth century, cf. C. K o e h n, *Justinian und die Armee des frühen Byzanz*, Berlin 2018. For a similar work to the present one (however, different in scope and focus, partially due to the much better source coverage of the period), but on the commanders of the sixth century, cf. D.A. P a r n e l l, *Justinian's Men. Careers and Relationships of Byzantine Army Officers 518–610*, London 2017.

be unwise to assume that the late Roman military order of battle did not undergo changes over the course of the fifth century. In fact, the evidence suggests that the Thracian *magisterium* was dismantled and reinstated at some point early in the reign of Theodosius II, which serves as proof of discrepancies between the document and the actual state of affairs in the East in the fifth century. More importantly, however, it appears that the title of *magister militum* of Illyria did not exist as part of the Eastern Roman chain of command for the majority of the described period[46]. It is most likely that the Illyrian army was disbanded when that territory was given to the Western Roman Empire, and, as opposed to the Thracian army, it was never permanently reinstated[47]. Thus, in the process of assigning generals to their posts, it is assumed that for most of the discussed period there were four permanent territorial offices of *magistri militum* with corresponding field armies[48].

The harsh reality of the fifth century sometimes called for greater flexibility on the part of the military command than the system of territorial offices allowed for. This could be achieved thanks to the practice of creating temporary military offices qualified as *vacantes*. *Magistri militum vacantes* were especially prominent in offensive operations, or any other campaigns which called for additional commanding officers, irrespective of territorial divisions. In addition, they could be appointed in an *ad hoc* fashion, which gave the emperor more room for political manoeuvres. In theory, if the ruler quarrelled with a general, he had the option to quickly to choose a loyal replacement, who could serve in the capacity of a *magister militum*. The position of *vacantes* in the hierarchy of offices was defined by the legislation of Theodosius II in 441, likely in the anticipation of the expedition against the Vandals[49].

The existence of such a practice constitutes another problem in assigning territorial offices to generals. In essence, there is often little evidence that would allow one to determine whether an individual held a permanent post or was assigned one as a *vacans*. In addition, usually there is little in terms of data to make any distinction between a *magister militum vacans* and a *comes rei militaris*. Thus, it is very difficult actually to determine how common such nominations were. It is, however, my assumption that they were at least not uncommon. We have direct evidence of the emperor Theodosius going to the trouble of clarifying the legal status of *magistri militum vacantes*; furthermore, considering the

---

[46] Alexander D e m a n d t (*Magister militum*, [in:] *RE*, t. XII suppl., 1970, p. 737) observes the relative silence and lack of information regarding the Illyrian mastery; however, he claims that it was likely due to the difficulties with keeping records in such uncertain times.

[47] There is a possibility that Leo tried to reinstate the office at some point in the 460s in order to appoint Marcellinus as one of the *magistri militum*, cf. p. 154 of the present work.

[48] Cf. Appendix 1.

[49] *CJ*, XII, 8, 2.

political and military realities of the period under discussion, such a tool would probably be too useful to pass up.

There are other examples of the changeability of the fifth-century Roman system of command. Because of the growing naval threat presented by the Vandals who terrorized the *Mediterraneum* with their corsair raids, the previously non-existent need to amass grand fleets in order to respond to such dangers had emerged. The command over those elements was also given to *magistri militum*, even if the naval forces were not normally attached to their units[50].

The Prerogatives of *Magistri Militum*

The generals of the Eastern Roman field armies were chosen to their office by the emperor. It is unknown whether there was a legally established term of service. There is no law or any other document that would indicate that; however, it neither seems that the emperor had a free hand in dismissing *magistri militum* from their offices. In addition, there seems to be an observable regularity to how much time Eastern Roman generals served in their positions. Arnold Jones claimed it was around three to five years, with which Evgeniy Glushanin agrees. Unfortunately, neither scholar sufficiently elaborated on those claims; nevertheless, their authority in such matters should not be disregarded. Thus, I assume that the tenures of *magistri militum* were time-limited and they lasted about 5 years; however, there was no limitation to extending service for another term. Even if that was not based on any specific law, it is highly probable that such was the political reality of the period. Considering that the protection of the Empire's borders was reliant upon a stable system of military command and that Rome had a long tradition of terms of office[51], such an approach would be very sensible. This is further supported by the existence of *magistri militum vacantes*. Such office would make little sense if the emperor could already make *ad hoc* staff decisions[52].

---

[50] On the Roman fleet in this period, cf. M. R e d d e, *Mare Nostrum. Les infrastructures, le dispositif et l'histoire de la marine militaire sous l'empire romain*, Roma 1986, p. 647–652; J.H. P r y o r, E.M. J e f f r e y s, *The Age of Dromon. The Byzantine Navy ca. 500–1204*, Leiden 2006, p. 123–161.

[51] Admittedly, the service of most Roman officials lasted one year. However, the need for stability could have led to the extension of the terms of military offices, and it indeed seems to have been the case across all ranks, cf. A.H.M. J o n e s, *The Later...*, p. 380–381.

[52] Cf. Appendix 1.

Service as a general of one of the Eastern Roman field armies brought considerable influence and status. *Magistri militum* received the highest honorary rank of the *illustres*, thanks to which they were eligible for holding the seats in the Senate and numerous privileges[53]. Imperial offices came with a considerable salary, and it would be highly unlikely for *magistri militum* to have been an exception. Its exact size is not known; however, it was probably substantial, considering that it was one of the highest offices of the state[54]. It is safe to assume that the generals possessed considerable wealth, and there are several examples which give evidence that this was the case. In a letter to Areobindus, Theodoret of Cyrrhus tries to intercede on behalf of the peasants working in the general's estates, referring to his being rich when asking for his kindness[55]. The wealth of the members of the military elite is also apparent in their funding of public utilities. The remains of a water reservoir built by Aspar can be seen in Istanbul to this day[56]. The inscription on the floor of a bath house in Seleucia in Isauria indicates that it was renovated by the wife of Flavius Zeno[57].

Magistri militum were commonly present at the court of the emperor, taking part in the *consistorium*[58] or otherwise advising the monarch. Anatolius was recorded counselling Theodosius on the policy directed towards Armenia and Persia; Aspar unsuccessfully tried to convince the emperor Leo not to intervene in a conflict between the barbarian tribes of the Pannonian Goths and the Sciri, and also to distance himself from the religious unrest in Alexandria. Service in such capacity was probably limited to those commanding the armies 'in the presence' of the emperor due to their proximity to the capital, which partially explains the prestige associated with this function, even if nominally all of the commanding posts were equal.

Furthermore, while the times of the Roman conquests may have been long gone, martial achievements were still held in high regard. Thus, successful generals were often rewarded with high honours, such as the consulate, in recognition for their service. Those who were able to achieve that would as a result become prominent members of the Senate and ranked high in the Imperial hierarchy.

---

[53] A.E.R. B o a k, *The Roman...*, p. 135–137.

[54] A. D e m a n d t, *Der spätrömische Militäradel*, Chi 10, 1980, p. 630–631; A.D. L e e, *Theodosius and his Generals*, [in:] *Theodosius II. Rethinking the Roman Empire in Late Antiquity*, ed. Ch. K e l l y, Cambridge 2013, p. 99.

[55] T h e o d o r e t, *Ep.* 23.

[56] *Chronicon Paschale*, a. 459.

[57] He is mentioned in the inscription as 'dear to Ares'. Cf. K. F e l d, *Barbarische Bürger: Die Isaurier und das Römische Reich*, Berlin 2005, p. 221; A.D. L e e, *Theodosius...*, p. 98.

[58] Cf. A.H.M. J o n e s, *The Later...*, p. 333–341. The *consistorium* was an assembly of the emperor and his officials. In the discussed period it seems that it had mostly ceremonial functions; however, the emperor still met with a select group of higher officials on a regular basis.

In addition, *magistri militum* prominently featured as envoys to foreign powers. It can be assumed that they were chosen for that role due to their experience in contacts with the Empire's neighbours, even if it was normally gained
on the battlefield, and the fact that they were high-ranking officials, who often
found themselves near the borders, whether due to a recent campaign or specific
territorial assignment[59]. This function certainly was a source of honours and influence, especially since it seems that the highly prestigious title of the *patricius*
was commonly bestowed on those who took part in diplomatic missions[60]. It
also undoubtedly allowed those generals who had an interest in foreign policy to
affect the outcome of negotiations.

There were other instances of Roman generals serving as representatives of the
emperor and enforcers of his will. A good example of this is their involvement in religious matters, both in the provinces and the capital. General Anatolius represented the emperor Marcian on the Council of Chalcedon. Ardaburious was tasked
with recovering the remains of the St. Simeon the Stylite and protecting them from
relic-hunters. Plintha mediated on behalf of the emperor in the conflict between
patriarchs John of Antioch and Cyril of Alexandria. *Magistri militum* were also
used as Imperial emissaries in various internal affairs, for example generals Arsacius
and Varanes were sent to appease the citizens of Constantinople during bread riots,
assumedly as a veiled threat of using military power against the rebellious mob[61].

Sources of Power and Influence

Many of the prerogatives that came with the office of *magister militum*
allowed some of the generals further to expand their power and influence and
become even more involved in other socio-cultural matters. It should be noted that each *magister militum* had an *officium* directly subordinate to himself,
which managed a variety of financial and judicial tasks[62]. It nominally numbered 300 officials, but repeated attempts in the legislation to limit it to this
number indicate that it must have often been larger than that[63]. That personnel

---

[59] Cf. B. C r o k e, *Anatolius and Nomus: Envoys to Attila*, Bsl 42, 1981, p. 165–166.

[60] Cf. R.W. M a t h i s e n, *Patricians as Diplomats in Late Antiquity*, BZ 79, 1986, p. 35–49.

[61] *Chronicon Paschale*, a. 412; *PLRE*, vol. II, p. 152, (s.v. *Arsacius 3*); *PLRE*, vol. II, p. 1149–1150, (s.v. *Varanes 1*).

[62] On that topic, cf. A.E.R. B o a k, *The Roman...*, p. 153–158; A.H.M. J o n e s, *The Lat-er...*, p. 597–599.

[63] Cf. A.E.R. B o a k, *The Roman...*, p. 147.

received salaries, privileges, and it was even exempt from any court proceedings outside of the jurisdiction of the *magister militum* himself[64]. In addition to this *officium*, Roman generals also had subordinates in the rank of *domestici*, who served as military officers or *aides-de-camp*[65]. Those functionaries were instrumental in managing all of the army matters: provisions, wages, and the martial courts. Not only did this allow the *magistri militum* to have immense control over the military, but also permitted them to create a loyal base of support within it, since all of those officials owed their superiors the status and careers they enjoyed.

The previously mentioned system of the *foedus* could also contribute to the power of the members of the military elite. Usually, it was *magistri militum* who were the intermediaries between the tribe and the emperor. This increased their influence and at times meant that a tribe developed a much closer bond with the general than with the Empire. This in turn allowed the generals to use such *foederati* as a political asset. In the East, this was most notably the case with the Thracian Goths and their relationship with Plintha and later Aspar[66].

It was also relatively common practice for powerful military commanders, who had such opportunities, to employ private retinues. Such forces were called *bucellari*[67] and they undoubtedly contributed to the status and power of those who owned them. Some powerful generals, most notably Flavius Zeno and Aspar, were known to have had large groups of loyal companions. It must have been an important asset, as emperor Leo forbade the possession of such armed bands after he had got into a conflict with Aspar[68].

The influence of the members of the military elite extended also outside of martial circles. The previously mentioned founding of public utilities certainly helped their popularity among common citizens. In one instance, Aspar was re-

---

[64] *CTh*, I, 7, 4.

[65] Cf. A.E.R. B o a k, *The Roman...*, p. 158–159.

[66] H.U. W i e m e r, *Theoderich der Große. König der Goten – Herrscher der Römer*, München 2018, p. 134; J.H.W.G. L i e b e s c h u e t z, *Barbarians...*, p. 43–47; A. U r b a n i e c, *Wpływ patrycjusza Aspara na cesarską elekcję Leona*, USS 11, 2011, p. 188–189; A. L a n i a d o, *Aspar and his Phoideratoi: John Malalas on a Special Relationship*, [in:] *Governare e riformare l'Impero al momento della sua divisione. Oriente, Occidente, Illirico*, ed. U. R o b e r t o, L. M e c e l l a, Roma 2016, p. 325–344; Ł. P i g o ń s k i, *Kilka uwag na temat kariery magistra militum Flawiusza Plinty i jego wpływów na dworze Teodozjusza II*, BP 28, 2021, p. 23–30; P. C r a w f o r d, *Roman Emperor Zeno. The Perils of Politics in Fifth-century Constantinople*, Barnsley 2019, p. 37; 43.

[67] H.J. D i e s n e r, *Die Bucellariertum von Stilicho und Sarus bis auf Aetius (454/455)*, K 54, 1972, p. 321–350; O. S c h m i t t, *Die Bucellari. Eine Studie zum militärischen Gefolgschaftwesen in der Spätantike*, Ty 9, 1994, p. 147–174; M. W i l c z y ń s k i, *Germanie...*, p. 475–482.

[68] *CJ*, IX, 12, 10. Cf. E.A. T h o m p s o n, *The Isaurians under Theodosius II*, Her 68, 1946, p. 25; J.H.W.G. L i e b e s c h u e t z, *Barbarians...*, p. 47.

corded on account of and praised for his role in mitigating the effects of the fire that ravaged Constantinople in 465[69].

Religion was another issue that was of major public interest during that time-period. The generals were at times involved in religious matters, not only in official capacity, as previously mentioned, but some happened to be personally invested. Flavius Dionysius, who was a devout Orthodox, was mentioned interfering in some Church proceedings and was reportedly deeply concerned with its unity[70]. On the other hand, generals Plintha and Aspar were influential leaders of the Arian religious minority[71]. Considering the uneasy situation of the followers of this 'heretical' creed, it would have been unsurprising if they have loyally supported their powerful protectors, thus further reinforcing the power-base of the generals. One, however, should not approach these matters cynically, as it is highly likely that both Plintha and Aspar were primarily motivated by sincere personal belief; besides, this support was a double-edged sword, as many devout orthodox Christians would probably hold it against these generals that they support the heretics.

There is also some evidence of the members of the military elite having been involved in the broader cultural life of the Eastern Roman Empire. Select generals exchanged letters with important intellectual figures of the time, as exemplified by several letters addressed to various members of the military elite by Theodoret of Cyrrhus[72].

The above overview shows that the military elite was a prominent group in late antiquity and that their involvement in the life of the Eastern Roman Empire was not limited to military service. Naturally, the examples given above do not exhaust all the ways in which generals impacted the workings of the Eastern Roman state. An exploration of the various venues through which members of the military elite amassed power and exercised their influence will constitute a major part of the narrative to follow.

[69] C a n d i d u s, fr. 1. On the fire, cf. E v a g r i u s, XII, 3.

[70] *PLRE*, vol. II, p. 365-366 (s.v. *Fl. Dionysius 13*).

[71] Aspar and his family were also known for their Church donations, cf. M. M c E v o y, *Becoming Roman? The Not-So-Curious Case of Aspar and the Ardaburii*, JLA 9, 2016, p. 496.

[72] T h e o d o r e t, *Ep.* 23; 34; 45; 65; 71.

The Military Elite during the Reign of Theodosius II

T he Eastern Roman Empire entered the fifth century facing a major political crisis which involved the military. The person at the centre of those events was a military commander of Gothic origins, Gainas[1]. It started with the revolt of the Goths in 399 in Phrygia, which grew serious due to the incompetent handling of the rebels by general Leo, who was sent to suppress it. This fact was used as a pretext by Gainas, who was the other commander sent to quell it, to dispose of the eunuch Eutropius, who was a grey eminence at the court since 395. Eutropius had enemies at the court, thus his fall came about with little issue; however, the next praefect who assumed power in Constantinople, a certain Aurelian, also had a falling out with the general and was accused of trying to limit the influence which the barbarians had in the army[2].

---

[1] For an in-depth reconstruction and analysis of the events in question, cf. G. A l b e r t, *Goten in Konstantinopel*, Wien 1984; J.H.W.G. L i e b e s c h u e t z, *Barbarians and Bishops. Army, Church, and State in the Age of Arcadius and Chrysostom*, Oxford 1991; A. C a m e r o n, J. L o n g, *Barbarians and Politics at the Court of Arcadius*, Berkeley 1993.

[2] Arnold H.M. J o n e s (*The Later Roman Empire 284–602. A Social, Economic and Administrative Survey*, vol. I–III, Oxford 1964, p. 202–203) claims that Aurelian was simply a staunch opponent of Gainas and the Goths in service of the Empire. According to J.H.W.G. L i e b e s c h u e t z (*Barbarians...*, p. 104–110) the matter was much more complicated and Gainas even co-operated with Aurelian at some point.

Gainas' next move was to join forces with the rebelling Goths and march with them at Constantinople. He managed to secure power for about six months, after which a popular revolt broke out in the city and resulted in the massacre of the Goths. Gainas escaped, but when he tried to retreat with some of his forces to Asia Minor, he was intercepted by a fleet commanded by Fravitta, who defeated the rebels. Fravitta was then appointed as *magister militum* in Gainas' stead.

The revolt of Gainas had far reaching consequences for the policy of the Eastern Roman Empire. From 401 to the end of Arcadius' reign no law was issued in the name of any *magister militum*[3]. Fravitta, seemingly for no reason, was accused of treason and executed, most likely falling victim to political paranoia, as it appears that there was a fear of any military commander gaining influence, no matter how loyal he may have been. Furthermore, as Evgeniy Glushanin points out, when Yazdigird I proclaimed himself the protector of Theodosius II's rights to the throne, the shah named only the Senate as a potential threat to the young emperor's rule, and, as the historian accurately observes, omitted mention of any military figures, which suggests that no member of the military elite wielded enough political power to be of note[4]. This was the background to Theodosius II' accession to the Eastern Roman throne.

The Regime of Anthemius

Theodosius was only seven years old when he became the sole *Augustus* of the Eastern Roman Empire[5]. Due to the emperor's young age the actual power rested in other people's hands. At first the most important man in the government was certainly the *praefectus praetorio* Anthemius. He originated from an Egyptian family which had reached the highest positions in the Empire only two generations ago, as Anthemius' great-grandfather was just a simple sausage-seller. His son Philippus, Anthemius' grandfather, made a great and quick career climbing the ranks of Imperial offices to reach the post of *praefectus praetorio* of the East[6]. Anthemius himself also showed a great administrative talent which

---

[3] Е.П. Глушанин, *Военная знать ранней Византии*, Барнаул 1991, p. 98.

[4] *Ibidem*, p. 98.

[5] He held that title since 402 alongside his father Arcadius, cf. R.C. Blockley, *The Dynasty of Theodosius*, [in:] *CAH*, vol. XIII, *The Late Empire A.D. 337–425*, ed. A. Cameron, P. Garnsey, Cambridge 1998, p. 128.

[6] A.H.M. Jones, *The Career of Flavius Philippus*, Hi 4, 1955, p. 229–233.

was reflected in his rapid advancement in hierarchy. Probably in 383 he took part in an embassy to Persia, in 400 he is known to have been the *comes sacrarum largitionum*[7]. In 404 he was already the *magister officiorum*, and from July 405 the praetorian praefect of the East[8]. He held that office for ten years, being the *de facto* ruler of the Eastern Roman Empire.

He was certainly a very gifted politician. To begin with, what probably should speak the most to our imagination, he was unequivocally praised for his rule[9], which stands in a stark contrast to the previous regime, as well as being a very rare case for a politician in general, since politics tends to be a rather contentious matter regardless of times. He seemed to bring peace among warring political factions. As Kenneth Holum remarks, there is no evidence of Anthemius' religious beliefs; however, it is most likely that he was a Christian, yet not a religious fanatic, and open to those who practiced the old Hellenic faith[10]. The popularity of his moderate rule was also helped by tax remissions[11].

The policies of Anthemius regarding the security of the Empire warrant a more in-depth look. Certainly, this was a major issue. Just after the accession of Theodosius II, the Eastern Roman Empire was in peril from two sides. Initially, general Stilicho, the executor of the will of emperor Theodosius the Great, wanted to set off to the East to re-establish himself as the guardian of a unified Empire[12]. Luckily for Anthemius' regime, Stilicho did not follow through with his plans because he was informed of dissent among the troops in Ticinum. Its cause were the false allegations spread by Olympius that the real motivations behind Stilicho's expedition were to make the his son, Euphemius, emperor in Constantinople. The situation deteriorated quickly, developing into a mutiny aimed against the general's supporters, who were slaughtered in the process. Despite the pressure from his soldiers, Stilicho did not allow them to take revenge and attack the mutineers. When he joined the emperor at Ravenna, he learned that Honorius had ordered his capture. Having found sanctuary in a church, he came out as soon as he was given a sworn promise that he would not be harmed. The emperor, however, broke his oath and ordered an immediate execution. Stilicho accepted the unjust judgement,

---

[7] A high ranking official responsible for financial matters. Cf. *ODB*, p. 486, (s.v. *Comes sacrarum largitionum*).

[8] *PLRE*, vol. II, p. 94 (s.v. *Anthemius 1*).

[9] K.G. H o l u m, *Theodosian Empresses: Women and Imperial Dominion in Late Antiquity*, Berkeley–Los Angeles–London 1982, p. 87–88.

[10] *Ibidem*, p. 86–87.

[11] *CTh*, XI, 28, 9.

[12] T. J a n β e n, *Stilicho. Das weströmische Reich vom Tode des Theodosius bis zur Ermordung Stilichos (395–408)*, Marburg 2004, p. 240; I. H u g h e s, *Stilicho. The Vandal Who Saved Rome*, Barnsley 2010, p. 203–205.

not allowing his soldiers to resist[13]. The death of the general had many far-reaching repercussions in the West, yet in the East the news of it must have been met with relief. After a period of tense relations, or even outright hostility, between both parts of the Empire, the situation finally calmed down.

This did not, however, mean the end of problems. In the same year a Hunnic leader Uldin crossed the Danube and invaded the Balkans[14]. The barbarians seized the opportunity, since most of the Eastern Roman troops were moved to the eastern frontier as the danger of Stilicho's invasion had passed. It seems that the government was aware of the danger, as an order to strengthen the fortifications in Illyricum had been issued[15]. It appears that the Romans wanted to rely on the walls of the fortified cities in the region, which were often enough to stop barbarians unskilled in the art of siege warfare. Unfortunately, Uldin managed to capture by treachery at least one of these settlements, Castra Martis in Dacia Ripensis. We do not know if other fortifications had also fallen, but it is likely that this forced the local commanders to hastily gather troops against the Hunnic menace, since a passage in the contemporary *Commentary on Isiah* by Jerome suggests that there was a battle which resulted in a defeat of the Roman army[16]. Regardless of whether the battle took place, the Roman forces were not able to deal with the invasion and attempts were made to solve the crisis diplomatically. Trying to reach any kind of agreement with Uldin himself, however, failed, and if we are to believe Sozomen, when the boastful barbarian met with the envoys, he pointed at the sun and asserted that he could conquer all the lands under it[17]. Luckily for the Romans, there was some kind of dissent among Uldin's warriors and numerous tribes defected to the emperor's side, which forced their former leader to retreat with his remaining loyal followers.

In both of the afore-mentioned situations the goddess Fortuna surely kept a vigil over Anthemius' regime, although it is almost certain that the dissent in Uldin's camp was instigated from the outside[18]. It would neither be the first nor

---

[13] T. J a n β e n, *Stilicho...*, p. 241–244; I. H u g h e s, *Stilicho...*, p. 207–209.

[14] S o z o m e n, XI, 5. On the invasion and its aftermath, cf. E.A. T h o m p s o n, *A History of Attila and the Huns*, Oxford 1948, p. 29–30; I. B ó n a, *Das Hunnenreich*, Stuttgart 1991, p. 23; T. S t i c k l e r, *Die Hunnen*, München 2007, p. 55–57; K. R o s e n, *Attila. Der Schrecken der Welt*, München 2016, p. 87–88.

[15] *CTh*, XI, 17, 4. The date of the edict has been disputed in the literature; however, I follow the interpretation of Otto Maenchen-Helfen. On that debate, cf. O. M a e n c h e n - H e l f e n, *The World of Huns. Studies in Their History and Culture*, London 1973, p. 64, n. 243.

[16] O. M a e n c h e n - H e l f e n, *The World...*, p. 64.

[17] S o z o m e n, XI, 5. Cf. P. H e a t h e r, *The Fall of the Roman Empire A New History of Rome and the Barbarians*, Oxford 2006, p. 196.

[18] Cf. E.A. T h o m p s o n, *A History...*, p. 29; T. S t i c k l e r, *Die Hunnen...*, p. 56.

the last operation by the agents of the Roman intelligence aimed against powerful barbarian leaders[19]. Unfortunately, due to the nature of those covert actions it
is impossible to tell without a doubt whether Anthemius had a hand in successfully dealing with Uldin. However, the solution of the third crisis that came up
as a result of the death of Arcadius was definitely orchestrated by Anthemius and
bears all semblance of his political excellence. As it has been mentioned before,
the transfer of troops to the east after the danger of the western invasion had
passed was dictated by the increased tensions along the Persian border. It was
of utmost importance that the Persian *Shahanshah* Yazdigird I accept the rule
of Theodosius II. The customary embassy announcing the accession of the new
emperor was dispatched to Persia and the diplomatic exchange seems to have resulted in a resounding success as Yazdigird turned out to be very receptive to Roman claims, and even announced that he would act as the executor of Arcadius'
will, guaranteeing Theodosius' rights to the throne and threatening war against
anyone who would challenge young emperor's claims[20]. To be sure, the Persian
ruler did not want the friendly Theodosian dynasty replaced. Furthermore, the
Romans reached out to Yazdigird for his assistance in settling the quarrels among
the Christians who lived in Persia. It seems that their expectations were surpassed: not only was the Persian Church permitted to hold a synod in 410, which
resulted in its self-regulation through the establishment of its own dogma, but
Isaac was also confirmed as the bishop of Ctesiphon.

All what that meant for Anthemius' regime was ensuring a lasting peace with
its most powerful neighbour and security on the eastern border. What is more,
the praefect learned a lesson from the now passed danger of an invasion from the
north and took several precautions. In the following years the crowning achievement of his reign was completed, a marvel of late antique architecture, the ring

---

[19] On the Roman intelligence gathering efforts in general, cf. M. H u m p h r i e s, *International Relations*, [in:] *The Cambridge History of Greek and Roman Warfare*, vol. II, ed. P. S a-
b i n, H. v a n W e e s, M. W h i t b y, Cambridge 2008, p. 250–253; A.D. L e e, *Information
and Frontiers: Roman Foreign Relations in Late Antiquity*, Cambridge 1997, p. 175; A. P i k u l-
s k a-R o b a s z k i e w i c z, *Funkcjonariusze służb specjalnych w późnym Cesarstwie –„agentes in
rebus”*, PK 37, 1994, p. 151.

[20] P r o c o p i u s, *History of the Wars*, I, 2.1–10; T h e o p h a n e s, AM 5900;
K.G. H o l u m, *Theodosian...*, p. 83; M. K u l i k o w s k i, *The Tragedy of Empire. From Constantine to the Destruction of Roman Italy*, Cambridge 2019, p. 172; B. D i g n a s, E. W i n t e r, *Rome
and Persia in Late Antiquity. Neighbours and Rivals*, Cambridge 2007, p. 95–97. Interestingly,
this event is not mentioned by contemporary sources. R.C. B l o c k l e y (*East Roman Foreign
Policy. Formation and Conduct from Diocletian to Anastasius*, Cairns 1992, p. 51) explains that
this is probably because shortly after the relations with Persia deteriorated, and it was not appropriate for historians to present the Persian monarch in a positive light. It was only after some time
had passed and both sides grew closer that this event could be revisited.

of fortifications protecting the city[21]. One cannot understate the importance of this project, especially if we consider that the so-called Theodosian Walls rendered Constantinople virtually unconquerable for the next eight hundred years. Further-more, Anthemius ordered the repair of walls of the towns in Thrace and called for the strengthening and renovation of the patrol craft fleet on the Danube in 412[22].

Undoubtedly, all these efforts were meant to prevent any further danger of an invasion from the north[23]. However, Kenneth G. Holum remarks that another possible consideration at play was to protect the government in Constantino-ple from the political ambitions of the military commanders and their using the field army as leverage[24]. This had already happened once during the revolt of Ga-inas, just several years ago in 400, so the memory was still fresh among the ruling civilian elite of the city. The scholar then goes on to point out that Anthemius' 'wall defended a new system of government, in which politicians could control a weak emperor in full security'[25]. Therefore, according to him, Anthemius so-ught to continue the policies of the previous regime in regard to dealing with the military elite, and even further limiting their influence.

On the other hand, Evgeniy Glushanin argues that Anthemius' policy was one of reconciliation[26]. Contrary to Eutropius[27], he did not try to concentrate central military offices in his own hands. Thanks to *Chronicon Paschale* we know of two *magistri militum praesentales* in the year 409[28], Varanes and Arsacius, both of an eastern, possibly Persian or Armenian, origin[29]. Anthemius also seems to

---

[21] *CTh*, XV, 1, 51; K.G. H o l u m, *Theodosian...*, p. 89; E.A. T h o m p s o n, *A History...*, p. 30.

[22] *CTh*, VII, 17, 1. While the law itself bears only the names of the emperor and *magister militum* Constans, it is unlikely that the eleven-year-old Theodosius would make the decision by himself. Therefore, it is reasonable to attribute it to Anthemius. cf. R.C. B l o c k l e y, *The Dynasty...*, p. 129; W. T r e a d g o l d, *A History of Byzantine State and Society*, Stanford 1997, p. 89.

[23] According to Peter H e a t h e r (*The Fall...*, p. 202–205) this was when the Huns moved to Pannonia.

[24] K.G. H o l u m, *Theodosian...*, p. 89.

[25] *Ibidem*, p. 89.

[26] Е.П. Г л у ш а н и н, *Военная...*, p. 99–100.

[27] Apart from the previously mentioned engagement of Eutropius in the Gainas' affair, the eunuch is also known to have lead a campaign himself. On that topic see: G. A l b e r t, *Stilicho und der Hunnenfeldzug des Eutropius*, Chi 9, 1979, p. 621–645.

[28] *Chronicon Paschale*, a. 412. The date in the chronicle is wrong; however, the correct dat-ing can be established thanks to the mention of the praefecture of Monaxius, which can be firmly placed in 409, as there is a law (*CTh*, XIV, 16, 1) addressed to him from that year. In addition, the same events are mentioned by M a r c e l l i n u s   C o m e s (a. 409) under the year 409. Cf. *PLRE*, vol. II, p. 764–765, (s.v. *Fl. Monaxius*).

[29] *PLRE*, vol. II, p. 152 (s.v. *Arsacius 3*); *PLRE*, vol. II, p. 1149–1150 (s.v. *Varanes 1*); A. D e m a n d t, *Magister militum*, [in:] *RE*, t. XII suppl., 1970, p. 745.

have expanded the authority of the regional masters of arms. As a matter of fact, the praefect created a new office of *magister militum per Thracias*, which was tasked with the afore-mentioned strengthening of the northern border. This seems to have been a contentious decision, opposed by the *duces* of Moesia and Scythia. Evgeniy Glushanin points out that the recent incursions by the Huns and the problems within the central government in Constantinople allowed them to enjoy a high degree of independence. The law concerning the reinforcement of the Danube mentions a threat to fine these officials if they disrupt the tasks of the *magister militum*; another one from 413 equates subordinates of regional masters of soldiers and the *duces*.

Despite undeniable evidence of strengthening the authority of regional *magistri militum* and the defensive system of the Empire, Holum's remarks should not be completely discounted. Certain actions and political motives of the praefect are open to question. It is possible that he decided to deal with external problems by employing diplomacy, and if that failed, subterfuge, simply due to the weakness of the military at the time. However, the fact that Anthemius decided on such a course of action was perhaps caused by his being hesitant to resort to the use of military force. It is likely that his political programme was affected by the looming shadow of Gainas' revolt and he preferred to deal with external problems by peaceful means.

Furthermore, relying on the regional masters of arms and diminishing the independence of the *duces*, Anthemius kept a closer watch on the Empire's frontier, effectively retaining more control over the military in his hands. During that time no powerful military figures are attested by the sources and only two *magistri militum in praesentis* are known, Varanes and Arsacius. They are both mentioned in relation to the Constantinopolitan bread riots of 409, where their successful intervention appeased the mob and resolved the crisis[30], for which it appears one of them, Varanes, received the consulate for the next year. After that they disappear from the sources, so it seems unlikely that any of them achieved a lasting position of importance. Therefore, there is no reason to think that Anthemius supported the military elite or even allowed it to exert any influence at the court.

He did, however, see the errors of the previous regime and the dangers which the course of action undertaken by it had caused, and understood that the Empire needed strong military force led by competent commanders in the coming turbulent times. It does not seem as though he enjoyed that prospect; more likely, he considered it a necessary evil. The chief fact was therefore that

---

[30] *Chronicon Paschale*, a. 412; *PLRE*, vol. II, p. 152 (s.v. *Arsacius 3*); *PLRE*, vol. II, p. 1149–1150 (s.v. *Varanes 1*).

the civil magistrates (and of course, by extension, Anthemius himself) possessed far more power and influence than any military figure could attain. Ultimately, it was about control over the government and Anthemius' priorities were not to allow any external or internal force to threaten the system.

The Fall of Anthemius and the New Regime of Pulcheria

Anthemius is last attested in his office in April 414[31]. This may be due to his death shortly afterwards; however, what is also within the realm of possibility is his downfall due to opposition within the court. The family of Anthemius acquired quite a lot of power, seeing as his son, Isidorus, became the praefect of Constantinople in 410. Kenneth Holum even claims that Anthemius' marrying his daughter to general Procopius[32], who apparently claimed the lineage of Constantine himself[33], revealed an ambition of reaching for the throne[34]. Whether it was true is difficult to say, however, it is very likely that this was how the aristocratic elite of the city perceived the actions of the praefect. The turning point, however, was the conflict which arose between him and the fourteen-year-old sister of Theodosius, Pulcheria[35]. As the young woman was reaching the age fit for marriage, finding a suitable husband was of utmost importance. Anthemius most likely had his own candidate in mind, his grandson Theophilus. This design was probably supported by the *cubicularius* Antiochus[36].

Pulcheria however would not agree to any of this. On the one hand she certainly enjoyed her independence and did not want her future to be dictated to her; on the other hand, she probably saw the danger which a further expansion of Anthemius' influence would pose to her brother. Just before her fifteenth birthday she proclaimed that she was devoting her virginity to God. Undoubtedly, it was a political move, the only one which could counter the plans of the all-powerful praefect. Sozomen clearly states that her decision was made to prevent other men from entering the palace and engaging in intrigues[37]. That move obviously forced Anthemius and Antiochus to abandon all their plans to have Pulcheria

---

[31] *CTh*, IX, 40, 22.

[32] Sidonius, *Carmina*, II, 94.

[33] Sidonius, *Carmina*, II, 68–69.

[34] K. Holum, *Theodosian...*, p. 95.

[35] The description of the events follows the interpretation of Kenneth Holum.

[36] *PLRE*, vol. II, p. 101–102 (s.v. *Antiochus 5*).

[37] Sozomen, IX, 1.3–4.

married. Furthermore, Antiochus was soon replaced and Isidorus lost his praefecture of the city. These events were not coincidental, and they clearly show how the power of Anthemius and his supporters slowly slipped from their hands.

Pulcheria might have been helped in her endeavours by some faction opposing the praefect, however, the ambition and capabilities of the young woman should not be underestimated. She took control of the government under the guise of asserting her brother's will[38]. In the place of Anthemius she designated an elderly associate of her mother, Aurelian[39]. On 4 July 414 Pulcheria was proclaimed *Augusta*, officially establishing her political authority[40]. She also had immense influence over her brother, which was not limited to educating him in religious matters and courtly behaviour.

Kenneth Holum mentions that Pulcheria's regime seems to have brought about a change in the policy of military nominations, returning to the practices of her grandfather, Theodosius I, who employed barbarian commanders and allowed them to gain significant political influence[41]. Similarly, Ronald A. Bleeker also assumes Pulcheria's involvement in appointing of military commanders during that time[42].

Notably, there is an apparent increase in the appearances of military commanders in the sources, which may be an indirect proof of their growing influence. Additionally, there is direct evidence in a specific source, as Sozomen mentions that general Plintha possessed great influence at the court[43]. The historian reports that in relation to the commander's involvement in religious matters, as he apparently was the one responsible for ending a thirty-five-year-long schism among the Arians. It is certainly a proof of his status, at least among his fellow believers.

Furthermore, as Doug Lee points out, the generals were actively using their influence to aid the careers of their family members[44]. Plintha was able to secure

---

[38] The sources clearly mention her personal involvement, cf. S o z o m e n, IX, 1.5–7; P h i l o s t o r g i u s, XII, 7. Furthermore, all evidence points to her being very able despite her young age, cf. A. C a m e r o n, J. L o n g, *Barbarians...*, p. 399–402.

[39] Once, in May of 414, another praefect is attested, a certain Monaxius, however, his tenure was ephemeral. Perhaps he did not agree with Pulcheria, so she had him removed in favour of a more amenable candidate. Cf. A. C a m e r o n, J. L o n g, *Barbarians...*, p. 400–402.

[40] *Chronicon Paschale*, a. 414; M a r c e l l i n u s C o m e s, a. 414.

[41] K. H o l u m, *Theodosian...*, p. 101–102.

[42] R.A. B l e e k e r, *Aspar and the Struggle for the Eastern Roman Empire, AD 421–71*, London 2022, p. 35–36.

[43] S o z o m e n VII, 17.14.

[44] A.D. L e e, *Theodosius and his Generals*, [in:] *Theodosius II. Rethinking the Roman Empire in Late Antiquity*, ed. Ch. K e l l y, Cambridge 2013, p. 101.

a commanding position for his son Armatius; similarly, it was the case for Ardaburious and his son Aspar. This phenomenon, however, was not limited to the
barbarian families, as general Procopius likely managed to do the same thing for
his son Anthemius.

A look at the legal sources, however, offers a different perspective. The law
of 415[45] addressed to the master of soldiers Florentius deals with the problem of
the issuing of commissions to the officials in command of the frontier forces[46].
This was traditionally in the area of the competence of the *magister officiorum*,
and the law stated that forty of those offices should be reassigned back to the master of offices. According to Evgeniy Glushanin, it was part of a concerted effort
to reassert government control over commissions of the middle command staff,
and, in turn, it reduced the practical influence of the military elite[47]. However,
Doug Lee claims that the afore-mentioned law should be seen in a different light.
As he points out, it did not reverse the existing situation but rather constituted
a compromise, reassigning only a portion of the commissions[48]. According to
him, this is a proof of the generals' influence, since they were able to encroach on
areas of competence traditionally belonging to other officials, and possibly, gain
all the benefits, funds, and political patronage that attached to them. However,
unless it can be pin-pointed when this began to happen, it is unwarranted to
make such claims regarding the political influence of the military elite in the
early reign of Theodosius II. If anything, the source material demonstrates that
the political capital of the generals was weak enough for the civil magistrates to
regain their long-lost authority.

This is further proved by another set of laws from the year 424 which followed through with the previous constitution, assigning all the posts to the master
of offices' sphere of competence[49]. It is therefore certain that the civilian officials
attempted to reduce the generals' influence over administrative matters.

There are several other arguments for the political weakness of the military
elite in the early reign of Theodosius. As Glushanin notes, it seems that the *magistri militum* were consistently kept in office for up to five years and rotated out
as their term was over[50]. Maintaining the temporary nature of the office therefore
prevented the commanders from building up political capital.

---

[45] *CTh*, I, 8, 1.

[46] The *laterculus minus* (lesser register), which included tribunes, praefects, and other minor military officers.

[47] Е.П. Глушанин, *Военная...*, p. 101.

[48] A.D. Lee, *Theodosius...*, p. 94–95.

[49] *CTh*, I, 8, 2–3. Interestingly, Doug Lee mentions these laws, but does not comment on
them, cf. A.D. Lee, *Theodosius...*, p. 95, n. 25.

[50] Е.П. Глушанин, *Военная...*, p. 102.

Moreover, the claims of Pulcheria's involvement in the military developments are based on very flimsy evidence. Even if the emperor's sister was an influential and politically savvy figure, it does not follow that she was personally
invested in developing the careers of certain military commanders, it is just as
much, if not more likely, that there was nothing extraordinary about the careers
of the generals during that time[51].

The sudden emergence of a new military elite can be explained differently, as
it seems to coincide with the new conflicts which followed the relatively peaceful
times. Firstly, it brought attention of the sources to the generals, who naturally
played important role in those events. This can sufficiently explain their 'sudden'
appearance in the pages of history. Bearing that in mind, nothing indicates that
any of them were somehow artificially elevated, with support from Pulcheria or
anyone else, or that their careers were not normally developing for years before
that point. In addition to that, the conflicts also helped the careers of many military commanders, as success in war allowed them to gain prominence. An example that illustrates this phenomenon is that of Plintha, who, in the rank of *comes*,
was responsible for suppressing the rebellion in Palestine in 418. For the successful resolution of the conflict he was awarded a consulate for the next year, along
with the title of *magister militum praesentalis*. Evgeniy Glushanin states outright
that the political significance of the military elite was directly correlated with
the situation on the international scene, namely whether the Empire needed to
project its force, and, in turn, required competent generals to lead its armies[52].

The War with Persia

The most important event was however the war with Persia that broke out
in 421. The relations between both countries had been deteriorating for several
years, mainly because of the religious unrest in Persia which involved conflicts
between Christians and Zoroastrians, as well as the hard-line policy against heretics and heathens (which included fire-worshippers) which was adopted in
the Roman Empire with the advent of Pulcheria's regime. For as long as the ruler of Persia was the moderate Yazdigird I, the tensions never escalated to the
point of war; however, he died in 420, possibly in an assassination ordered by

---

[51] Contrary to what Ronald A. B l e e k e r (*Aspar...*, p. 35) claims, it may just as well be that
the rise through the ranks of the generals like Ardaburious under Pulcheria's regime was, in fact,
a coincidence.

[52] Е.П. Г л у ш а н и н, *Военная...*, p. 105–106.

conspiring Persian nobles, with one of the plausible motivations being Yazdigird's failure to address the religious unrest and growing opposition among
the worshippers of Zoroastrianism. His successor, Bahram V, began to openly
persecute Christians, who in turn started fleeing and seeking asylum in the
Roman Empire. Since the Romans allowed them to seek refuge inside their
borders and refused to comply with Persian demands for their return, Bahram
responded by mistreating Roman hired workers and tolerating the plundering
of Roman merchants[53].

The Roman response to that was war. Their forces seem to have been well
prepared for conflict and in the beginning they achieved numerous successes.
The war obviously presented a chance for military figures to rise to prominence,
so a more in-depth look is warranted.

The command structure of the Roman forces is, however, somewhat unclear. There were several commanders who were involved in the fighting: the Alan
Ardaburious; the already mentioned Procopius, a Roman of aristocratic lineage;
possibly Anatolius; a certain Vitianus, otherwise unknown; and the Goth Areobindus. Out of these, only the rank held by Areobindus during the conflict is
known without a doubt, and it was *comes foederatorum*.

To begin with, many complications arise because in 420 the commander of
the eastern forces, Maximinus, was killed by his soldiers in a mutiny[54]. Unfortunately, we do not know what exactly the practice was in such cases, especially
since the tensions on the eastern frontier were already increasing and the war
was on the horizon.

Therefore, it is unclear who, if anyone, served as *magister militum per
Orientem* in the war. As far as sources go, John Malalas claims that Procopius,
who by then had borne the title of *patricius*, was appointed the commander
of the east and sent with expeditionary forces against the Persians[55]. He does
not mention, however, the successful campaign by Ardaburious at all and only
writes of Areobindus out of the commanders involved in the conflict. These te-
stimonies stand in contrast with another source, the panegyric on the emperor
Anthemius by Sidonius Apollinaris, the author of which claims that Procopius,
the emperor's father, was rewarded with the office for his achievements in the
war, along with the title of patrician. Even though he is a Western source, Sidonius was notoriously well informed, and, considering the official status of his

---

[53] R.C. B l o c k l e y, *East Roman...*, p. 56–57.

[54] M a r c e l l i n u s   C o m e s, a. 420. It cannot be stated with certainty that Maximinus
held the Eastern *magisterium*, cf. A. D e m a n d t, *Magister...*, p. 740.

[55] M a l a l a s, XIV, 23: βασιλεὺς Ρωμαίων ἐποίησεν στρατηλάτην ἀνατολῆς τὸν πατρίκιον
Προκόπιον καὶ ἐπεμψεν αυτον μετὰ εξπεδίτου πολεμῆσαι.

work (panegyrics were recited in front of the emperor and the court, so any glaring mistakes would be easily spotted), this piece of information should not be disregarded. Alexander Demandt proposes a rather straightforward explanation of the discrepancy in the sources and claims that Procopius was appointed *magister militum per Orientem* before the war and rewarded with the patriciate afterwards[56]. According to John Martindale, Procopius was still either a *comes* or *dux* during the war, however, his achievements gained him both the *magisterium* and the title of *patricius*[57], and the historian posits that the commander of the east over the course of the war was Ardaburious[58]. Evgeniy Glushanin generally agrees with Demandt's claims; however, he disagrees on who was the commander-in-chief of the Roman forces involved in the fighting[59]. He assumes it was Procopius, while according to Demandt this general was either commanding only part of the forces alongside Ardaburious or even was his subordinate, as the German scholar claims that the Alan commander occupied the post of *magister militum praesentalis*. In Glushanin's view, on the other hand, Ardaburious was likely still a *comes rei militaris* during the war.

Another contentious matter is the case of Anatolius. It is even debatable whether he took part in the war at all. Kenneth Holum has arrived at the conclusion that it was Anatolius who held the eastern command and there are certain researchers, such as Brian Croke or Roger Blockley, who follow his interpretation[60]. The primary source for that is the passage on the war with Bahram in the *History of the Wars* by Procopius[61], where the historian specifically mentions his rank. Furthermore, there are other sources that seem to confirm the general's involvement in the conflict[62]. Holum also takes into consideration the possibility that the Anatolius involved in this war was an otherwise unknown relative (likely the father) of the *magister militum per Orientem*, who was appointed to the office in 433[63]. Glushanin and Demandt do not mention Anatolius in the context of the war of 421–422, and the latter attributes the passage in Procopius to a later conflict in the forties[64].

---

[56] A. D e m a n d t, *Magister...*, p. 741.

[57] *PLRE*, vol. II, p. 920 (s.v. *Procopius 2*).

[58] *PLRE*, vol. II, p. 137 (s.v. *Ardabur 3*).

[59] Е.П. Г л у ш а н и н, *Военная...*, p. 104.

[60] K.G. H o l u m, *Pulcheria's Crusade A.D. 421–22 and the Ideology of Imperial Victory*, GRBS 18, 1977, p. 156; 167–169; B. C r o k e, *Dating Theodoret's Church History and Commentary on the Psalms*, B 54, 1989, p. 70, n. 45; R.C. B l o c k l e y, *East Roman...*, p. 200, n. 31.

[61] P r o c o p i u s, *History of the Wars*, I, 2.

[62] T h e o p h a n e s, AM 5921; C y r i l o f S k y t h o p o l i s, *Life of Euthymius*, 10.

[63] K.G. H o l u m, *Theodosian...*, p. 101, n. 102.

[64] A. D e m a n d t, *Magister...*, p. 742. Cf. also B. D i g n a s, E. W i n t e r, *Rome...*, p. 136.

Fortunately, the case of Vitianus is much simpler, as it is very unlikely that he could have held any *magisterium*; instead, he might have been either a *dux* or *comes rei militaris*. John Martindale remarks that the nature of his independent military actions seems to point to the latter[65].

A look at the course of the war may however clarify certain unknowns. The most comprehensive account was relayed by Socrates Scholasticus, according to whom the forces of Ardaburious were the first to be involved in the fighting. The general marched through Armenia and invaded the province Arzanene in which he encountered a Persian army commanded by Narses. In the following battle the Persians were soundly defeated, which allowed the Romans to press on into Mesopotamia, towards the fortress of Nisibis. Upon learning of the failures of his armies, the shah decided to call upon his Arabic allies. According to Socrates, a great army was assembled; however, thanks to Divine Providence, the Arabs were overcome with fear and a great number of them drowned in the Euphrates during their flight. What happened exactly is unknown, however, the drowning of a hundred thousand Arab auxiliaries is rather unlikely to say the least, especially because the news of the reinforcements was enough to force the Romans to abandon the siege of Nisibis and withdraw. However, the following Persian counter-attack failed, since the Persians were not able to conquer the fortress of Theodosiopolis-Resaina[66]. Afterwards, both sides seem to have been looking for a resolution to the conflict. For that reason, Helion, the *magister officiorum* himself was sent by the emperor to sign a peace treaty. The peace talks were conducted by Helion's intermediary, an assessor of Ardaburious, Maximinus. King Bahram, convinced by some of his generals, decided to look for one last opportunity. He held Maximinus captive and launched a surprise attack upon the Roman forces, splitting his own army and attempting to encircle them. Luckily, the arrival of Procopius' detachment resulted in the flanking Persian unit's being spotted and attacked from the rear, which resulted in a defeat for the shah.

One of the most vivid elements of this campaign is how well prepared and quick to act the Romans were at the beginning of the war. Thus, whatever the rank of Ardaburious may have been, he was present in the east and in command of a ready fighting force on the eve of the war. The supposition that was the *magister militum praesentalis* in command of the forces which were sent from the capital to the war is very unlikely, considering how quickly he was able to seize the initiative. The march of the praesental army across the whole Anatolia would undoubtedly cost precious time which would have made the rapid advance into

---

[65] *PLRE*, vol. II, p. 1178 (s.v. *Vitianus*); Alexander D e m a n d t (*Magister...*, p. 753) claims he might have been *magister militum vacans*.

[66] T h e o d o r e t, *HE*, V, 37.

the Persian territory improbable[67]. Such forces eventually did arrive and there are two accounts that point to at least one praesental army being involved in the fighting: John Malalas mentions some expeditionary forces, while Theophanes tells a story from the early life of the future emperor Marcian about how he marched to war with Persia through Anatolia; then also the successful Hunnic invasion of Thrace in 422 was very likely enabled by the Romans' pulling out too many forces from the Danube frontier for the war with Persia. Those forces therefore arrived at a later date; possibly even as a response to Bahram's gathering the enormous army and marching against the Roman lands. Therefore, considering the urgency of the situation in 420–421, it is very likely that the command of the Roman armies of the east was decided *ad hoc*, and, as a temporary measure, Ardaburious was appointed *magister militum*. It is conceivable that he received the eastern office, but it is equally, if not more, likely that he was granted the title of *magister militum vacans*. Such a course of action would allow the Roman government to avoid making hasty decisions about military nominations, while not compromising the war effort at the same time. It is most probable that Ardaburious was chosen for the task because he was present at the site, perhaps in the rank of *comes rei militaris*, and as a former subordinate of the murdered Maximinus. He was probably tasked with reorganization of the army of the east, and after the war had broken out, he effectively served as the commander-in-chief of the Roman forces. Ardaburious almost certainly stayed at the front till the very end of the war, considering that his own subordinate was conducting the peace negotiations[68].

Procopius was likely not involved in fighting from the very beginning, since the account of John Malalas clearly mentions Procopius at the head of the expeditionary forces[69]. He must have, therefore, arrived later at the head of the praesental army. His exact rank is thus unclear. Seemingly, it would have made the most sense if he were *magister militum praesentalis*, however, it seems unlikely. It is known for a fact that Procopius held the rank of *magister militum per Orientem* after the war had ended, so it would have been improbable for him essentially to become demoted despite his commendable conduct during the conflict. It is also quite doubtful for him to have been just a *comes* and to have led the whole

---

[67] A victory over the Persians was announced in Constantinople on 6 September 421 (cf. *Chronicon Paschale*, a. 421), which most likely refers to Ardaburious' success in Arzanene against Narses. Cf. K.G. H o l u m, *Pulcheria's...*, p. 168. This would mean that it took between the beginning of the war and 6 September for the forces of Ardaburious to set out and march through Armenia, plunder Arzanene and destroy the Persian army, and the information to travel back and reach Constantinople.

[68] S o c r a t e s, VII, 20; *PLRE*, vol. II, p. 741 (s.v. *Maximinus 3*).

[69] M a l a l a s, XIV, 23.

praesental army, so it leaves two possibilities. Since Procopius was sent in a later phase of the war, most likely when the news of Bahram's assembling his large army and the Romans' abandoning the siege of Nisibis arrived in Constantinople, it is possible that the decision to appoint Procopius as the commander of the east had already been made. While it was uncommon for the *magister militum per Orientem* to lead a praesental army, an exception could have been made since the forces of the east were already engaged in combat against the Persians. The other equally likely possibility is that Procopius was also sent as *magister militum vacans*. This interpretation seems to accommodate the differing sources best, since it would mean that he could have both held a high rank during the war and been awarded the *magisterium* of the east alongside the title of *patricius* upon its conclusion, exactly as Sidonius reports.

It should be recognized that Anatolius was also involved in the war with Persia. His efforts to fortify Karin-Theodosiopolis[70] and diplomatic activity are proved by numerous sources[71]. It is also possible that he was present during the negotiations with Bahram which eventually settled the peace, as Procopius claims, albeit it is very unlikely that his role was so pronounced and heroic[72]. There is however no need to assume that Anatolius held a rank of *magister militum*. Firstly, it would be very unlikely for a commander to receive an appointment to territorial command for a duration of one year, and then being replaced by another person. While Anatolius' achievements during the war probably fade in comparison with the exploits of Ardaburious or Procopius, we know nothing of any signs of incompetence, insubordination, or anything that would justify him being demoted. Neither is it the case of him abandoning the military service, since Anatolius' career would flourish later[73]. Thus, Anatolius being *magister militum per Orientem* during the war is highly doubtful. It is more probable that he also received command free of territorial boundaries as *magister militum vacans*, but this would also mean that he held the highest military offices for more than thirty years, which was not unheard of, but very unusual nonetheless. It should be therefore taken into consideration that Anatolius might simply have held a lower rank at the time of the war, possibly that of *comes rei militaris*. Nothing is known of his military exploits; it appears that his activity was primarily diplomatic in nature. That seems to further strengthen the

---

[70] Moses of Khoren, III, 59.

[71] Procopius, *History of the Wars*, I, 2; Theophanes, AM 5921; Moses of Khoren, III, 57; Cyril of Skythopolis, *Life of Euthymius*, 10.

[72] It is very likely that Procopius merged the events of 422: the name of the Persian shah, Bahram V, and the clauses of the treaty, and 441: the fact that Anatolius led the negotiations, first making truce with the Persians and then signing a binding treaty.

[73] Unless the commander Anatolius known from 30s and 40s and the one who took part in the Persian war of 421 were different people, which Kenneth Holum takes as a possibility.

hypothesis that he was a subordinate commander, serving as an envoy, likely being placed in such a capacity in the east even before the war[74].

The situation of the Roman forces in the east was quite complicated on the brink of the war. We do not know the exact course of the events, but a mutiny of soldiers and the resulting murder of the eastern commander must have been considered a major danger to the security of the eastern border, when the war with Persia seemed inevitable. It appears very likely that the Roman government was forced to improvise the military nominations for the war, resorting to appointing commanders Ardaburious and Procopius as *magistri militum vacantes* for the duration of the campaign, to avoid making a decision with long-lasting consequences in a hurry.

The numerous successes and victories in the field of both masters of arms probably even surpassed the expectations of the government and propelled their and other distinguished commanders' careers. Ardaburious became *magister militum praesentalis*, Procopius became *magister militum per Orientem* and received the title of *patricius*, Areobindus was rewarded with the consulate.

Thus, the war with Persia laid the groundwork for a certain measure of continuity. In the preceding period, the masters of arms seemed to serve their term and then to be rotated out of their offices, and there is no evidence of their returning to their posts or receiving promotions to different positions of command. From now on, the same names would continue to appear repeatedly over the course of the following decades.

The Campaign against the Usurper John

Shortly after the war with Persia had been concluded, the Empire faced another crisis. In the West, after death of Honorius, a certain John[75] proclaimed himself emperor. Theodosius did not accept that, likely because he

---

[74] He negotiated a treaty with a certain Aspebetus, an Arab chieftain who fled the persecution under Yazdigird II. Cf. C y r i l o f S k y t h o p o l i s, *Life of Euthymius*, 10; I. S h a h i d, *Byzantium and the Arabs in the Fifth Century*, Dumbarton Oaks 2006, p. 40–49.

[75] Cf. *PLRE*, vol. II, p. 594–595 (s.v. *Ioannes 6*). For more information on John and the subsequent power struggle between generals Flavius Felix, Bonifatius, and Aetius, which led to the latter establishing his dominant position, cf. P. H e a t h e r, *The Fall...*, p. 258–262; T. S t i c k l e r, *Aetius. Gestaltungsspielraume eines Heermeisters im ausgehenden Westromischen Reich*, Munchen 2002, p. 25–58; R. M a t h i s e n, *Sigisvult the Patrician, Maximinus the Arian, and political strategems in the Western Roman Empire c. 425–40*, EME 8, 1999, p. 173–196; J. W i j n e n d a l e, *The early career of Aëthius and the murder of Felix (c. 425–430 CE)*, Hi 66, 2017, p. 468–482; M. P a w l a k, *Walka o władzę w Rzymie w latach 425–435*, Toruń 2004.

considered the members of the Theodosian dynasty to be the only rightful heirs to the Roman throne[76].

He dispatched an army to take down the usurper led by Ardaburious, freshly appointed as *magister militum praesentalis*. Accompanying him were the general's son, Aspar, and Flavius Candidianus. It is possible that they both had the rank of *magister militum vacans*[77], but it is also possible that Aspar, who must have been quite young at that point, was a junior officer[78]. According to the sources, he led the cavalry. The expedition reached the city of Salona in Dalmatia where the forces were split into two detachments. Ardaburious embarked with some of his troops to cross the Adriatic, while Candidianus and Aspar proceeded on land through Dalmatia. Unfortunately, the expedition was put in jeopardy because the forces of Ardaburious were caught in a sudden storm, which swept his ships ashore, resulting in the capture of the general himself. The usurper treated the general well and did not keep him in confinement, as he wished to sue for peace. This, however, proved to be a mistake, since Ardaburious made use of his freedom to plot against John and sway some of his officers to his own side. In the meantime, the remaining forces of the expedition under Candidianus and Aspar pushed into the Italian Peninsula, capturing the important fortress of Aquileia on their way. Their exploits seem to have helped Ardaburious in his efforts, since soon after usurper John was betrayed and murdered in Ravenna, which allowed the Eastern Roman forces to enter the city. Afterwards, Helion was dispatched to Rome to oversee the enthronement of Valentinian. Even though the campaign seemed to have been concluded successfully, just before his downfall, John sent out a supporter of his, a young general Aetius, to gather an army from the friendly Hunnic tribes[79]. He arrived in Italy too late to affect the course of the war, but soon enough to create a problem for the newly established government. What followed is disputable. According to Philostorgius, the Hunnic army led by Aetius was met on the field of battle by Aspar and his forces. In the encounter that ensued, neither side was able to gain the upper hand and both suffered great casualties. For Aetius it was, however, pointless to pursue further conflict, and thus he made a deal with Placidia to secure his standing after the change of regi-

---

[76] T. S t i c k l e r, *Aetius*..., p. 30–31; M. P a w l a k, *Walka*..., p. 82–83.

[77] Е.П. Г л у ш а н и н, *Военная*..., p. 105.

[78] Possibly a *vicarius magistri militum*, cf. A. D e m a n d t, *Magister*..., p. 748.

[79] T. S t i c k l e r, *Aetius*..., p. 32–35. In his youth, Aetius was sent as a hostage to the Hunnic court. Cf. G r e g o r y o f T o u r s, II, 8; M e r o b a u d e s, *Carmina*, IV, 42–46; M e r o- b a u d e s, *Panegyrici*, II, 1–4; 127–143; Z o s i m u s, V, 36.1; T. S t i c k l e r, *Aetius*..., p. 23–25; 87–88; I. B ó n a, *Das Hunnenreich*..., p. 20. The army he gathered was reportedly 60,000 strong, cf. P h i l o s t o r g i u s, XII, 7. However, it is likely this number is inflated, cf. J. W i j n e n d a l e, *The early career*..., p. 471, n. 23.

me. The Hunnic warriors were paid off to return to their lands[80]. Interestingly, Olympiodorus, the other source, informs of no such incidents.

It is not the only discrepancy between the two sources. Philostorgius mentions Aspar's efforts as fundamental to the success of the campaign: the capture of Aquileia, reaching Ravenna, and facing off against Aetius, while the fragments of Olympiodorus claim it was Candidianus' capturing of cities which contributed to the outcome, while Aspar succumbed to despair after his father had been captured[81]. There is a possible explanation to some of these differences. The fragments from Olympiodorus are less detailed than the account of Philostorgius, although such an important event as the battle between Aetius' Huns and the Eastern Roman expeditionary forces undoubtedly would not have been omitted. The editors of Philostorgius came up with a probable explanation in that the historian might have confused certain accounts critical of Theodosius II's Hunnic policy and made up a course of events which seemed plausible to him[82]. Thus, it is much more likely that there was no battle, but instead Aetius used the Hunnic mercenaries at his disposal as leverage in his deal with Placidia, and afterwards the Huns were paid off to return home. It is possible that such events were not considered relevant enough for Olympiodorus or, what is more likely, the compiler of the fragments.

Even though the climactic show-down between the two future *generalissimi* most likely did not occur, the campaign against the usurper John, despite all its set-backs, was another success of the Eastern Roman military. Taking all of the sources into account, it seems that both Candidianus and Aspar distinguished themselves in the campaign. Ardaburious, despite the accident that could have led to the failure of the whole mission, was also reported to have accomplished much when plotting against the usurper while in his captivity. Overall, all of the goals set out for the expedition were met successfully.

It is not known whether Candidianus got rewarded for his service in Italy[83], however, he remained an influential political figure which is exemplified by his being chosen to serve as emperor's representative at the Council of Ephesus in 431[84]. Ardaburious, as he was leaving his post in 427, received a consulate, undoubtedly in recognition of his service. Aspar's exploits seem to have been noticed, considering how quickly his career developed over the following years.

---

[80] On the campaign, cf. R.A. B l e e k e r, *Aspar...*, p. 44–47.

[81] O l y m p i o d o r u s, fr. 43.

[82] P h i l o s t o r g i o s, *Kirchengeschichte*, ed. B. B l e c k m a n n, M. S t e i n, Bd. II, Paderborn 2015, p. 617.

[83] Which lends more credibility to the reasoning that not only his, but also Aspar's exploits contributed to the success of the campaign.

[84] A. D e m a n d t, *Magister...*, p. 748.

After 427 there is no more mention of Ardaburious in the sources. Evgeniy Glushanin argues that this must mean that he somehow lost his influence[85]. There is, however, a more mundane explanation which also seems more likely, and it is that at some point soon after 427 Ardaburious died. Especially since the person who received the *magisterium* after him was his own son, Aspar.

The First Vandal Expedition

In 428 yet another crisis arose in the West. A Germanic tribe of the Asdingi Vandals, joined by the remnants of their Sillingi brothers and allied Alan tribes, crossed the straits of Gibraltar from the Iberian Peninsula and proceeded towards the rich Roman province of Africa. The forces of the African *comes* Bonifatius were insufficient to deal with the threat. In 430 the barbarians besieged Hippo Regius, the second most important city in Africa. In the battle which ensued outside the city walls the Roman forces were defeated. The city managed to hold out for fourteen months and only after the inhabitants were allowed to leave did the Vandals capture it. Nevertheless, the situation in the province was critical[86].

The perspective of losing Africa would have dire consequences to the Roman Empire, especially its Western part. The province provided a steady supply of grain, much needed by the Italian cities. Furthermore, it used to be relatively rich and easy to defend, contributing much to the Imperial budget, while not requiring a lot of expenses to secure the flow of revenue. With the coming of the Vandals, it would all change[87]. It seems that Theodosius II was aware of these consequences. In his policies, he considered himself responsible for both parts of the Empire. Therefore, when the local forces proved insufficient, Theodosius decided to intervene. Organizing such an expedition was a complicated and time-consuming process, not to mention the need to wait for good sailing conditions, so the help could not have been sent immediately.

---

[85] Е.П. Глушанин, *Военная...*, p. 106.

[86] On the Vandal capture of Africa, cf. Ch. Curtois, *Les Vandales et l'Afrique*, Paris 1955, p. 155–164; P. Heather, *The Fall...*, p. 268–272; H. Castritius, *Die Vandalen. Etappen einer Spurensuche*, Berlin 2006, p. 76–90; R. Steinacher, *Die Vandalen. Aufstieg und Fall eines Barbarenreichs*, Stuttgart 2016, p. 92–95, 98–101; Y. Modéran, *Les Vandales et l'Empire Romain*, Arles 2014, p. 95–117.

[87] P. Heather, *The Fall...*, p. 272–281.

Next year, in 431, Aspar was dispatched with expeditionary forces to Carthage to help fight off the Vandal menace[88]. This time, however, the general met a worthy opponent in the person of the Vandal king Geiseric. The combined remnants of the provincial forces of Africa commanded by Bonifatius and the Eastern Roman expeditionary forces met the Vandals on the field of battle; however, they were bested[89]. Many Roman soldiers were captured, among them Marcian, Aspar's *domesticus* and future emperor of the East. Despite the Vandal victory, the situation in Africa remained a stalemate. After two major defeats, the Romans were in no position to contest the Vandals in combat and attempt to force them out or otherwise to subjugate them. The Vandals, however, due to their lack of competence in siege warfare[90], could not assault Carthage, the capital of the province, which was firmly held by Aspar and the remainder of his troops.

After two years of an *impasse*, it seems that both sides tried to reach some kind of agreement. It is likely that Aspar negotiated a temporary settlement regarding a return of captives and possibly laid ground for future peace talks[91]. A treaty was concluded in 435 by the envoy Trygetius that allowed the Vandals to settle around Hippo Regius in exchange for a tribute[92], which most likely meant that the Romans wanted to secure the *annona* tax from the province.

Aspar's return to Constantinople was certainly not as glorious as after his previous campaign. He was rewarded with the consulate, but the nomination came from the Western court. Evgeniy Glushanin claims that Aspar returned in disgrace[93], but this seems like an overstatement. While tactically and militarily the campaign in Africa was not successful, in the end its outcome probably seemed satisfactory[94]. It should be recognized that at that point in time no one had the power of hind-sight to know that the peace of Trygetius would be broken by 439. Furthermore, some kind of settlement with the Vandal side was probably an outcome for which the Romans had aimed; however, they had likely hoped for a more favourable one. The concept of total war was foreign to the ancients[95], and the complete extermination or expulsion of the tribe undoubtedly was not taken into consideration, especially since at that point the Vandals had not yet become such a thorn in the Romans' side. Regardless,

---

[88] Cf. Ch. Curtois, *Les Vandales...*, p. 164, n. 2.

[89] Helmut Castritius (*Die Vandalen...*, p. 88–90) has doubts whether the grand battle actually took place, or if the fighting was limited to skirmishes near the gates of Carthage.

[90] *Ibidem*, p. 97.

[91] Y. Modéran, *Les Vandales...*, p. 118–119; R.A. Bleeker, *Aspar...*, p. 58.

[92] Prosper, 1321.

[93] Е.П. Глушанин, *Военная...*, p. 107.

[94] R.A. Bleeker, *Aspar...*, p. 59.

[95] Y. Modéran, *Les Vandales...*, p. 196–197.

the consular nomination of Aspar in 434 proves that, at least in the West, his efforts were considered sufficient[96].

Following his interpretation, Glushanin also claims that Aspar lost his command over the army, which was instead given to Areobindus[97]. Alexander Demandt argues that Areobindus was appointed as *magister militum praesentalis* in 433 or 434 as well, which coincided with his consular nomination alongside Aspar. However, he claims that Areobindus was nominated together with Aspar and Plintha, therefore as a third general of the same rank.

It should be noted, however, that this whole discussion was based on an incorrect dating of a law in *Codex Justinianus* and a resulting erroneous placement of Apollonius at the post of *magister militum praesentalis* as the successor of Plintha. Alexander Demandt places the afore-mentioned law between 435 and 440[98], however, it is much more likely that it was issued in 443.

This means that there is a much simpler explanation. Aspar was not superseded by Areobindus but rather by Flavius Dionysius, who had just finished his five-year service as master of the east. This is proved by a passage in Priscus who mentions him and Plintha as being interested in the diplomatic mission to the Huns and strongly implies the parity in their political standing[99]. Furthermore, Flavius Dionysius is independently mentioned by the acts of the ecumenical Council alongside another general who was the master of the east. John Martindale assumes that Dionysius must, therefore, have been a *magister militum vacans*[100], but there is no reason why he could not have been a *magister militum praesentalis* instead.

When Plintha's tenure had ended in 435, it was his office to which Areobindus received his appointment The fact that Areobindus received consulship does not necessarily mean he had held the rank of *magister militum* at that point. It should be noted that it is not exactly known what he did receive this honour for, however, the earlier example of Plintha shows that it was entirely possible for a *comes* to become a consul before receiving an appointment to the office of *magister militum*[101].

---

[96] Roland S t e i n a c h e r (*Die Vandalen...*, p. 100) supposes that the consular nomination was just an elegant way of saying 'Thank you' to the East for the intervention.

[97] Е.П. Г л у ш а н и н, *Военная...*, p. 107.

[98] A. D e m a n d t, *Magister...*, p. 746.

[99] The historian mentions that both were proconsuls and generals, but he does not specify which office either of them held, however, we know for certain that Plintha was a *magister militum praesentalis*, so it makes the most sense that Dionysius held an equivalent post, cf. P r i s c u s, fr. 2.

[100] *PLRE*, vol. II, p. 366 (s.v. *Dionysius 13*).

[101] A similar case is the consulship of Aspar's son, Ardaburious, who certainly did not serve as a *magister militum* when receiving the nomination, and would not receive such an office for several years more. It is possible that he was being prepared for it; however, the perceived failure of his father in the war of 447 caused the government to stop backing the Ardaburii and to look for other candidates for military offices.

Plintha and the Huns in the Twenties and the Thirties

As it has already been discussed earlier in the chapter, the security of the Empire's northern border was challenged by the Hunnic tribes led by Uldin. The danger was contained by skilful employment of diplomacy and possibly an involvement of the Roman secret service, but it does not mean that the danger from the Huns had passed. In 422, when the Roman forces had been moved from the Balkans to support the war effort against Persia, the Huns led by king Rua invaded Thrace. A detailed analysis of all the sources regarding the invasion of 422 was made by Brian Croke who proposed the following course of events: in 421, when a large portion of the troops from the European provinces was relocated to the east, Thodosius pre-emptively settled the tribe of the Goths in Thrace to bolster the security of the local borders against a potential Hunnic invasion. In spite of these efforts, the Huns circumvented the Roman defences and attacked Thrace. To deal with the threat, Theodosius decided to pay off the Huns, agreeing to an annual tribute of 350 pounds of gold[102].

It has to be said that the interpretation of Croke is very well put together. He offers a comprehensive analysis of multiple sources in support of his hypothesis. There are, however, some aspects of his reasoning that can be disputed.

Firstly, he assumes that the Goths were resettled in Thracian provinces as a precaution. This implies a great deal of political forethought on the part of the government in Constantinople. We do not know how much time resettling a whole tribe took, but certainly it was not something that could have happened overnight. If we accept Croke's dating, it would mean that the decision to settle the Goths in the Thracian provinces must have been made very early, probably even before the start of the war with Persia. That is not impossible, however, the course of the said conflict suggests that the Romans did not expect their enemies to gather such numerous armies, nor that they would need all possible reinforcements to stop Bahram's counter-attack.

Secondly, according to Croke, the tribute of 350 pounds of gold was paid to the Huns in exchange for their retreat from Thrace. The tribute paid to king Rua is supported by a very reliable account of Priscus[103], however, many scholars differ on when he received it. There are three major dates which are taken into consideration: 422, 424, and 431[104]. The arguments of Croke for the year 422

---

[102] B. C r o k e, *Evidence for the Hun invasion of Thrace in 422*, GRBS 18, 1977, p. 347–367.

[103] P r i s c u s, fr. 2.

[104] Some agree on the year 422, cf. M. R o u c h e, *Attila. La violence nomade*, Paris 2009, p. 120; A.H.M. J o n e s, *The Later...*, p. 193. John B. B u r y (*History of the Later Roman Empire*

amount to the fact that he deems it unlikely for the Romans to have given tribute to the Huns in any other instance than following an invasion. This assumption, however, is incorrect. It was a relatively common practice of the period to supplement diplomatic agreements with barbarians with annual payments of this kind[105]. Such tribes were then bound as *foederati* and in exchange for gold (or very often the equivalent in other goods) they served the Roman emperors. The extortion conducted by the Huns in the 430s and 440s, which Croke uses as an example, was actually anomalous and related to the aggressive policy of Attila. Furthermore, the sums agreed upon with Rua were in fact not 'so large', as 300 pounds of gold was the usual sum attached to a *foedus*. It should be noted that despite all these arguments it is not entirely improbable that the Huns received the tribute as early as 422. It would, however, mean that for twelve years till 434 the diplomatic relations between the Romans and the Huns remained unchanged, and that the involvement of Rua's Huns in Italy during the war with the usurper John in 424, the expulsion of the Huns from Pannonia in 427, and the Eastern Roman support in the war against the Vandals in the 430s did not affect them at all. In 424, the fact that the Huns were paid off to leave Italy is confirmed by the sources, and even though it involved the Western part of the Empire, Eastern Roman officials were present and involved in those matters.

In addition to the previous dates, another one could be proposed. In 427 the Huns were expelled from Pannonia and the tribute (probably accompanying a *foedus*) might have been a means to stabilize the diplomatic relations. Therefore, each of the proposed dates has some merit and it is not possible to state without any doubt when and under what circumstances the payments began. As such, information regarding the tribute should not serve as a basis for an interpretation of the events in question.

Thirdly, both Brian Croke and Kenneth Holum (who was the first to came up with that idea) seem to overestimate the importance of the law from March 422, which forced the civilians who occupied the towers forming part of the walls of Constantinople to quarter the soldiers[106]. According to these historians, it proves that Theodosius started to pull troops back from the war with Persia to deal with the Hunnic menace. Croke even claims that the capital itself was

---

from the Death of Theodosius I. to the Death of Justinian, vol. I, London 1958, p. 271) claims that Rua received the tribute beginning from 424. Edward A. T h o m p s o n (*The Foreign Policies of Theodosius II and Marcian*, Her 76, 1950, p. 62) posits that the ruler of the Huns was granted the tribute as a result of an embassy in 431, when he threatened war if his demands were not met.

[105] Е.П. Г л у ш а н и н, *Военная...*, p. 108–109; E. L u t t w a k, *The Grand Strategy of the Byzantine Empire*, Cambridge 2009, p. 55.

[106] *CTh*, VII, 8, 13.

in danger[107]. On the other hand, the significance of the law may be much more mundane. Due to the escalation in the east, the constant need for reinforcements and men being transferred from the European to Asiatic provinces meant that they needed lodging in Constantinople. The fact that the inhabitants of the city walls assumed immunity from the usual practice of *hospitalitas* certainly caused problems. The law might have therefore been an attempt to clarify the situation, but it does not necessarily imply that soldiers were stationed in Constantinople to protect it from an impending Hunnic attack.

It is important to set up the background to the invasion of 422, since it too seems to have been an important factor in the emergence of the military elite in the 420s, alongside the Persian war. Even though there is no direct information stating it, all the evidence points to Plintha being closely involved in the resolution of the conflict against Rua. We do not know who the commander of the Thracian forces was at that point in time[108]; however, Plintha, being the *magister militum praesentalis* not involved in the war with Persia, in case of Hunnic invasion, he would have been the leader of the Roman armies sent to deal with the threat. That being said, most of the forces were engaged in the east. In that case the decision to employ the tribe of the Goths, bound by a *foedus* to serve the Roman Emperor, seemed very reasonable. The Goths who were resettled by Thodosius were undoubtedly the same group who appear later in the sources as the followers of Theodoric Strabo[109]. It is very likely that Plintha had some kind of influence over them, and possibly was an intermediary in resettling them to Thrace as a counter-measure against the Huns[110]. If this plan proved successful and the Hunnic raiders were driven out of Thrace by the Goths, then the influential position of the general at the Constantinopolitan court of which Socrates informs, and his twice prolonged tenure as *magister militum praesentalis* would be much easier to understand. Glushanin, on the other hand, explains Plintha's extraordinary position simply by noting the fact that the forces under his command were those tasked with the defence of the capital; and twice, when his tenure was about to end, the other army was either away on a campaign (between 424 and 425 in Italy) or preparing to set out on one (around 429 and 430 to

---

[107] He references T h e o d o r e t (*HE*, V, 37).

[108] There is, however, solid evidence for that to have been a certain Macedonius, otherwise unknown. He is named as a *magister militum* in 423, and since we know the occupants of the other positions, by a process of elimination he must have been *magister militum per Thracias*, possibly still in office in 425. Cf. *CJ*, III, 21.2; *PLRE*, vol. II, p. 694 (s.v. *Macedonius 5*).

[109] Cf. P. C r a w f o r d, *Roman Emperor Zeno. The Perils of Politics in Fifth-century Constantinople*, Barnsley 2019, p. 34–35.

[110] It would not be too far-fetched of an idea to assume that Plintha might have had blood-ties with this tribe.

Africa against the Vandals)[111]. His arguments, however, do not seem convincing. Nothing prevented the emperor from appointing another officer to serve as the leader of the army which was stationed near Constantinople. Glushanin's arguments could have some merit if the capital were under immediate danger in both of those instances, as changes in leadership could potentially influence the army's effectiveness, however, that was not the case. Therefore, there must be another explanation for Plintha's case, and his military achievements combined with the support of an important group of *foederati* which bolstered the defences of the Empire seem like a sufficient reason for the emperor to keep Plintha in his post.

In 427 there was another conflict with the Huns; unfortunately, the sources are even more scarce than before. There are just two short passages, one by Marcellinus, who mentions that the Romans drove the Huns away from Pannonia after 50 years[112], and a similar one by Jordanes, who adds only one detail, namely that the Romans were helped by the Goths[113]. Due to the scarcity of information, there is a multitude of interpretations of the events of 427. A comprehensive overview of the scholarship on this matter was presented by Hrvoje Gračanin[114]. Firstly, it is unclear who the 'Romans' spoken of in the sources were, since even though Marcellinus claimed that he wrote a history of the Eastern part of the Empire[115], as Otto Maenchen-Helfen perceptively points out, he described events pertaining solely to the West several times in his work[116]. It is, then, debatable what group of the Huns do the sources mention. Many scholars assume, it was the so-called tribe of the Great Huns from beyond the Danube; however, as Laszlo Varady has accurately observed, they disregard the information that these Huns held Pannonia for 50 years, in which case the tribe in question must have been the Hunnic *foederati* settled there earlier in the fourth century[117].

All things considered, it is more likely that the events of 427 involved a military action on the part of the Eastern Roman forces. The West had barely any reason to get involved in Pannonia, and, considering the limited resources at the disposal of its government, it would have been foolish for it to do so. The Eastern Roman Empire, however, might have acted on the basis of a preliminary agreement from 424 which involved the cession of western Illyricum by the West[118]. The Huns who got expelled were Western *foederati*, with whom the East

---

[111] Е.П. Глушанин, *Военная...*, p. 105–106.

[112] Marcellinus Comes, a. 427.

[113] Jordanes, *Getica*, 166.

[114] H. Gračanin, *The Huns and the South Pannonia*, Bsl 64, 2006, p. 47–49.

[115] Marcellinus Comes, praefatio.

[116] O. Maenchen-Helfen, *The World...*, p. 78.

[117] L. Varady, *Das Letzte Jahrhundert Pannoniens (376–476)*, Amsterdam 1969, p. 281.

[118] B. Croke, *Evidence...*, p. 361, n. 25.

had no binding agreements. It is, however, not entirely unlikely that the Huns of Rua were involved in some way. It is possible that the vicinity of such a powerful enemy might have prompted the Romans to employ major forces, which include the allied Gothic tribes, very likely the same ones who had fought against the Huns five years earlier. Additionally, since Plintha was still a *magister militum praesentalis* in 427, he probably was the Roman commander-in-chief for the Pannonian campaign, which is even more plausible considering that the Goths were involved[119].

Unfortunately, we know nothing beyond these two laconic remarks, and any details regarding the military operations, battles, and the extent of the Romans' victories are shrouded in mystery. Regardless of the scope of the campaign, it was nonetheless successful, and if the assumption that Plintha was in command is correct, it explains why his stint would be extended for yet another term.

In 430s, the tensions between the Eastern Roman Empire and the Huns rose again. Several tribes belonging to the Hunnic confederacy sought co-operation with the Romans[120]. Rua decided to make war on the dissidents and sent his envoy to Constantinople, demanding that every refugee be sent back. Interestingly, when the Romans were deciding on sending an embassy to Rua, Priscus mentions that both Plintha and Dionysius, who both were *magistri militum praesentales* and ex-consuls at that time, wished to go. Apparently the former was so determined that he resorted to concocting a plot to secure his membership in the embassy. He sent his retainer, Sengilach, to accompany the Hunnic envoy with orders to convince the king that he speak only with Plintha. What exactly motivated the general remains obscure. Otto Maenchen-Helfen assumes that Plintha must have used the Huns as leverage in court politics, similarly to what Aetius did in the West[121]. Evgeniy Glushanin claims that in such a way Plintha attempted to secure command for himself for another term, as diplomatic functions were usually bestowed upon those who held high military or civilian offices[122].

---

[119] Vladislav P o p o v i ć (*Die süddanubische Provinzen in der Spätantike vom Ende des 4. Bis zur Mitte des 5. Jahrhunderts*, [in:] *Die Völker Südosteuropas im 6. bis 8. Jahrhundert*, hrsg. B H ä n s e l, Berlin 1987, p 102) claims that it was Aspar who commanded those forces, however, he provides no sources for it.

[120] P r i s c u s (fr. 2) mentions several tribes: Amilzuri, Itinmari, Tounsures, and Boisci. He seems to indicate that whole tribes were fleeing to join the Romans, cf. O. M a e n c h e n--H e l f e n, *The World*..., p. 90. However, Roger B l o c k l e y (*Fragmentary Classicising Historians of the Later Roman Empire*, t. I, Liverpool 1981, p. 379–380, n. 3) rightfully points out that it is more likely that those were large groups of individuals who fled into Roman territories rather than the whole tribes.

[121] O. M a e n c h e n - H e l f e n, *The World*..., p. 91. Cf. K. R o s e n, *Attila*..., p. 99–100.

[122] Е.П. Глушанин, *Военная*..., p. 107.

There may be another explanation for this altogether; regardless, it is unknown if anything came out of it, since Rua died and was succeeded by the brothers Attila and Bleda. When an embassy to them was being assembled in Constantinople, the Senate recommended Plintha; however, it cannot be ascertained whether this choice was affected by his previous intrigue. The general was accepted to be an envoy by the emperor and he chose a certain Epigenes to accompany him, following which he set out to meet the kings of the Huns near the city of Margus. There a treaty was agreed upon which doubled the tribute that the Huns had been receiving from the Romans[123], prohibited the latter from allying themselves with tribes hostile to the Huns, and forced them to relinquish all the fugitives. The Roman prisoners of war were to be ransomed for eight *solidi* each. Additionally, markets with equal rights for the Huns and the Romans were to be established on the frontier[124].

The Second Vandal Expedition (441)

In 439 Geiseric, the king of the Vandals, broke his treaty with the Romans and in a sudden attack managed to capture Carthage[125]. This event caused great distress in both parts of the Empire. The fall of the capital of the province of Africa sealed the fate of a whole region which was instrumental in sustaining the struggling economy of the Western Roman Empire. Economic factors aside, it also meant that any attempt at retaking Africa in future campaigns would be much more difficult, as the Romans had lost their primary foothold in the area. Furthermore, Geiseric gained access to the multitude of vessels docked in Carthaginian ports, which significantly bolstered the strength of the Vandal navy[126].

This event made the Romans realize that the Vandal threat was much more serious than they had originally thought. Soon after, they took hasty precautions to defend themselves from an attack that seemed imminent. In the West, the

---

[123] This clause may have been added simply because of the fact that treaties with barbarian tribes tended to be agreed upon with its rulers, rather than tribes themselves; since from then on there were two of them, both needed to receive payments. Cf. R.C. B l o c k l e y, *East Roman...*, p. 203, n. 8. Cf. K. R o s e n, *Attila...*, p. 108.

[124] K. R o s e n, *Attila...*, p. 110–111; I. B ó n a, *Das Hunnenreich...*, p. 55; T. S t i c k l e r, *Die Hunnen...*, p. 66.

[125] P r o s p e r, 1339. Cf. Ch. C u r t o i s, *Les Vandales...*, p. 171; Y. M o d é r a n. *Les Vandales...*, p. 119–130; R. S t e i n a c h e r, *Die Vandalen...*, p. 120–125.

[126] R. M i l e s, A. M e r r i l l s, *The Vandals*, Oxford 2010, p. 111.

commander Sigisvult created a system of early warning to inform of approaching Vandal fleets, and the right to bear arms was restored[127]. Additionally, in the East the sea-side walls of Constantinople were renovated[128].

The fears were not unsubstantiated, as just the next year the Vandal forces appeared on the coast of Sicily. The whole country-side was ravaged, Lilybaeum fell, and Panormos endured a prolonged siege[129]. Whether it held or fell in the end is not certain, however, Hydatius mentions some persecutions of orthodox Christians instigated by the local Arian leaders which followed the incursion[130]. Despite some limited successes of the local forces in fighting off the barbarians, the situation on the island was dire[131].

Valentinian's pleas for help must have been heard by Theodosius, as the Western emperor reassures in his *Novellae* that the forces from the East would be coming soon[132]. Indeed, Theodosius decided to act against the Vandals, however, this expedition proved to be an endeavour costly in both resources and the time it took to prepare. The official responsible for the logistics of the operation, Pentadius, was rewarded by the emperor for his efforts[133]; yet, it still took until the next year for the expedition to set out. The strength of the forces involved was reported by Theophanes to be 1,100 ships, which is probably an overstatement, however, likely to a lesser extent than it is usually assumed. This would translate into about 30,000 soldiers and 70,000 sailors, which would have put this force on par with the later famous expedition of Basiliscus in 468. What supports these high numbers of the Roman soldiers is the number of the commanders involved[134]. The commander-in-chief was Areobindus, who at that point had the rank of *magister militum praesentalis*. Another commander mentioned by three independent sources is Germanus, who was *magister militum vacans*. Both Prosper and Theophanes mention Ansila, who is, however, otherwise unknown. Only the latter account informs of two more, namely Innobindos (unknown) and Arintheus, who was probably synonymous with Agintheos, a commander

---

[127] *Novellae Valentiniani*, IX. Cf. R. M a t h i s e n, *Sigisvult...*, p. 184–185.

[128] *Chronicon Paschale*, a. 439.

[129] E. K i s l i n g e r, *Sizilien zwischen Vandalen und Römischem Reich im 5. Jahrhundert: Eine Insel in zentraler Randlage*, Mil 11, 2014, p. 241; A. G o l t z, *Sizillien und die Germanen in der Spätantike*, Kok 53/54, 1997/98, p. 215–217.

[130] H y d a t i u s, 112. Cf. A. G o l t z, *Sizillien...*, p. 215–216.

[131] C a s s i o d o r u s (*Variae*, 1, 4, 14) mentions his great-grandfather successfully organizing the local resistance. Cf. E. K i s l i n g e r, *Sizilien...*, p. 242; A. G o l t z, *Sizillien...*, p. 217.

[132] *Novellae Valentiniani*, IX.

[133] *PLRE*, vol. II, p. 858 (*s.v. Pentadius 2*).

[134] Cf. P. H e a t h e r, *The Fall...*, p. 290; M. W i l c z y ń s k i, *Gejzeryk i „czwarta wojna punicka"*, Oświęcim 2016, p. 121.

in Illyria mentioned by Priscus in 449[135]. Both Demandt and Glushanin assume that all of the four commanders, besides Areobindus, held the titles of *magistri militum vacantes*[136], yet there is evidence for that only in the case of Germanus, so it is certainly a possibility that the others were lower ranking officers[137].

That being said, in that year a new legislation was promulgated in Constantinople which established a flexible system of offices with a clear hierarchy[138]. The law was linked with the expedition of 441 and mentioned Pentadius and Germanus; undoubtedly, it was created to give the government the ability to quickly appoint officials to temporary functions as the need arose[139]. The institution of the law might have meant that the government was going to make full use of it and appoint multiple *magistri militum vacantes* for this one expedition.

It is also not improbable that the unusual number of commanders involved in one combat theatre directly contributed to the failure of the expedition. The Eastern Roman forces arrived on Sicily when the warriors of Geiseric had already retreated. Prosper claims that it was caused by the arrival in Africa of a certain Sebastianus[140], who was a Western Roman commander, a rival of Aetius, and later a councillor to the Vandal monarch[141]. It is difficult to guess what Prosper might have exactly had in mind, or whether his account is accurate in this regard; however, it is much more likely that the direct reason for the invaders' withdrawal was the news of the Eastern Roman reinforcements approaching Sicily[142]. The Vandals rarely engaged in field battles in their raids and Geiseric cannot have liked the odds of fighting a whole armada.

---

[135] Priscus, fr. 11.

[136] Е.П. Глушанин, *Военная*..., p. 108; A. Demandt, *Magister*..., p. 790. Demandt does, however, recognize the fact that there is hard evidence only for Germanus' case. Cf. A. Demandt, *Magister*..., p. 753. Edward A. Thompson (*The Foreign Policy of Theodosius II and Marcian*, Her 76, 1950, p. 64; 66) posits that Aspar also took part in the expedition and even commanded it, but that claim is unsupported and most certainly wrong.

[137] Cf. M. Wilczyński, *Gejzeryk*..., p. 121.

[138] *CJ*, XII, 8, 2.

[139] Е.П. Глушанин, *Военная*..., p. 107.

[140] Prosper, 1342. On Sebastianus, cf. *PLRE*, vol. II, p. 983–984 (s.v. *Sebastianus 3*); R. Mathisen, *Sigisvult*..., p. 187–188; Ł. Pigoński, *Wpływ czynników religijnych na relacje rzymsko–wandalskie w latach 429–474*, ChrA 8, 2016, p. 106–107.

[141] Victor of Vita, I, 19.

[142] Ralph Mathisen (*Sigisvult*..., p. 187–188) puts forward an interesting thesis that the rumours of Sebastianus' arrival were spread by Sigisvult as part of a disinformation campaign. This is very much possible and would explain why such a seemingly unimportant and unconfirmed event features so prominently in the sources. Whether the rumours were truly that effective or Geiseric learned of the approach of the very real Eastern fleet, it is impossible to determine.

If the goal of the expedition was to force the Vandals to retreat, Areobindus accomplished it before he had even reached the coast. There are, however, several possible interpretations of what followed. According to Prosper, the Eastern Roman troops stayed on the island for a prolonged duration, to the distress of the already struggling local population, which had to procure supplies for the allied forces[143]. Theophanes, on the other hand, mentions that the forces waited for Geiseric to send an embassy and sue for peace[144]. Furthermore, around the time of the expedition against the Vandals, the Eastern Roman Empire became engaged in a conflict with Persia and had to defend against the raids of Isaurian and Tzani tribes in Anatolia, as well as having to deal with a major Hunnic invasion in Thrace[145]. The fact that the Roman homeland was in danger was without a doubt a contributing factor in the eventual retreat of the expedition and is often presented by scholars as the explanation for the failure of the campaign[146].

This fact, however, does not explain the protracted stay on the island related by Prosper[147]. If Theodosius was indeed content with forcing the Vandals to retreat, then keeping the forces on the island and overseeing the peace negotiations would have made little sense. Considering the cost and effort required to send the expedition, it seems unlikely that it had such limited goals. Sicily, due to logistical reasons and the technique of sailing at the time had to be a station *en route* to Africa; thus, it is not outside the realm of possibility that Areobindus was tasked with striking at the heart of Geiseric's kingdom[148]. Certainly, it seems that such were the expectations of the inhabitants of Sicily. One likely reason for the Roman army to linger on the island for an extended period was the problem of divided command. As has already been said, there were as many as five commanders present, and it is in fact possible that most of them held the rank of *magister militum*. It can be assumed that this allowed for all kinds of disputes over competence, especially if some controversial matter arose (for example making a decision whether to gather

---

[143] Prosper, 1344.

[144] Theophanes, AM 5942.

[145] Marcellinus Comes, a. 441.

[146] E. Stein, *Histoire du Bas-Empire*, t. I: *De l'état romain à l'état byzantin (284–476)*, Paris 1959, p. 291; E.A. Thompson, *The Foreign...*, p. 62; R.C. Blockley, *East Roman...*, p. 62. Ewald Kislinger (*Sizilien...*, p. 242) thinks that Aspar also had a hand in making the decision, but while the scholar accurately presents the general's political convictions, Aspar probably was not so powerful at that point as to force the emperor's hand in that matter. It is, however, possible that he might have advised a retreat.

[147] It should be noted that Prosper was likely well informed of the events on Sicily since he was a member of the papal offices, and it is known for a fact that the pope corresponded with the members of the Church on Sicily.

[148] P. Heather, *The Fall...*, p. 290–291.

troops and sail to Africa or consider Geiseric's peace proposals). In fact, the king used such a strategy several times, sending out his envoys with agreeable peace proposals to delay his opponents and buy himself more time. In this instance he did not seem to have any specific plan, but instead was simply lucky. Eventually, the expedition tarrying on Sicily learned of the problems in the homeland, particularly of the dangerous incursions. The Eastern Roman forces were needed in the Balkans, so they hastily accepted the terms offered by Geiseric and returned home.

The expedition of 441 was in the end a complete failure. This time the treaty signed by the Romans and the Vandals gave away most of the rich and fertile parts of the province to the barbarians; as Roger Blockley accurately states, 'Geiseric remained secure in his possession of Carthage and a powerful fleet'[149], and even though the tensions died down for several years, the Vandal power was there to stay and would be a thorn in the Romans' side.

The Developments in the East

In 428 the last king of Armenia from the Arsacid dynasty, Ardashir, was deposed by Bahram at the request from the local aristocracy. The Persian king appointed a *marzaban* to govern the province, effectively incorporating it into his Empire. At the same time the *catholicos* of Armenia, Sahak, was removed from his office[150]. Little is known of the Roman response to that. Apparently, the *magister militum* of the east, Flavius Dionysius, who succeeded Procopius in 428, was sent on an embassy to Persia which was probably related to those events, however there are no details regarding its goals or outcome[151].

In 433 Anatolius received a nomination for the position of *magister militum per Orientem*, succeeding Flavius Dionysius. The choice was likely not coincidental, as Anatolius seems to have been relatively well versed in Armenian matters. The case of Sahak was still open, as the Armenian nobles petitioned to Bahram to restore the bishop to his function. The king refused, to which Anatolius responded by requesting that Sahak be transferred to the Roman-controlled part of Armenia, yet he met with another refusal. Apparently, the Romans must have wanted to keep a peaceful relationship with Persia, as no further action on their part followed[152].

---

[149] R.C. B l o c k l e y, *East Roman...*, p. 62.

[150] Roger B l o c k l e y (*East Roman...*, p. 61) argues that the latter was potentially more impactful.

[151] *PLRE*, vol. II, p. 366 (s.v. *Fl. Dionysius 13*).

[152] R.C. B l o c k l e y, *East Roman...*, p. 61.

In 438 Bahram V died. His successor, Yazdigird II, was occupied by a rebellion against his rule in the first years of his reign and a war with the Kidarite Huns which broke out afterwards. However, around 441 he turned his attention to the West, invading Roman Mesopotamia. The pretext for that incursion seems to have been the fact that the Romans had stopped making the previously agreed upon payments towards maintaining the defences of Caspian Gates.

The war was very brief and not much is known about the battles, if any had even place. It is very likely that the only goal of the shah was the projection of power, and it seems he succeeded, as the Romans were in a reasonably conciliatory mood at that time. This was mostly due to the fact that Theodosius II was preparing the expedition against the Vandals since 439. Secondly, the Isaurian and Tzani tribes had just raided Anatolia, which also required an intervention of the Roman army. Thus, Anatolius was dispatched as an envoy who first negotiated a year-long truce and later signed a peace treaty which most likely upheld most of the clauses from 422[153].

The War against the Huns of 441–442

In 441, when the Roman forces were already occupied in the east against Persia and in the west against the Vandals, up in the north on the Danubian frontier the Huns provoked an incident, attacking the Romans during a time of market. In the course of the negotiations that followed the Huns claimed that it was a retaliatory strike for the transgressions of the bishop of Margus, who, according to them, robbed some of their royal tombs. Regardless of how much credibility there is to these assertions about an alleged grave-robbing bishop, whether there was another reason for the aggression, or whether the Huns just took advantage of the temporary defencelessness of the Eastern Empire and its military predicament, they demanded that the bishop be turned in to them, along with any fugitives whom the Romans were prohibited from accepting as refugees under the existing treaty[154]. Since mediation had failed, the Huns invaded the Roman territory. Viminacium, Margus[155], Singidunum[156], and Sirmium

---

[153] Marcellinus Comes, a. 441; Procopius, *History of the Wars*, I, 2. Cf. P. Heather, *The Fall...*, p. 301.

[154] And even Priscus admits that the Romans broke that clause, as there were many fugitives who were accepted into the Roman territory. Cf. Priscus, fr. 6.

[155] Margus was eventually betrayed by the bishop, who allowed the invaders inside in exchange for his own safety, cf. Priscus, fr. 2.

[156] Marcellinus Comes, a. 441.

fell to the barbarians[157], who in the end advanced as far as Naissus, which was also conquered after a siege described in detail by Priscus[158]. To face the enemy, the emperor dispatched *magister militum praesentalis* Aspar[159]. It is unknown what forces he had at his disposal, however, considering on how many fronts the Roman soldiers were engaged in 441, they were likely insubstantial[160]. Most likely, he did not even attempt to fight the enemy, and instead secured a year-long truce, which gave the forces on Sicily time to return home[161].

In 442 the hostilities were resumed with another Hunnic invasion. This time the barbarians advanced into Thrace[162]. Otto Maenchen-Helfen wonders why the Huns were stopped and assumes it might have been due to a plague or a tribe of Sorosgi raiding their territories[163]; however, there is a much simpler explanation, which is that the forces of Areobindus had finally returned from Sicily and could contain the Hunnic menace. At this point Attila and Bleda agreed to a peace, which was preliminarily negotiated with the Roman general and then ratified by the *magister officiorum* Nomus[164].

Interestingly, there is another event related to the Eastern Roman generals in 441. According to both Marcellinus Comes and the *Chronicon Paschale*, one Arnegisclus murdered John the Vandal[165], who likely was at that point the *magister militum per Thracias*[166]. The reason for it is unknown; the assumption of John Martindale is that it was a political assassination motivated by John's ethnicity and the imminent conflict with the Vandals; however, his argumentation does not seem convincing. We should not overlook the fact that Arnegisclus re-

---

[157] O. M a e n c h e n - H e l f e n, *The World...*, p. 116; M. M e i e r, *Geschichte der Völkerwanderung. Europa, Asien und Afrika vom 3. bis zum 8. Jahrhundert n.Chr*, München 2019, p. 412.

[158] P r i s c u s, fr. 6. Cf. M. W h i t b y, *Siege Warfare and Counter–Siege Tactics (ca. 250–640)*, [in:] *War and Warfare in Late Antiquity*, ed. A. S a r a n t i s, N. C h r i s t i e, Leiden 2013, p. 445.

[159] Ronald A. B l e e k e r (*Aspar...*, p. 71–76) argues that Aspar was a *magister militum per Illyricum*, however, the only place where one could find any traces of an Illyrian army in 441 were probably the Imperial archives, which contained the dusty pages of *Notitia Dignitatum*. There is no reason why Aspar could not have received a mastery in presence after Flavius Dionysius.

[160] R.C. B l o c k l e y, *East Roman...*, p. 62.

[161] B. C r o k e, *Anatolius and Nomus: Envoys to Attila*, Bsl 42, 1981, p. 164–165; B. C r o k e, *The Context and Date of Priscus Fragment 6*, CP 78, 1983, p. 308. K. R o s e n (*Attila...*, p. 121–122) assumes Aspar that suffered a defeat because of the anecdote recorded in *Suda* (Z 29), which mentions the capture of his slave Zerkon by the Huns.

[162] M a r c e l l i n u s C o m e s, a. 442; *Chronicon Paschale*, a. 442.

[163] O. M a e n c h e n - H e l f e n, *The World...*, p. 116.

[164] B. C r o k e, *Anatolius...*, p. 167–170. The tribute likely increased to 1400 pounds of gold a year, cf. P. H e a t h e r, *The Fall...*, p. 307.

[165] M a r c e l l i n u s C o m e s, a. 441; *Chronicon Paschale*, a. 441.

[166] A. D e m a n d t, *Magister...*, p. 744–745.

ceived the office of his victim shows that it was approved by those in power[167]. Interestingly, there is another account, written by Theophanes, who, admittedly, confused the general John with the usurper in Rome, thus its credibility is dubious; notwithstanding, he links *spatharius* Chrysaphius to the murder[168]. The infamous eunuch, Chrysaphius-Ztoummas, which was his original, Armenian name, became a close advisor to Theodosius and an influential person at the Constantinopolitan court[169] precisely around that time. It is difficult to determine why he would be involved in ordering a murder of one of the generals. Arnegisclus and John might have been conflicted[170], and Chrysaphius allowed a bloody resolution to the feud, to secure loyalty of the former. It is certain that the eunuch sought the support of the army[171] and he was not getting it otherwise, on the account of how unpopular his policy of appeasement towards the Huns was among the military elite. This is why he might have decided to go for such a drastic solution, but it probably did not do him any favours with the other generals.

The year 441 was in more than one respect a turning-point of Theodosius' reign. Primarily, however, it signalled a major failure of his foreign policy, and the emperor was at least partially to blame. The fact that he engaged in such a costly campaign, while there were several potential flash-points on the Empire's borders only resulted in his forces being stretched so thin that it led to difficult concessions in all of the theatres of war. The unfavourable peace with Persia and the *de facto* acceptance of the Vandal dominion over Africa were at this point a done deal. The settlement with the Huns, however, was the outcome of that ill-fated year which Theodosius could have turned around. It is clear that the emperor did not fully recognize the danger posed by the invaders from beyond the Danube up to that point, but this was about to change. In 443 he ordered to reinforce the *limitanei* troops and restore them to their original numbers, rebuild the river flotilla on the Danube, threatened to punish all instances of corruption in which funds assigned to strengthening the military forces of the Empire were embezzled, and announced a system of oversight and annual inspections to make sure that the reforms would be implemented correctly[172].

---

[167] *PLRE*, vol. II, p. 597 (s.v. *Ioannes the Vandal 13*).

[168] T h e o p h a n e s, AM 5943.

[169] He was also a *cubicularius*, an attendant of the Imperial bedchambers. While on the surface this office appears unimportant, in reality it implied immense power due to an unrestricted access to the emperor. F. M i l l a r, *A Greek Roman Empire. Power and Belief under Theodosius II 408–450*, Berkeley 2007, p. 226.

[170] Their sons were feuding well into the 460s, which might have been caused by this event, but it is possible that the conflict predated it and the murder just reignited the matter.

[171] The elevation of Flavius Zeno supports that claim.

[172] *Novellae Theodosiani*, XXIV; O. M a e n c h e n - H e l f e n, *The World...*, p. 117; P. H e a t h e r, *The Fall...*, p. 308.

The Road to the Next War

Perhaps beginning with the following year, 444, the emperor decided that no more payments of the tribute would be made to the Huns. The barbarians at this point were first involved in the West, in a limited conflict which was concluded with a peace negotiated by Aetius[173], and soon after, in 445, Attila murdered his brother and co-ruler Bleda[174]. This move had made Attila the sole leader of the Huns, but obviously he needed to pacify dissidents and the former followers of Bleda. Subsequent to that, he also became engaged in a war with another Hunnic tribe called Akatziri. Naturally, considering all of these struggles, he was unable to challenge the Roman Empire about the cessation of the payments.

For the next three years it seemed like Theodosius' policy was a success. After the payments were withheld, Attila seems to have threatened the emperor with war[175]; however, considering the bolstered defences on the Danube, it would have been rather unlikely for the Huns to be able to face the concentrated might of the Roman armies in the Balkans.

Unfortunately, it appears that on this occasion the goddess Fortuna favoured the barbarians. In 446 and 447 the province of Thrace was struck by an earthquake which was followed by a plague and famine[176]. Considering the sorry state in which the struggling Balkan provinces of the Empire were at that point,

---

[173] I follow the interpretation of Otto M a e n c h e n - H e l f e n (*The World*..., p. 95–107), who provides a detailed analysis proving a rise in tensions between the Huns and the Western Roman Empire, which was pacified by Aetius. For additional commentary, cf. T. S t i c k l e r, *Aetius*..., p. 116–122.

[174] M a r c e l l i n u s   C o m e s a. 445; I. B ó n a, *Das Hunnenreich*..., p. 62; O. M a e n - c h e n - H e l f e n, *The World*..., p. 104–105.

[175] P r i s c u s, fr. 9. Attila sent Theodosius a message saying that without the gold he would not be able to hold back his warriors from invading. Otto M a e n c h e n - H e l f e n (*The World*..., p. 118) interprets this information as proof that within the Hunnic confederation there were some restless, warlike groups which decided to raid the frontier on their own, before the war had started. Gerhard W i r t h (*Attila. Das Hunnenreich und Europa*, Stuttgart 1999, p. 69–70) claims that Attila was sincere when informing the emperor that he urgently needed the gold to keep his men in check, as the stability of his realm was in jeopardy after the murder of Bleda. These interpretations are well reasoned and certainly interesting; it is unarguable that Attila was facing some dissent, possibly from hawkish parties among his followers, and needed the gold from the tribute as a tool in governing his realm. However, there might be another, simpler explanation, namely that this passage relays a threat disguised in diplomatic language, with the actual purport being that the attacks would continue if the gold were not sent.

[176] M a r c e l l i n u s   C o m e s, a. 447. Cf. B. Croke, *Two Early Byzantine Earthquakes and their Liturgical Commemoration*, B 51, 1981, p. 131–140.

it was a perfect time for the Huns to strike. Undoubtedly, the Roman attention was focused on dealing with the calamities, and the ability of local forces to withstand the invasion, despite Theodosius' previous efforts to strengthen it, was at its lowest. To make matters worse, the earthquake severely damaged the walls of Constantinople itself, which rendered the capital, usually impervious to any barbarian horde, exceptionally vulnerable[177]. It must have caused a great distress at the Imperial court as the news of Attila's attack reached the capital.

The War of 447: A Conflict Shrouded in Mystery

The war of 447 could be considered one of the most important conflicts of the fifth century, and it has a special significance for the topic explored in the present work. Unfortunately, the data at our disposal is extremely scarce and spread across multiple sources.

Marcellinus Comes claims the war was even greater than the previous one, informing us that Attila reached as far as Thermopolis[178]. He mentions one major battle which took place at the Utus river, in which *magister militum* Arnegisclus fought bravely against the forces of Attila; however, he was struck down just when the encounter was turning in the Romans' favour[179]. This clash is related by two other sources; Jordanes in his *Romana* elaborates how the general was killed because his horse collapsed under him and he was surrounded as a result; in addition to these minor details, he tells us that Arnegisclus set out to meet the enemy from Marcianopolis[180]. The death of the general in the field is also recorded in the *Paschal Chronicle*, which also adds that Marcianopolis fell to the invaders in the aftermath of the battle[181].

Another account of the events can be found in Theophanes' *Chronicle*, however, his work is very confused chronologically. The historian seems to have combined the war of 447 with the previous conflicts, and as such, it is unclear which information pertains to which year. He mentions Arnegisclus by name, as well as

---

[177] Apparently fifty-seven towers collapsed alongside the certain sections of the wall, cf. M a r c e l l i n u s   C o m e s, a. 447. According to *Chronicon Paschale* (a. 447), the results of the earthquake were much less lethal since people had managed to escape the towers before they crumbled.

[178] *Attila usque ad Thermopolim infestus advenit* – M a r c e l l i n u s   C o m e s, a. 447.

[179] M a r c e l l i n u s   C o m e s, a. 447.

[180] J o r d a n e s, *Romana*, 331.

[181] *Chronicon Paschale*, a 447.

Aspar and Areobindus, and laconically reports that the generals suffered defeats in the battles that occurred. Then he writes of several cities which fell to the Huns and Attila reaching the fort Athyras, before describing the conditions of the peace[182].

The most important source for those events, the *History* of Priscus, is unfortunately severely lacking, as the passages concerning the conflict itself are missing[183]. Some details which he mentions in passing indicate that the Huns first invaded Ratiaria and he refers to a battle at the Chersonesus, however, the fragment did not specify its outcome. The historian also brings up Flavius Zeno's role in the war, the destruction caused by the Huns, as well as praising the resolve of the defenders of the fortress Asemus, who apparently managed not only to successfully to fend off the Huns, but also sallied forth, engaging some raiding parties in the field and dealing them serious losses. An interesting passage exists in the *Gallic Chronicle of 452*, the author of which enumerates the cities destroyed in the war and blames the Western government for not intervening to help its brethren[184].

As such, much of the war of 447 is shrouded in mystery and the interpretations of the scholars vary widely. Adding to the over-all confusion, previously some parts of the conflict were erroneously dated to the year 443[185]; this does not necessarily render the observations of the otherwise renowned historians who made that mistake useless, however, the confused chronology certainly does detract from their treatment of the topic. As far as the evaluation of the conflict is concerned, there is some difference of opinion as to how successful the Huns were when facing the Roman army[186]. Many claim that it was an utter disaster

---

[182] T h e o p h a n e s, AM5942; Since it is known from other sources that Aspar and Areobindus were involved in the war of 441–442, it is impossible to tell whether Theophanes meant this conflict or actually reported on their taking part in the war of 447. Ronald A. B l e e k e r (*Aspar and Attila: The Role of Flavius Ardaburius Aspar in the Hun Wars of the 440s*, AWo 3, 1980, p. 25) assumes that Theophanes adhered a chronological continuity and since the information on the war comes after the mention of the murder of Bleda, he claims that all of it pertains to the war of 447. However, the account on Bleda's murder is a digression, since the chronicler follows it up with a part about an earlier treaty with Geiseric, after which Areobindus returned to the Balkans and fought the Huns, saying that all this took place in 442.

[183] This is likely due to the character of those fragments, which were recorded in the later compilation of the excerpts from embassies. In the original work Priscus undoubtedly specified the outcomes of the battles and elaborated on them; however, the copyists of the *Excerpta de legationibus* were interested specifically in parts directly detailing the diplomatic negotiations and embassies, omitting the war itself.

[184] *Chronica Gallica a. 452*, 132.

[185] J.B. B u r y, *History*..., p. 275; A.H.M. J o n e s, *The Later*..., p. 193; E.A. T h o m p s o n, *A History*..., p. 85.

[186] Interestingly, no source, barring Theophanes, explicitly states that the Romans suffered defeats in the field besides the battle of Utus.

in military terms for the latter and that the warriors of Attila crushed the forces sent against them, allowing the king of the Huns to dictate his terms to the Romans[187]. Others draw attention to the presence of many coinciding factors which allowed the Huns to achieve the favourable result; however, it was at a cost[188]. Interestingly, there are even singular voices claiming that the campaign of 447 was a defeat for Attila[189].

When it comes to the course of the campaign, outcomes of the battles, and the leadership, the historiography generally refrains from delving into much detail. It is understandable if we consider the limited data afforded by the sources. The Battle of Utus, being the most widely reported event, has, however, been given some interpretations. Scholars such as Evgeniy Glushanin and Karl Feld claim, supposedly following Theophanes, that all the Roman forces in the Balkans joined together to resist the Huns[190]. The battle of the Chersonesus is rarely discussed at all, and generally it is assumed that it was another defeat for the Roman army[191]. There is also a common mistake that repeatedly appears in the literature, the mistaking of Marcellinus' Thermopolis as the famous Thermopylae passage[192].

The Course of the War

The foregoing overview should demonstrate how complicated the question of the conflict of 447 is. The safe approach, therefore, is to avoid interpretations based on anecdotal evidence and rely only to information which is confirmed by the sources. This may be the right approach as far as a general overview of the era is concerned; however, considering the importance of the affairs under discussion to the issues central to the present work, it simply does not suffice to just

---

[187] J.B. B u r y, *History...*, p. 275; A.H.M. J o n e s, *The Later...*, p. 193; A. D e m a n d t, *Geschichte...*, p. 140; H.J. K i m, *The Huns, Romans and the Birth of Europe*, Cambridge 2013, p. 71.

[188] E.A. T h o m p s o n, *A History...*, p. 92.

[189] G. W i r t h, *Attila...*, p. 74.

[190] Е.П. Г л у ш а н и н, *Военная...*, p. 109; K. F e l d, *Barbarische Bürger: Die Isaurier und das Römische Reich*, Berlin 2005, p. 214.

[191] E.A. T h o m p s o n, *The Isaurians under Theodosius II*, Her 68, 1946, p. 20; M. M e i e r, *Geschichte...*, p. 419; P. H e a t h e r, *The Fall...*, p. 309; H.J. K i m, *The Huns...*, p. 72.

[192] Concerning this misconception, see: J. K a r a y a n n o p u l o s, *Byzantinische Miszellen*, [in:] *Studia in honorem Veselini Beševliev*, ed. V. G e o r g i e v, Sofia 1978, p. 490; J. P r o s t k o - P r o s t y ń s k i, *Attila and Novae*, [in:] *Novae. Legionary Fortress and Late Antique Town*, vol. I, *A Companion to the Study of Novae*, ed. T. D e r d a, P. D y c z e k, J. K o l e n d o, Warsaw 2008, p. 137, n. 24.

attest to the uncertainty of the data at our disposal. Thus, an attempt at puzzling out the course of the events is critical; however, it needs to be stressed that the interpretation attempted below, despite my the best efforts to take into account and properly analyse all the information available, no matter how disjointed and fragmentary, is liable to mistake and largely subjective in its nature.

In the first place, it is important to keep in mind the strategic situation of the Romans on the brink of the war. The Huns had thus far decided to make war against the Eastern Roman Empire only when its forces were occupied elsewhere and the defences of the northern border were not at full strength. The earthquake and other calamities from which the Empire suffered before the commencement of the hostilities undeniably diminished its ability to defend itself to such a point that Attila must have felt ready to attack. This means that the recently reorganized forces of the *limitanei* on which Theodosius had based his policy, were just a couple years later in 447 no longer able to hold the back king of the Huns for any substantial amount of time. Additionally, the normally impervious city of Constantinople had its walls seriously damaged and the barbarians, who usually had problems dealing with sieges, would have been able to enter and plunder the city.

If we take the factors outlined above into consideration, there could have been only one immediate goal for the Roman army in 447, and that was to stop the Huns from reaching the capital, or at least to delay them long enough for the defences to be rebuilt. If the motivations of the Romans are relatively easy to speculate on, how they went about stopping the enemy is unfortunately unknown. We can, however, theorize on what might have been regarded as the best course of action at the panicked court of Theodosius.

At the outset, we can discount the idea that the entire army was stationed near Constantinople. Sources clearly describe how the capital was saved by the forces coming from the east; thus, the majority of the troops in Thrace must have been sent to meet the Huns in the field. A probable reason for such a course of action was the fear of defeat by the walls of Constantinople, which could not have been rebuilt in time if the Huns had been allowed to invade the Empire unimpeded. The outcome of a field battle was always uncertain. If one were to take place further up north, there would always be a chance to slow down the approaching enemy, even if fortune were not on the Romans' side.

It can be, therefore, safely assumed that the majority of the Roman forces in Thrace, consisting either of both of the praesental armies or of one reinforced with supporting units from the other, were dispatched against the invading Huns. The fastest route connecting the capital and the endangered frontier was *Via Militaris*. Attila had already chosen this approach to invade Thrace in the past and all likelihood that was where the Roman soldiers were sent to intercept the approaching opponent. It is up for speculation who commanded these forces. It is probable that one of the commanders was Aspar, which is evidenced not by the faulty passage in Theophanes' chronicle, but rather by the coinciding fact that Aspar's son, Ardaburious, was granted consulship for 447. Evgeniy Glushanin justifiably notes that it was likely a 'gift' to the clan of Ardaburii to secure their loyalty, since Aspar was presumably considered an important asset in the new policy of the emperor against the Huns. Thus, he must have been in a position of command around that time, likely replacing Areobindus in 445; incidentally, it was exactly around that time when the relations with the Huns turned sour. It may be that Aspar's good use of the limited resources he had at his disposal in the wars of 441–442 was the reason why it was decided that he would be the commander in the future conflicts. The other commander was possibly Apollonius, but the evidence in support of that is even more uncertain. All that we know is that he is attested to have been in command in 443 and to have taken part in an embassy in 452, which would have been unlikely if he had held no office at the time. This would amount exactly to two terms in office[193]. Furthermore, simply by a process of elimination there is no other name unaccounted for which would be referenced around that time, save for that of Areobindus; however, there is nothing which would indicate he held the office during the conflict, since the account of Theophanes cannot be taken as proof of that. He might have taken part in the war as a *magister militum vacans*[194]. Having said that, there is also a possibility of sudden nominations and dismissals, which we have no way to account for.

Whoever was in charge of the Roman field armies had the difficult task of intercepting the Hunnic forces in the Balkans. This time, however, Attila, after the capture of Ratiaria, which most likely held out much shorter than the Romans had hoped it would and needed it to, turned eastwards in parallel to the course of the Danube, while the army of the *magister militum per Thracias* Arnegisclus was marching from the opposite direction. It is plausible that the general did not plan to confront the invaders, but instead intended to join forces with the army dispatched from Constantinople. Whether or not he was reinforced is difficult to ascertain, and there is no evidence in the sources which would point one way or the other. However, for that to have been the case, his forces would either have to have been strengthened by some detachments from the field

---

[193] The fact that Apollonius managed to build a close relationship with Flavius Zeno after the war, presumably based on similar views on the Hun policy, may also suggest that they were both commanders in the war of 447.

[194] However, it bears mentioning that Areobindus must have been fairly old, since he died of natural causes just two years later, cf. M a r c e l l i n u s   C o m e s, a. 449. He might have been no longer fit for military service.

armies prior to the Hunnic invasion, or the praesental forces (or their elements) would have had to cross the Hemos mountains to join him. Furthermore, of all the sources relating the course of the battle, none mentions any commanders other than Arnegisclus, and only Theophanes (whose credibility in this case is, as it has been pointed out, highly questionable) names him alongside Aspar and Areobindus, but does not mention the Battle of Utus itself.

In the engagement which followed, Arnegisclus valiantly opposed the Hunnic forces, but was ultimately defeated. The sources at our disposal seem to indicate that the battle was going favourably for the Roman side, and it was only the death of the commander, who was bravely leading his troops in the midst of the fighting, turned the tide. It might have been so, but it is equally probable that the Battle of Utus was later considered by the Romans a necessary sacrifice of the numerically inferior army of Thrace to slow down the Hunnic hordes. It was certainly the most famous event of the whole war, which is indicated by the survival of three accounts, which describe it. Its actual tactical and strategic aftermath is, however, difficult to evaluate.

It is not known what happened to the other Roman armies in the Balkans. It is simply assumed in the historiography that they were destroyed, but, as it has previously been established, it is not even likely for them to have taken part in the Battle of Utus. Regardless of that, the Huns pressed on into the Roman territory, eventually capturing Marcianopolis. The destruction of the Roman armies would be a reasonable explanation for the quick successes of the Huns. That being said, if by turning east the barbarians evaded the main force that was sent to meet them, the subsequent news of the catastrophe at Utus and Arnegisclus' demise could have been a major blow to the Roman morale, even to the point that the armies were rendered effectively useless for military purposes[195]. Furthermore, those soldiers were now in a very difficult situation. We obviously do not know at what points they learned of the fall of Ratiaria, the route taken by the Huns, and eventually the fate of the army of Thrace and its general, but, undoubtedly, they were always a couple of steps behind. As the enemy pressed on, it might have become clear that they were neither able to chase him nor cut him off because Hemos mountains standing in the way.

The only sensible course of action must have been to retreat to Constantinople as quickly as possible, because even if the walls could be rebuilt in time, there were not enough defenders in the capital to man them. Apart from that, it might have been too late to do so anyway.

---

[195] It needs to be noted that the events preceding the war of 447 could also have had a detrimental effect on the morale, considering that they could have been interpreted as bad omens or a sign of divine wrath.

Similar fears must have been going through the minds of the emperor and his court. The Romans did not have many options to choose from when deciding how to deal with the threat. Unfortunately, this is also the part of the war which is the most obscure due to the lack of sources, a problem which explains the tendency to avoid making any claims regarding these events in the scholarship.

The only clues at our disposal are the fragments of Priscus, especially the second passage in the excerpts from the Roman embassies[196]. The short, laconic note mentions the mission of Flavius Senator to Attila and an army commander Theodulus who was stationed in Odessos. The first piece of information should not be a surprise. The use of diplomacy either to stop an opponent or at least gain time when facing a serious threat was a common practice. In this case however, as Priscus bluntly states, the envoy achieved absolutely nothing. What is more interesting is how he decided to reach the Huns. As the historian remarks, Senator was unsure if he could travel by land, therefore he decided to sail to Odessos. This must mean that at that point the Hunnic vanguard must have already been moving south, parallel to the coastline of the Black Sea, towards Constantinople, and thus the envoy did not want to risk capture.

The fact that Priscus names Theodulus at that point is curious as well. He specifically mentions that the general was sent to Odessos. It is clear, therefore, that as soon as the news of the tragic fate of Arnegisclus and the army of Thrace had reached Constantinople, the emperor immediately dispatched Theodulus to reorganize the dispersed units in the north. The commander did not manage to prevent the fall of Marcianopolis, nor could he oppose the Huns in the field. He probably gathered the remnants from Arnegisclus' army and the survivors from the siege of Marcianopolis and prepared to hold Odessos, successfully, as we know that the town did not fall during the war.

When Senator's embassy failed, the emperor was truly helpless. Luckily, the walls of the city were rebuilt at incredible speed in just three months' time due to the extraordinary efforts of the urban praefect Constantine, who, thanks to his cunning, employed the circus factions and ensured their engagement by making the opposing factions compete against each other[197]. All of this would have been for naught had it not been for the eventual arrival of Flavius Zeno with his Isaurian troops[198]. The Huns most likely managed to reach the fortress of Athyras[199] located just on the outskirts of Constantinople. Having had no chance to conquer the rebuilt walls defended by the Isaurians, it seems that the Huns either tried to

---

[196] Priscus, fr. 9.
[197] Marcellinus Comes, a. 447. Cf. *PLRE*, vol. II, p. 317 (s.v. *Fl. Constantinus 22*).
[198] P. Crawford, *Roman...*, p. 27.
[199] Theophanes, AM5942.

plunder the lands to the west of the capital or attempted to cross the Dardanelles, since the next major event of which we know was the battle at the Chersonesus.

This engagement, known only in passing from a reference in the *History* of Priscus, its details, significance, and even the outcome are all a matter of speculation. The location of the battle could mean that the Huns were facing, among other units, the reinforcements from the east led by Anatolius. Such a conjecture is further supported by the fact that this general was later responsible for the peace negotiations, which was often the prerogative of the military commander who was the closest to the theatre of operations[200]. Furthermore, it is possible that the forces of Flavius Zeno took part in the clash, considering how close they were to the location of the battlefield. Whether the praesental armies of the Empire took part in it is uncertain, however, it cannot be ruled out. Nevertheless, it is likely that the Huns met the concentrated Roman force at the Chersonesus.

The outcome of the battle is another unknown. As it has already been pointed out, the scholarship generally assumes that it was another defeat for the Roman side; however, there are several counter-arguments to that. Firstly, the fact that the Huns retreated from Thrace and did not even attempt to lay siege to Constantinople indicates that the Roman army had not been routed. Secondly, several Roman commanders, with the saviour of Constantinople, Flavius Zeno, at the forefront wanted to continue the war at all cost. The reasons behind their determination will be explained in detail in following chapters; however, they had to estimate their chances highly against the Huns of Attila if they were willing openly to push for a military resolution of the conflict. It would be unlikely for that to have been the case if the Roman forces had been completely obliterated in the encounters with the barbarians. Thus, it is quite probable that the battle of the Chersonesus was a stalemate[201]. Neither did the Huns manage to break the Roman forces nor did the Imperial army defeat the invaders. In such a situation Theodosius was left with the decision whether to pursue further conflict.

While the outcome of the war hung in the balance, the fortified town of Asemus located on the northern border, witnessed, like many other Roman cities at the time, raiding and pillaging of the surrounding country by the Huns. The Asemuntians, however, stood out among the rest due to their courage and mar-

---

[200] P r i s c u s, fr. 9.

[201] Christopher K e l l y (*The End of Empire. Attila the Hun and the Fall of Rome*, New York 2009, p. 137–138) recognizes the battle at the Chersonesus as something more than just another defeat; he suggests that it was rather a costly military effort that saved the capital, which it probably was. Some aspects of his overview of the campaign of 447 are interesting, however, he confuses the chronology, placing the battle of Utus after Attila's march into Thrace. Cf. *ibidem*, p. 130–139.

tial prowess, as they not only defended the walls, but also managed to set out to the field and defeat some of the raiding parties. Doing that, they freed many prisoners and captured Hunnic baggage trains with spoils. There is no doubt that the episode of Asemus serves a specific purpose in the story of the war in Priscus' work, and it may have been slightly exaggerated. It is, however, also an example that the Huns suffered set-backs in the campaign of 447 and that the outcome war itself was not one-sided[202].

The Peace of 447

The clash at the Chersonesus was the last engagement in the war. As Priscus reports, peace negotiations followed, even before Attila retreated from the Roman territory, and the envoys who were chosen to negotiate were Anatolius and Theodulus, two commanders who operated in the area[203]. It seems to indicate that the subject of the talks was an armistice rather than a lasting peace. For the emperor, an imminent cessation of hostilities must have been a priority in this situation.

The price that the Romans had to pay for it, however, was steep. An annual tribute of 2,100 pounds of gold was agreed upon. In addition, the Romans had to pay the arrears of 6,000 pounds of gold, and relinquish all of the refugees and prisoners, while the Roman prisoners of war were subject to a ransom of 12 *solidi* per capita. To add insult to injury, Theodosius also was forced to pay for prisoners whom the Huns claimed to have captured, but who escaped on their own.

Priscus adds that Attila demanded a strip of land stretching from Pannonia to Novae, which was five days' travel deep into the Roman territories. It used to be commonly accepted that Anatolius indeed ceded some territory to the Huns to create a demilitarized buffer zone[204]. This would have been a temporary measure, as just two years later another embassy would negotiate a return of those lands under full Roman control. It has to be understood that considering the difficult situation the Empire was in, such a decision would not have been

---

[202] When Hyun Jin K i m (*The Huns...*, p. 72) presents his interpretation of the course of the war, describing Roman armies suffering defeats, one after another, and all of Thrace being over-run, he conveniently omits the story of Asemus and its valiant defenders.

[203] P r i s c u s, fr. 9.

[204] A.H.M. J o n e s, *The Later...*, p. 194; O. M a e n c h e n - H e l f e n, *The World...*, p. 124; R. H o h l f e l d e r, *Marcian's Gamble. A Reassessment of Eastern Imperial Policy toward Attila AD 450–453*, AJAH 9, 1984, p. 55; T. S t i c k l e r, *Aetius...*, p. 123.

entirely unreasonable, especially since the Romans, as Priscus states explicitly, were desperate to make peace at all cost. However, other scholars interpret the source differently, positing that Attila's demands were not grounded in any previous agreement and just constituted his usual extortions and threats, which was probably the case[205].

The consequences of the war of 447 and the ensuing peace are hard to gauge and have been subject to much discussion. Priscus paints an apocalyptic picture of the Roman populace becoming subject to exorbitant taxes, which ruined their livelihoods, leading some to starvation or even suicide from despair. Some from the formerly rich senatorial class were forced to sell their belongings, even furniture or their wives' jewellery. Furthermore, some of the refugees, who were to be handed over, refused to comply and were thus killed by Roman hands. The historian certainly attempts to present this peace as a political catastrophe, a disgrace to the Roman state, and a huge strain on the budget. The latter part is disputable, however. Some scholars have noted that the sums that were demanded by Attila were relatively insignificant considering the economic capacity of the Roman Empire[206]. They tend to attribute bias to Priscus and to point to his allegiance to the senatorial class as the motivation behind his criticism, and propose an interpretation to the contrary: considering their enormous wealth, the additional taxes imposed on the higher classes could not have harmed their well-being, and were rather a sound decision because they prevented burdening the general population with additional taxes. However, what these considerations fail to take into account is that the taxes were collected from the people who had previously been exempt from them. A usual practice was to grant exemptions to those who were affected by natural disasters or enemy raids. It also has to be recognized that the additional taxes had to cover the expenses of a state that was first hit by natural disasters, then had to wage a war, and finally pay tribute. If we take all of that into account, suddenly the sums which were the subject of the treaty become more significant[207]. In addition, Priscus does not say that it was only the senators

---

[205] B. C r o k e, *Anatolius...*, p. 169; J. P r o s t k o - P r o s t y ń s k i, *Attila...*, p. 139.

[206] A.H.M. J o n e s, *The Later...*, p. 206–207; E.A. T h o m p s o n, *The Foreign...*, p. 73. See also: Ch. K e l l y, *The End...*, p. 141–142.

[207] Furthermore, Doug L e e (*The eastern empire: Theodosius to Anastasius*, [in:] *CAH*, vol. XIV, *Late Antiquity: Empire and Successors, AD 425–600*, ed. A. C a m e r o n, B. W a r d - P e r k i n s, M. W h i t b y, Cambridge 2008, p. 45, n. 77) brings up an interesting argument that the quick collection of vast financial reserves by the successor of Theodosius, Marcian, could be attributed to his different policies regarding tribute, and could indicate how much of a strain on the Empire's resources the appeasement of Attila was. For other scholars who accept the severity of the taxes, cf. C.D. G o r d o n, *The Age of Attila. Fifth-Century Byzantium and the Barbarians*, Michigan 1961, p. 66–67; O. M a e n c h e n - H e l f e n, *The World...*, p. 114; N. L e n s k y, *Captivity*

who were affected by the additional obligations and his allusions to their leading to starvation and suicides among some people seem to suggest that the common man was not spared by the tax collector either.

Therefore, it seems that the terms of the peace of 447 were controversial to say the least, not only among the rich senatorial class, but with other groups as well. Furthermore, its conclusion did not put an end to the tensions. It appears that the Romans were not particularly willing to turn over the fugitives and prisoners, and were acting in an obstructive way. The dissatisfaction must have been common, and one sphere of the society which seems to have been particularly upset with the outcome of the war was the military elite.

The Straw that Broke the Camel's Back: The Conflict over the Hunnic Question

There is some evidence that certain members of the Eastern Roman military command were not happy with how the Hunnic problem was being dealt with. Naturally, we do not have their own statements criticizing the policies of the emperor; however, their attitudes can be discerned with the help of an analysis of their activities just after the war. Luckily, the aftermath of the conflict of 447 and the diplomatic talks with Attila are among the most detailed and credible descriptions of historical events from the fifth century which can be found in the whole corpus of the sources.

The most vocal opponent of the Imperial policy regarding the Huns was doubtlessly the hero of the war, Flavius Zeno, the Isaurian. His willingness to continue the fight was apparent, considering the political scandal he was willing to create only to make his point[208].

As it has already been stated, Theodosius was desperate to conclude peace with Attila. When the Hunnic embassy, at some point after the armistice of 447, had reached Constantinople, one of its members, a Western Roman named Constantius who was the king's secretary, offered the emperor to ensure that a lasting peace would be made on the condition that he receive a wealthy, noble-born

---

among the Barbarians and Its Impact on the Fate of the Roman Empire, [in:] The Cambridge Companion to the Age of Attila, ed. M. M a a s, Cambridge 2015, p. 235–238; H.J. K i m, The Huns..., p. 71–73; P. H e a t h e r, The Fall..., p. 312.

[208] P r i s c u s, fr. 14; K. F e l d, Barbarische..., p. 218–219; R. K o s i ń s k i, The Emperor Zeno. Religion and Politics, transl. M. F i j a k, Cracow 2010, p. 61; M. M e i e r, Geschichte..., p. 421.

bride for his efforts. Theodosius happily agreed to the request, offering a daughter of a wealthy senator named Saturninus. She was under the emperor's care
ever since her father had been killed by the order of the empress Eudocia[209]. It
is not stated in the sources how Constantius planned to achieve the promised
lasting peace, whether he had Attila's ear or had some other way in mind. According to the Huns, the issues that prevented a conclusion of an agreement were
primarily the sly and deceptive attitude on the part of the Romans when they
had to turn over the fugitives and prisoners. Consequently, Attila refused to relinquish the territories on the Danube which he had occupied. However, knowing how most issues in Roman-Hunnic relations were resolved, the answer was
probably money. As Priscus reports, Constantius agreed to split the dowry he
would receive with the king. It is possible that this was a way of appeasing Attila
with yet more gold, and an alternative to straining the Imperial treasury even
further, as it was already in dire straits[210].

Unfortunately for Theodosius, this is when Zeno decided to step in and take
matters in his own hands. He kidnapped Saturninus' daughter, hid her away,
and ordered her to marry one of his subordinates, a certain Rufus. Whatever
arrangements the emperor had with Constantius, they were no longer binding.
The Roman protested his case to Attila, and the king took a personal interest in
the matter[211]. As a result, just after the costly treaty of 447 had been settled, the
diplomatic relations changed for the worse yet again, and over an issue that was
not at all something the emperor was willing to fight for.

Even though there are plausible reasons why the generals might have wanted
to continue the war with the Huns, Zeno's fervour seems exceptional for a mere
difference of opinion, even if the well-being of the Empire was at stake. Perhaps
the Isaurian was just fierce in his convictions, but a certain letter he received from
Theodoret may hint to other reasons. The bishop of Cyrrhus expresses in it his
sympathy for the loss of Zeno's brother. Considering that the letter is dated for
448, it is conceivable that he might have died in the war, perhaps even in the field
of battle[212]. Could Zeno be motivated not only by political calculations but also
the feelings of grief and vengeance? It is impossible to ascertain; however, the
above consideration should serve as a reminder of the humanity of the people
involved in the historical events and the fact that their individuality also contributed to shaping them.

---

[209] R.C. Blockley, *The Fragmentary*..., vol. II, p. 388, n. 86.

[210] Idem, *East Roman*..., p. 66.

[211] The issue was brought up during the meeting of Maximinus and his embassy with Attila,
cf. Priscus, fr. 14.

[212] Theodoret, *Ep.* 65. Cf. *PLRE*, vol. II, p. 1199–1200 (s.v. *Fl. Zenon 6*).

The Curious Case of Berichus

Even though it appears that there is little evidence implying the political alignment and common goals of the military commanders beyond what has already been stated, there is an important clue hidden in the narrative of Priscus which could serve as a basis for new interpretations. The story in question is part of the historian's report from his diplomatic mission to the Huns and concerns an argument with a certain Berichus, a Hunnic nobleman, who was sent with the returning Roman envoys to conduct negotiations on behalf of Attila. As they were travelling together, Berichus suddenly appeared resentful for no apparent reason: he refused to communicate or even ride along with the Romans. When finally asked about what had caused his behaviour, he accused Maximinus, the head of the embassy, of claiming in front of Attila that Aspar and Areobindus were unreliable barbarians and had no say at the emperor's court. Unfortunately, Priscus is not clear as to why this infuriated the Hun so much, and it is just as likely that the diplomat himself did not understand what had caused the barbarian's ire. There are many possible explanations, and some (which I consider to be the most probable) may be relevant to the questions at hand[213].

There are two main problems with the case of Berichus: why did Maximinus make such statements about Aspar and Areobindus, and why did that fact anger the Hun so much. There are two possible ways of accounting for Maximinus' words: the envoy made the observation that Aspar and Areobindus had no power because after the war with the Huns they were no longer held the offices of *magistri militum*. This would mean that the tenure of Aspar was cut short, which, from what we know, was not a common occurrence, even if the commander in question could be accused of failures in his service. Of course, it is possible that the war of 447 was a special case, but it is impossible to say whether Aspar could have been guilty of any misconduct, cowardice, or incompetence. However, considering the humiliation that was the peace of 447, it is not unlikely that the commanders leading the army who failed to deliver a victory over the Huns made have made convenient scapegoats[214]. It does not, however, explain why would Attila need to know that and why would it infuriate Berichus.

The other possibility is that Maximinus wanted Attila to name specific persons as future envoys. The king of the Huns was very selective and sometimes refused to speak with the Romans when he considered them not illustrious

---

[213] Cf. Ł. P i g o ń s k i, *Berichus and the Evidence for Aspar's Political Power and Aims in the Last Years of Theodosius II's Reign*, SCer 8, p. 247–251.

[214] Cf. R.A. B l e e k e r, *Aspar...*, p. 81–82.

enough. In this instance, it appears that he named people he had already trusted and had dealings with: Anatolius, Nomus, Senator, Aspar, and Areobindus[215]. Out of these five, Maximinus clearly tried to convince Attila not to ask for Aspar nor Areobindus; for some reason both of those commanders were somehow inconvenient to the Roman envoy or the people he represented. This might have been simply due to their no longer holding any offices at that time, which would have made them ineligible for such an important diplomatic task. There is, however, another possibility to consider, namely why did Berichus get so offended after learning of the actions of Maximinus?

If we accept the seemingly straightforward interpretation that the envoy informed Attila of Aspar and Areobindus being unable to represent the emperor, the only explanation for Berichus' outburst is that it was a misunderstanding, since he perceived the words of Maximinus as blunt and insulting towards the commanders[216]. It is possible, however, that the envoy did indeed use such uncompromising language, and did so for a reason. There could have been a reasonable fear in 448, when the embassy took place, that the military might interfere in the diplomatic process. In fact, that had already happened when Zeno orchestrated the scandal involving the daughter of Saturninus. A more direct intrusion was also possible, and it would not have been unprecedented if we remind ourselves of the example of Plintha. Thus, Maximinus could have reasonably suspected it to happen and employed counter-measures by convincing Attila of the value of conducting negotiations only with select people. For that interpretation to make sense there is, however, yet another assumption that needs to be made: Aspar and Areobindus must have been viewed as opponents of the governmental policy regarding the Huns[217]. This is indeed quite likely, especially in the case of the former who would later on play a crucial role in the accession of Marcian, the emperor who initiated a change in the course of the Hunnic policy. Having been directly on the front and experiencing first-hand the consequences of the inconsistent foreign policy of Theodosius, they had every reason to disagree with it.

The wars of Theodosius were justified in a strategic sense and from the perspective of the well-being of the whole Roman Empire. However, it is unlikely that the Eastern Roman generals of barbarian origin cared much for the other

---

[215] B. C r o k e, *Anatolius...*, p. 166.

[216] Berichus probably took part in the fighting against the Romans; it is not unlikely that it was against the forces led by Aspar or Areobindus. Therefore, demeaning the commanders, especially in front of Attila, could have undermined his own exploits and hurt his prestige.

[217] Christopher K e l l y (*The End...*, p. 121, 137) correctly observes that about Aspar. Also, cf. R.A. B l e e k e r, *Aspar...*, p. 70.

half of the Empire; nonetheless, they probably did care for their own country. Thus, when its security was being put in jeopardy in order to save the West from the Vandals, it is unlikely that they were in support of such a course of action. If, additionally, their status and influence had also suffered, it should be no wonder why they were strongly dissatisfied with Theodosius' and Chrysaphius' policies.

The Developments of 448–450

Maximinus' embassy involved yet another attempt by Theodosius to manage the situation. One of its members, Vigilas, the interpreter, was provided with money by Chrysaphius in order to facilitate organizing a plot on Attila's life; however, the conspiracy has been uncovered[218]. Since the king of the Huns learned that who was responsible for it, he demanded that Theodosius hand over the eunuch. It seems that the emperor's line of defence was to deny accountability, claiming he had no hand in Zeno's and Chrysaphius' intrigues, which was very unlikely in the case of the latter; however, Attila would not be fooled. The barbarian replied to Theodosius' excuses quite wittily as he offered to send a military intervention to 'help' the emperor if he was unable control his subordinates. Diplomatic jargon aside, it essentially meant that another war, just after the destructive conflict of 447 had ended, was a marked possibility.

Theodosius was clearly not in control of the situation. Furthermore, Priscus informs us that Zeno too was seeking Chrysaphius. It is unfortunately difficult to say what exactly the historian meant by that. Zeno, as a *magister militum*, had no right nor means to apprehend Chrysaphius or seek retribution. Next, Priscus follows with an ambiguous statement that the eunuch had an almost unanimous support, and thus an embassy by Anatolius and Nomus in 449 was dispatched to appease Attila and solve the problems. Knowing Priscus' disdain for Chrysaphius, this comment is often considered to be sarcastic, but Blockley rightly remarks that it is possible that even his usual political opponents, save for Zeno, decided that it was preferable to defend the minister on this occasion rather than hand over a high Imperial official to a hostile barbarian ruler[219]. To make amends for the assassination plot, Theodosius agreed to send even more money, and to

---

[218] Priscus, fr. 11; R.C. Blockley, *East Roman...*, p. 66.
[219] R.C. Blockley, *The Fragmentary...*, vol. II, p. 389, n. 96.

keep the promise given to Constantius, another suitable bride was found, the widow of the late son of Plintha.

Interestingly, as Holum observes, it is likely that this woman was under Aspar's care, due to his familial relations to the Gothic general[220]. It must have meant that Aspar was willing to offer his support to avoid a crisis. Holum claims that it was part of a wider political change at the court: Pulcheria's gaining influence and Chrysaphius' falling out of favour[221]. However, there is only one source that supports such a case; the chronicle of Theophanes which is at odds with other evidence. Thus, it is quite unlikely that such a dramatic political change occurred, especially since an alternative explanation to the chronicler's claims could be argued for[222].

Ultimately, Chrysaphius stayed in power and Zeno was forced into hiding because of his schemes. The sources state that the emperor feared his open rebellion and an expedition was mounted to bring the insubordinate commander to justice[223]. The superior of Priscus, Maximinus, even though he was mostly known for his diplomatic service, was chosen as the commander and ordered to capture Isauropolis, where Zeno was expected to seek support[224]. It is interesting that no other known military officer was selected for the task. While it might have been due to their being needed at their stations, there is a possibility that it was because the other commanders either tacitly supported the Isaurian or were considered not loyal enough to lead such a mission. This could be seen as another piece of evidence for the existence of widespread opposition to the eunuch in the military.

In general, as it has been suggested previously, there is little direct information about the political conflict at the end of Theodosius II's reign. Each of the pieces of evidence which has been brought up may be on its own not convincing enough to challenge the established narrative which can be found in the literature. However, all of them combined can create a basis for a compelling argument that there was indeed major dissent in the military elite. The main cause of that seems to have been the failure of the foreign policy of Theodosius.

---

[220] K.G. H o l u m, *Theodosian...*, p. 207, n. 157.

[221] *Ibidem*, p. 207. This opinion is upheld by Michael K u l i k o w s k i (*The Tragedy...*, p. 187), but even he admits that we do not know how that might have happened. Chrysaphius was involved in some high-level corruption, which could in theory have brought about his downfall; however, his accomplice was Nomus who remained influential even after the change of the regime, cf. F. M i l l a r, *A Greek...*, p. 192–196.

[222] Cf. p. 92 of the present work.

[223] P r i s c u s, fr. 15–16; Е.П. Г л у ш а н и н, *Военная...*, p. 110; H. E l t o n, *Illus and the Isaurian Aristocracy under Zeno*, B 70, 2000, p. 396.

[224] P r i s c u s, fr. 16; K. F e l d, *Barbarische...*, p. 219.

Conclusion

Theodosius II acceded to the throne shortly after the Eastern Roman Empire had to face a major political crisis involving the military elite, Gainas' revolt. It is difficult to say if the memory of it stayed with the young emperor, but it is a fact that Theodosius in many ways tried to keep the members of the high command in check, reshuffling the appointments to high ranks regularly. However, his reign was marked by many wars, which led to the emergence of powerful individuals among the successful commanders. Theodosius' attempts at limiting their growing influence were futile and seem to have led to an opposite outcome, the consolidation of a new military elite. This and the emperor's failed foreign policy[225], as well as other contributing factors, inflated taxation for instance, contributed to the rising dissent among the commanders. It culminated after the war of 447, when disagreements over the resolution of the conflict with the Huns pushed the country to the brink of civil war. In the end, the emperor died in a horse riding accident before that could happen. However, at the conclusion of Theodosius' reign, because of its shared grievances, the military elite, despite otherwise having little in common, united under one banner against the emperor's minister, Chrysaphius. This meant that when Theodosius passed away, it was in a position to bring forth its own candidate, one who would align closer with its convictions: the the choice fell on an otherwise little-known military tribune, Marcian.

---

[225] That being said, in the end he managed to maintain the integrity of the borders, cf. F. M i l l a r, *A Greek...*, p. 82–83.

The Military Elite during the Reign of Marcian

The reign of Marcian in the Eastern Roman Empire is one of the most curious periods during the fifth century. It is difficult to properly evaluate it, since the sources which chronicle his rule are scarce and fragmentary, and the modern historiography tends to focus on the dramatic events in the West, which sowed the seeds of the eventual fall of the Empire. For the present work, however, the reign of Marcian is of utmost importance, especially considering his unique relationship with the military elite.

The Perception of Marcian by his Contemporaries and in the Scholarship

In the eyes of his contemporaries Marcian was, almost universally, regarded as a good emperor. It seems that in the seven years of his reign he managed to refill the treasury after the financial disaster brought upon by the last years of Theodosius' rule and left enough in the reserves to fuel adventurous policies of his successor, Leo. Moreover, Robert Hohlfelder accurately points out that Marcian was considered an emperor who exhibited traditional Roman martial virtues[1], since he took part in military campaigns and ceased sending the humiliating tribute to the Huns. Thus, his foreign policy was much more popular among the common people and the educated elite. Secondly, he lowered the taxes, which, unsurprisingly, also brought him universal acclaim. Thirdly, he ordered the assembly of the Council of Chalcedon in 451, which resolved some of the ongoing religious conflicts and brought him support of the Orthodox populace. In that case, however, those of opposing religious views would judge the emperor differently[2].

In the modern historiography there seems to be more disagreements on Marcian. The general works and textbooks that overview the history of the period tend to focus not on the emperor, but rather on the happenings in the West, which often seem to be of more consequence to the history of late antiquity. Thus, they tend to follow the judgement of the ancients, without any in-depth commentary.

There is also an opposing view on Marcian, which seems to have originated from the works of a prominent American scholar, Edward Thompson, and is still being upheld by his students. Thompson criticized Marcian's foreign policy as unnecessarily risky. According to him, the emperor was simply lucky that his decisions did not backfire and the Empire did not end up in a destructive war with the Huns[3]. Thompson also discounted the successes of Marcian, especially his fiscal achievements, as they benefitted the elite and the rich; According to the historian, since they were the ones who wrote history, Marcian was being praised not for any objective reasons, but rather because he supported interests of a specific group[4]. Due to Thompson's prominence in the Western scholarship, many later works were at least partially influenced by this outlook[5].

Interestingly, within the research into the military elite, the reign of Marcian is not generally recognized as notable, which is apparent from its inclusion with

---

[1] R. H o h l f e l d e r, *Marcian's Gamble, A Reassessment of Eastern Imperial Policy toward Attila AD 450–453*, AJAH 9, 1984, p. 63.

[2] Cf. R.W. B u r g e s s, *The Accession of Marcian in the Light of Chalcedonian Apologetic and Monophysite Polemic*, BZ 86/87, 1994, p. 59–60.

[3] E.A. T h o m p s o n, *A History of Attila and the Huns*, Oxford 1948, p. 135; i d e m, *The Foreign Policy of Theodosius II and Marcian*, Her 76, 1950, p. 69. Such views still exist in recent scholarship, for which a most vivid example would be the overview of Marcian's policy by Hyun Jin K i m (*The Huns, Romans and the Birth of Europe*, Cambridge 2013, p. 83–84).

[4] E.A. T h o m p s o n, *A History...*, p. 191.

[5] Primarily A.H.M. J o n e s (*The Later Roman Empire 284–602. A Social, Economic and Administrative Survey*, vol. I, Oxford 1964, p. 318–319), whose monumental work disseminated Thompson's ideas even further.

that of Leo's into a single chapter and the latter receiving more attention[6]. It is probably because of the general lack of prosopographic information on the generals of Marcian and an overall scarcity of the sources; however, a thorough analysis of the events pertaining to his reign can fill in the blanks and paint a clearer picture of the emperor's unique relationship with the military. It can be argued that Marcian's reign is instrumental in understanding the military elite in the fifth century and it significantly differs from that of his successor.

Accession to the Throne...

Marcian ascended the throne of the Eastern Roman Empire on the 25 August 450, a month after Theodosius' death. Before that point, however, there had been little in his life that would have indicated this happening. Marcian came from a family with military traditions and followed the same path, joining the army early in his life[7]. In 421 he took part in the Persian campaign commanding a troop[8], likely in the rank of *tribunus*[9]. Perhaps, it was at this point, or soon after, that he became a *domesticus* of general Ardaburious; however, no details of his service in this capacity are known. Later on, possibly when Ardaburious, for one reason or another, disappeared from the records, Marcian exercised the same function under the general's son, Aspar. Under his command he took part in the African expedition, where he was taken captive following the lost battle with the Vandal king, Geiseric[10].

Up until the year 457, every single piece of evidence points to the fact that Marcian was just a regular middle-rank officer. However, if we are to believe John Malalas, he was specifically chosen by Theodosius II on his deathbed to be his successor[11]. Other accounts, of Evagrius, Hydatius, and Theophanes, present a different story, namely that Marcian was chosen for his virtue by Pulcheria, the emperor's sister, and presented to the Senate, which accepted his candidacy on her advice[12]. While Hydatius' remark is rather laconic, both Evagrius and

---

[6] Е.П. Глушанин, *Военная знать ранней Византии*, Барнаул 1991, p. 113–136; A. Demandt, *Magister militum*, [in:] *RE*, t. XII suppl., 1970, p. 763–781.

[7] Priscus, fr. 18.

[8] Theophanes, AM 5943.

[9] Malalas, XIV, 27; Theodor Lector, *Epitoma*, 354.

[10] Evagrius, II, 1; Procopius, *History of the Wars*, III, 4, 2–10.

[11] Malalas, XIV, 26–27. The same story is repeated by *Chronicon Paschale* (a. 450).

[12] Evagrius, II, 1; Theophanes AM 5943; Hydatius, 139.

Theophanes add that Pulcheria had one condition. She required that Marcian respected her vows of virginity, which he agreed to do. The events presented thus far do not provide a reasonable explanation why it was specifically Marcian who was chosen for that role. Nothing is known of his involvement at the court or any connections to either member of the Imperial family; it begs a question how would Theodosius or Pulcheria even know of him. Furthermore, it would have been rather unlikely for a regular army officer to be selected to ascend the throne, regardless of how virtuous of a man he was. There was no natural successor to the throne in the East, but undoubtedly there were many who were more influential, powerful, and connected to the court.

... and Its Presentation

A person acquainted with the previously mentioned sources could have noticed my purposeful omission of much additional information regarding Marcian's past. The reason for that was to paint a realistic picture of the emperor's early career and explain how unlikely his accession to the throne was, if we were to fully accept the course of events presented by the sources. It would have been just as suspect for the ancients themselves, were it not for the fantastical elements that explained how Marcian was destined to rule[13].

According to Evagrius, when Marcian enlisted in the military he found a dead body *en route* to the camp and wished to do the honourable thing and bury it. While doing so he was spotted and wrongfully accused of murder; however, thanks to divine intervention, the murderer was identified and the future emperor was saved. This event indicated that Marcian was always favoured by the Divine Providence and protected from the consequences of bad fortune. In the unit he enlisted in, he was enrolled in a commanding rank due to a vacancy in the register because the previous holder of the office was recently deceased. As Evagrius notes, it just so happened that the name of the soldier was Augustus, hence Marcian was registered as 'Marcian who is also Augustus', foreshadowing his Imperial future, since *Augustus* was an Imperial title[14].

---

[13] Most likely they originated from Imperial propaganda, cf. R.W. B u r g e s s, *The Accession...*, p. 59.

[14] E v a g r i u s, II, 1. Even though Evagrius used Priscus as his source, those prophetic events regarding Marcian likely originated elsewhere, cf. D. B r o d k a, *Priskos von Panion und Kaiser Marcian. Eine Quellenuntersuchung zu Procop. 3,4,1–11, Evagr. HE 2,1, Theoph. AM 5943 und Nic. Kall. HE 15,1*, Mil 9, 2012, p. 159.

Evagrius follows that up with a story from Marcian's captivity among the Vandals, which is also recorded in Procopius' *History of the Wars*. The prisoners were gathered in an open field where they were being guarded. Marcian wished to rest, however, when he lied down in the scorching sun of the desert, an eagle flew over him, covering him with its shadow while he slept. Geiseric, the king of the Vandals, noticed this occurrence and considered it prophetic, meaning that Marcian was destined to become an emperor, and thus he decided to let him go[15]. Another version of this story is recorded in Theophanes' chronicle, in which it is said that this event happened in Lycia when Marcian had fallen ill on the way to war with Persia. The eagle's shadow shielding his body from the sun was noticed by two brothers who were taking care of him, and they interpreted this event in the same way as the king of the Vandals did. Convinced that Marcian was destined to rule the Empire, they convinced him to go back to Constantinople, gave him some money, and asked him to promise that he would reward them after the prophecy came true. Naturally, when it did, Marcian did not forget and kept his word[16].

It is not uncommon for historical sources of the time to include such prophetic events. However, the sheer number of them in relation to Marcian is out of the ordinary. In fact, it can be argued that this is the best preserved aspect of his reign. There is only one reasonable explanation to this phenomenon. Marcian's claims to the throne were weak. Weak enough, in fact, that they needed broad justification. It is unknown to what extent the above mentioned stories were devised by the historians and chroniclers, but it is not outside of the realm of possibility that they were encouraged or even actively proclaimed by the state. The story of Theodosius choosing Marcian as his successor with his dying breath, Pulcheria picking him on account of his virtue, and the unanimous support of the Senate for such a decision; they all likely have more to do with how the accession of Marcian has been presented officially, rather than what really went on behind the scenes[17].

---

[15] Evagrius, II, 1; Procopius, *History of the Wars*, III, 4. 2–10. Evagrius managed to make this event even more miraculous, implying that the unrelenting heat of the sun was extraordinary for the season (Procopius claimed it was summer).

[16] Theophanes, AM 5943.

[17] Cf. R.W. Burgess, *The Accession...*, p. 59. There is another side to this overview, provided by the Monophysite tradition, which also claims that Marcian was chosen by Pulcheria, not on account of his virtue, but rather her uncontrollable lust. The source of those slanderous accusations is obvious, and it is Marcian's religious policy. Contrary to most secular or Orthodox sources, Marcian is presented there as a wicked tyrant. What is important here, however, is that they ultimately accept a similar course of events, only with a much differing interpretation of their nature and the motivations of people involved. For the detailed synopsis of Monophysite authors' view of Marcian, cf. *ibidem*, p. 50–54.

It is possible that the story of Theodosius seeing through Chrysaphius' 'villainy' and the banishing of the eunuch towards the end of his reign, described by Theophanes, was also a part of Imperial propaganda[18]. After all, the marriage with Pulcheria has connected the new emperor with the Theodosian line, yet the political alignment of the Imperial couple was starkly opposed to the eunuch. All of the calamities and misfortunes that plagued the previous government were to be presented as Chrysaphius' responsibility. It certainly was beneficial for Pulcheria, and by extension, Marcian, to absolve her late brother of them. To justify the execution of the eunuch, a new narrative has been presented, which went as follows: in the last years of his reign, Theodosius has gotten away from under Chrysaphius' treacherous influence and he intended to punish the eunuch, yet, did not manage to deliver justice due to his untimely death. Thus, by executing Theodosius' minister the Imperial couple have fulfilled the late emperor's will, or so they claimed.

The Month of Power Struggle

Theodosius II died in a riding accident on 28 of July 450. If we are to believe John Malalas, he did not die on the spot, but survived long enough to be transported back to Constantinople and pick Marcian as his successor on his deathbed; however, it took almost a whole month between the death of Theodosius and the accession of Marcian. If, as many sources want us to believe, the line of succession was clear and universally accepted, whether due to the emperor's decision or his sister's, then there was no reason to leave the Empire for a whole month without a head of state. Normally, it was paramount to have the throne occupied at all times and to maintain an unbroken line of succession. Theodosius II himself was crowned *Caesar* in his father's lifetime, just as his father, Arcadius, had become *Caesar* when his father, Theodosius the Great, still had been alive. Thus, such a system could have ensured that any potential usurpers would have been discouraged, any disputes due to power vacuum would have been avoided, and it would have allowed for the transfer of power to be fast and clear; however, that did not happen in Marcian's case. Certainly not because he had no need to secure the indisputable right to rule[19].

---

[18] Theophanes, AM 5942.
[19] R.W. Burgess, *The Accession...*, p. 59.

Lawfully, if such a term can even be used in regard to the Roman succession system, there was a male member of the Theodosian dynasty who could have claimed the throne in Constantinople. Valentinian III, when the emperor Theodosius had died, technically should have become the *Augustus* of the whole Empire. While it was unlikely that he would have been able to rule directly over both parts[20], he could have expected to have a say in choosing a successor of his late elder cousin[21]. We ought to remember that when an analogous situation had happened after the death of Honorius, Theodosius did not hold back and sought military resolution to secure the succession within his dynasty and support Valentinian's rights. There is also some evidence confirming Valentinian's displeasure with the situation, as the Eastern consuls of 451 and 452 were not recognized in the West; thus, indicating that the emperor did not consider Marcian's regime to be legitimate[22].

Considering all of the above, if we take into account the situation Marcian was in, it would have been extremely unlikely for him to voluntarily delay his accession to the throne[23]. There had to have been another reason for it to happen. The most likely explanation is that it took time to establish Marcian's candidacy. After all, Chrysaphius was still powerful and likely had some support, so the establishing of the new regime could not have been accomplished in an instant.

Unfortunately, any details of the process are lost and all we can do is speculate. The most likely course of events was the consolidation of an alliance between influential members of the military, the other officials who were dissatisfied with Chrysaphius' regime, and Pulcheria. The emperor's sister certainly was not influential enough at that point to pick her own candidate, and if she were, there would have been no reason for him to be specifically Marcian. However, she still was a capable politician and her approval was needed. Even though the Empire had no formal laws of succession through inheritance, after 72 years of Theodosian dynasty's rule in the East there must have been a certain sense of loyalty towards. For that reason, Pulcheria's role was essential since she had the ability of giving the new emperor the much needed legitimacy[24].

---

[20] Michael K u l i k o w s k i (*The Tragedy*..., p. 187) is much more direct in claiming it was simply impossible, and the Eastern elites perceived the West at that point as some sort of 'failed state'.

[21] J.B. B u r y, *History of the Later Roman Empire from the Death of Theodosius I. to the Death of Justinian*, vol. I, London 1958, p. 235; E. S t e i n, *Histoire du Bas-Empire*, t. I, *De L'état romain à l'état byzantin (284–476)*, Paris 1959, p. 311; R.W. B u r g e s s, *The Accession*..., p. 49; 63.

[22] *CLRE*, p. 436–439.

[23] R.W. B u r g e s s, *The Accession*..., p. 59.

[24] *Ibidem*, p. 64.

Aspar's Right Hand Man

Considering all of the above there is an important question to be answered: how does a modest officer of the Imperial army suddenly become an emperor? Marcian had no status, influence, or political connections excluding one thing, namely his service as a *domesticus* of Aspar. Even though such a title could designate a wide range of officials, both civil and military, and it evolved through history[25], thanks to Procopius there is no doubt on Marcian's function; as the historian explains, he served as an advisor, an *aide-de-camp* of Aspar[26]. Certainly he must have been both loyal and very close to the commander and likely those qualities decided that it was Marcian who was chosen by the general. In fact, the elevation of Marcian is what directly implicates Aspar as the primary force behind the discussed events. Even though the faction opposing the previous regime had many other powerful figures, Aspar was likely the most influential opponent of Chrysaphius who happened to be present in the city of Constantinople when the news of the emperor's accident arrived. Furthermore, there is some secondary evidence which indicates Aspar's involvement in the succession, such as Malalas singling him out from those present at Theodosius' deathbed when the emperor supposedly chose Marcian as his successor[27], a detail which is also repeated by the *Chronicon Paschale*[28], and finally, Procopius implying that Marcian was destined to the throne not only due to the prophetic signs, but also his connection to Aspar and the latter's political influence in Constantinople[29].

Flavius Zeno, who was the most vocal opponent of Chrysaphius, was hiding in Isauria from the expedition sent against him, led by Maximinus. The whereabouts of Apollonius and Anatolius are unknown; however, as masters of arms they could have been in the field; and regardless, Apollonius probably lacked the political network of Aspar, and Anatolius did not seem to have such strong political convictions as to actively interfere with the succession. The fact that both of those commanders stayed influential figures after Marcian's accession may also indicate that they were not opposed to his candidacy.

This leaves only the late emperor's sister Pulcheria. Even though she is named as the person responsible for choosing Marcian, all the evidence points to that not being the case. Pulcheria, despite her talents, likely lacked the actual backing

---

[25] *ODB*, vol. I, p. 646 (s.v. *Domestikos*).
[26] P r o c o p i u s, *History of the Wars*, III, 4. 7.
[27] M a l a l a s, XIV, 26–27.
[28] *Chronicon Paschale*, a. 450.
[29] P r o c o p i u s, *History of the Wars*, III, 4. 8.

to choose her own candidate. Nevertheless, it seems that Marcian was acceptable to her due to his apparent piety; thus, it is likely that she supported Aspar's pick.

As for Chrysaphius, there is no evidence of him being able to mount any serious opposition, gather his supporters, or present a counter candidate[30]. The animosity towards the eunuch was what truly unified the fledgling political alliance and it can be assumed that his capture was of a highest priority, probably preceding even the political arrangements between Pulcheria and the generals. Chrysaphius' fate was recorded in several sources, however, the accounts differ slightly. Most claim Pulcheria had him murdered[31], John Malalas, on the other hand, claims that Chrysaphius faced accusations under Marcian and was officially executed[32]. However, the most detailed account of those events is presented by Theophanes, who mentions that Pulcheria allowed Jordanes, the son of John the Vandal, to kill Chrysaphius[33]. It bears reminding that the eunuch was most likely responsible for the murder of John; thus, Jordanes was granted by the empress the right to take vengeance. Interestingly, this is yet another piece of evidence, even if minor, that indicates the existence of a political alliance between Pulcheria and the military elite. It also directly names another general who opposed the eunuch, in this case for a very personal reason.

Thus, it seems that Marcian was Aspar's personal candidate, one who was in the end chosen due to the general's combined influence and being in a fortunate position at an opportune time. It is likely that Pulcheria and Zeno eventually supported this choice[34], possibly with the approval of wider circles in the

---

[30] Some people who were likely Chrysaphius' supporters still remained somewhat influential even after his downfall (eg. Nomus, Maximinus). It can mean that they did not help Chrysaphius in the critical month of the power struggle, so no retribution was needed. There is however one official, who disappears from the sources after Marcian's accession, *prefectus praetorio* Hormisdas, who is not even present in the lists of dignitaries at the Council of Chalcedon. Cf. *PLRE*, vol. II, p. 571 (s.v. *Hormisdas*). His falling out of favour is however one of many explanations, maybe he died or was not allowed on the Council for other reasons (could have been a monophysite, considering his name suggest eastern origins).

[31] Marcellinus Comes, a. 450; Theodor Lector, *Epitoma*, 353; Priscus, fr. 3. *Chronicon Paschale* (a. 450) only informs that Chrysaphius was killed, while Prosper (1361) informs of his death without mentioning the cause.

[32] Malalas, XIV, 32.

[33] Theophanes, AM 5942.

[34] The idea that Aspar, Pulcheria, and Zeno created an *ad hoc* political alliance against Chrysaphius to put their own candidate on the throne was proposed by some scholars. Cf. C. Zuckermann, *L'Empire d'Orient et les Huns. Notes sur Priscus*, TM 12, 1994, p. 176; R.A. Bleeker, *Aspar and the Struggle for the Eastern Roman Empire, AD 421–71*, London 2022, p. 58; *The Ecclesiastical History of Evagrius Scholasticus*, ed. et. transl. M. Whitby, Liverpool 2000, p. 60, n. 12; A.D. Lee, *Theodosius and His Generals*, [in:] *Theodosius II. Rethinking the Roman Empire*

military. As such, on 25 August 450 a new reign began. Marcian became the emperor in Constantinople; however, he owed his elevation to the throne to several influential people who made an alliance to gain control over the Imperial policy. Those people most likely still stood behind the throne, seeing to it that their interests were fulfilled. Marcian most likely did not make his decisions completely independently, on the contrary, he had to cooperate with a number of immediate associates, and the resulting, complex political scene is crucial to understanding his reign.

All Marcian's Men

When researching Marcian's personal policy there is one asset that is of immense help. The Council of Chalcedon lists dignitaries who took part in it and shines a little light on the internal workings of the state just after Marcian's accession. Even though it focuses mostly on civil servants, it mentions names, offices, and who was the representative of the Emperor and who represented the Senate[35].

Interestingly, the first official, who was the representative of the emperor and present at the Council was the *magister militum* Anatolius. It indicates that despite the previous government's trust in him, the general must have not supported Chrysaphius, at least not to the point of refusing close cooperation with Marcian. Consequently, the emperor clearly considered him a trustworthy associate, if he decided to rely on him as his representative in religious matters that were of utmost importance. This relationship is further corroborated by Arme-

---

in Late Antiquity, ed. C. K e l l y, Cambridge 2013, p. 95–96. Others take only Aspar and Pulcheria into account, of whom some underscore the former's power and influence as *Kaisermacher*: G. V e r n a d s k y, *Flavius Ardabur Aspar*, SF 6, 1941, p. 53; A.H.M. J o n e s, *The Later...*, p. 218; B. B a c h r a c h, *A History of the Alans in the West. From Their First Appearance in the Sources of Classical Antiquity through the Early Middle Ages*, Minneapolis 1973, p. 44; A. D e m a n d t, *Geschichte der Spätantike*, München 2008, p. 152, while some put more emphasis on Pulcheria's role: J.B. B u r y, *History...*, p. 235–236; E. Stein, *Histoire...*, p. 311. There has also been a trend to put Pulcheria in the absolute forefront, claiming the general lost much influence prior to the events of 450. Cf. R.A. B l e e k e r, *Aspar and Attila: The Role of Flavius Ardaburius Aspar in the Hun Wars of the 440s*, AWo 3, 1980, p. 23–29; K.G. H o l u m, *Theodosian Empresses. Women and Imperial Dominion in Late Antiquity*, Berkeley 1981, p. 206–209. Those views have been rightfully criticized by R.W. B u r g e s s (*The Accession...*, p. 27–63), who, however, probably goes a little too far discounting Pulcheria's political talents and not recognizing the importance of Flavius Zeno.

[35] R. D e l m a i r e, *Les Dignitaires Laics au Concile de Chalcedoine: Notes sur la Hierarchie et les Preseances au Milieu du Ve siecle*, B 54, 1984, p. 141–175.

nian sources which claim that Anatolius was still influential at the court and that the emperor often sought his guidance when deciding on the policy towards the Empire's eastern neighbours[36]. In fact, both Yeghishe and Ghazar accuse the general that it was his advice which convinced the emperor to not help the cause of Vardan Mamikonean's rebellion against the Persians[37].

Anatolius is the only high-ranking military official included in the list. Besides him there was a *comes domesticorum peditum* Sporacius. *Comites domestici* were captains of the Imperial guard, thus he certainly was a military official; however, little is known of his career besides the fact that he was awarded consulship in 452, although the reasons for which he received such an honour are unknown[38]. According to John Martindale, another one of the *comites* was Flavius Aetius, not to be confused with the famous Western general. The acts of the Council call him *magnificentissimus comes domesticorum et sacrarum stabulorum*, a title that does not exist in this form anywhere else. Therefore Martindale claims that Aetius must have either been a *comes domesticorum equitum*, and his title was just expanded in that instance, or that he combined the post of *comes domesticorum equitum* with that of *comes sacri stabuli*[39]. However, according to Roland Delmaire, Aetius' place on the list is not appropriate for the office he was supposed to hold. The historian argues it is much more likely that he wielded an honorary rank, that of *vacantes*, likely a *magister militum vacans*[40]. This seems to fit well with what is known about his later career.

Those three names exhaust the list of the officials that could be considered members of the military. However, among the names of the civil servants there is one that can lead to more conclusions about Marcian's relationship with the military, namely certain Flavius Areobindus Martialis. The name suggests that he was related to the late general of the Theodosian era, possibly being his nephew[41]. He was the *magister officiorum* around the time of Priscus' embassy, as the historian informs that he was notified by Theodosius of the plot to take the life of Attila[42]. He, however, was no longer in the office in 451. According to Gereon Siebigs

---

[36] Ł. Jarosz, *Kariera Flawiusza Anatoliusza*, [in:] *Florilegium. Studia ofiarowane profesorowi Aleksandrowi Krawczukowi z okazji dziewięćdziesiątej piątej rocznicy urodzin*, red. E. Dąbrowa, T. Grabowski, M. Piegdoń, Kraków 2017, p. 441.

[37] Ghazar P'arpec'i, 41; Yeghishe, III. On the rebellion and the events surrounding it, cf. N. Garsoian, *The Marzapanate (428–652)*, [in:] *The Armenian People from Ancient to Modern Times*, vol. I, ed. R.G. Hovannisian, New York 1997, p. 98–101.

[38] *PLRE*, vol. II, p. 1026–1027 (s.v. *Fl. Sporacius 3*).

[39] *PLRE*, vol. II, p. 29–30 (s.v. *Fl. Aetius 8*).

[40] R. Delmaire, *Les Dignitaires...*, p. 163–164.

[41] *PLRE*, vol. II, p. 729 (s.v. *Fl. Areobindas Martialis*).

[42] Priscus, fr. 11.

this indicates Marcian was trying to reduce Martialis' influence and stripped him of his dignities[43]. However, the German scholar omits Placitius, also an attendee of the assembly, who served as the *magister officiorum* after April of 449[44]; that is when Martialis is last recorded in office[45]. Thus, if Martialis faced some political backlash, it was by Theodosius II's hand[46]. The previous argument could have been extended to Martialis' successor; that being said, Placitius is also listed as one of the representatives of the emperor, who certainly would not have entrusted someone he considered disloyal or whom he wanted to isolate politically with such an important assignment[47]. The details of Placitius' deposition and the elevation of John Vincomalus, the *magister officiorum* as of the time of the assembly of the Council of Chalcedon, are unknown. Perhaps other factors were at play; since Vincomalus was very pious, maybe he was considered a better candidate for the office when the Chalcedon Council was being prepared, or, he might have been Pulcheria's choice[48].

Regardless of the intricacies of court politics, of which we unfortunately know very little, there is no evidence that Flavius Aerobindus Martialis has been an opponent of the emperor or of his policy, in spite of his no longer having served as the *magister officiorum*. All that being said, another assessment of Siebigs is certainly correct. Marcian, after his accession, reshuffled the cabinet[49]. The list of the representatives of the Senate includes mostly dignitaries who have not served in an office anymore, and names associated with the regime of Theodo-

---

[43] G. S i e b i g s, *Kaiser Leo I. Das oströmische Reich in den ersten drei Jahren seiner Regierung (457–460 n. Chr.)*, Berlin 2010, p. 73.

[44] R. D e l m a i r e, *Les Dignitaires...*, p. 163. The mistake probably originates from following Manfred C l a u s s (*Der magister officiorum in der Spätantike. Das Amt und sein Einfluss auf die kaiserliche Politik*, München 1980, p. 184) who mistakenly assumed Placitius was in office before Martialis, however, the order of the dignitaries in the Chalcedon lists proves that to have been impossible.

[45] R. D e l m a i r e, *Les Dignitaires...*, p. 162.

[46] There is an interesting notion in how P r i s c u s (fr. 11.) describes the emperor relating information to Martialis. The historian says that Theodosius confined in him by 'necessity'. This might simply mean that the emperor was doing his due diligence by informing a senior official of his plans, but it might also mean that Martialis was unlikely to support this plan, or maybe the relationship between the emperor and his functionary was tense. We have to remember it was after 447, when Martialis' uncle, Areobindus, supposedly 'carried no weight with the emperor' and was 'an unreliable barbarian'. It is impossible to know what the convictions of Martialis were, but it is not unreasonable to assume that he was an opponent of Chrysaphius as well.

[47] R. D e l m a i r e, *Les Dignitaires...*, p. 143, 163.

[48] He became a monk later in his life, however, would still visit the palace as a senator, but return humbly to all his menial tasks back at the monastery, cf. T h e o p h a n e s, AM 5957.

[49] G. S i e b i g s, *Kaiser Leo I...*, p. 73.

sius, such as Nomus or Senator, can be found among them. It is likely that at least some of them could have lost their influence after the accession of Marcian. Instead, the emperor seems to have brought new people in, the previously mentioned Vincomalus as *magister officiorum*, Palladius, who became the new *praefectus praetorio per Orientem*, and Tatianus, who became the praefect of the city of Constantinople[50].

It bears explaining why certain people who were previously mentioned as firmly in support of Marcian do not appear on this list of dignitaries. An avid reader may claim such a fact to be evidence to the contrary of the line of argumentation presented so far. However, the absence of most military officials is easy to explain. Apollonius, who was likely the other *magister militum praesentalis* serving alongside Anatolius, was needed in the field. While the Council was being assembled, some fighting was being reported in Illyricum, and even Marcian excused himself for being late to the assembly due to the need to inspect the troops at the front[51]. He claimed that the situation was already under control and that the religious matters were of primary importance to him, so that he was willing to postpone any further campaigning[52]; however, it would have been a logical decision to have an army commanded by Apollonius to remain stationed in the threatened territories to keep the situation in check, which is probably what happened. Regardless, Apollonius was a fresh convert in 448, previously a pagan, likely he neither had any interest in the *minutiae* of the Christian doctrine, nor was he qualified to dispute it. Consequently, the reason for Aspar's absence would have been very similar. As an Arian, a heretic, there was no place for him at the Council which was to decide the Orthodox dogma. That cannot indicate any falling out with the emperor, or the diminishing of his influence. Same can be said about the absence of Flavius Zeno, since he was a pagan.

In fact, all the evidence indicates that Marcian intended to keep the *status quo* in the military high command. All the generals have been serving their terms and there was no reshuffling done. Anatolius, who was likely the least convinced of Marcian's policy towards the Huns, was kept in the office and the emperor heeded his counsel in the matters of eastern foreign policy as well as involved him in his religious dealings. Apollonius seems to have served his full term up until 452 when he was rewarded with patriciate and sent to conduct diplomatic

---

[50] Tatianus was one of the brothers from T h e o p h a n e s' (AM 5943) story that foreshadowed Marcian's accession to the throne. In it, Marcian had promised to reward Tatianus and his brother if the prophecy came true, which, as is exemplified above, he did [Tatianus' brother, Julius, became the governor of Lycia, cf. *PLRE*, vol. II, p. 624 (s.v. *Iulius 4*)].

[51] *The Acts of Council of Chalcedon*, ed. R. P r i c e, M. G a d d i s, Liverpool 2005, p. 107.

[52] *The Acts...*, p. 109–110.

talks with the Huns. Flavius Zeno was also granted the title of *patricius*, however, not much can be said about his proceedings with Marcian, since he died at some point during the emperor's reign[53]. It is unknown whether Aspar served in any office, but, his son, Ardaburious, was chosen as a *magister militum per Orientem*, after Flavius Zeno, who had served in that office, had died[54]. Thus, the claims of Gereon Siebigs that Marcian tried to isolate Aspar are unsubstantiated.

Firstly, if there were any kind of conflict between the new emperor and his former superior, it is reasonable to assume that there would be some evidence for that being the case in the sources, especially if it were to happen in the early stages of his reign when Marcian's achievements did not yet contribute to his popularity and he was not recognized as the rightful ruler in the West. The conflict between Aspar and Marcian's successor, Leo, was a major point of interest in most sources of the period. That being said, the fragmentary nature of the surviving texts might mean that information on their quarrels simply could be lost to the time; however, if such conflicts were a pronounced aspect of Marcian's reign, it would at least be likely that some references should exist. Instead, there are none, on the contrary, it appears that Aspar's family grew in power, especially Aspar's son.

Secondly, considering the indisputable fact that Aspar was involved in elevating Marcian, and taking into account the relative weakness of the emperor's political position, being dependent on the people he owed the throne to (not to mention his other political problems of being unrecognized by Valentinian III and having to deal with Chrysaphius), it would have been an incredibly foolish move to start a quarrel with one of his benefactors. Even a Roman emperor could not have ruled alone, and Marcian needed the support of his associates to govern the country and realize his policy. This seems to have been the reason why he reshuffled most of the high civil offices; he wanted them to be occupied by people who were loyal and reliable. However, as Siebigs himself observes, Marcian did not touch the military offices[55]. This might have been due to his not being able to overcome the influence of those occupying them, or not wanting to, because they comprised his base of support. The second variant is much more likely, but even if the former were the case that would still mean that Marcian simply could not have isolated the powerful general he owed his throne to.

---

[53] J o r d a n e s, *Romana*, 333. Zeno is last attested as *patricius* in late 451, cf. *The Acts...*, p. 174–175; *PLRE*, vol. II, p. 1199–1200 (s.v. *Fl. Zenon 6*). It is likely he died soon after.

[54] P r i s c u s, fr. 19 = *Suda*, A 3803. No other *magister militum* of the east is attested during that time so a nomination just after Zeno's death is most likely. It is known that Ardaburious was already in the east before 453, so his nomination should be placed around 451 or 452.

[55] G. S i e b i g s, *Kaiser Leo I...*, p. 73.

The Wars of Marcian

In the previous chapters on the predecessor of Marcian, I have presented the idea that the failure of the foreign policy of Theodosius was a major factor which contributed to the dissent among the generals, especially towards the end of his reign. Thus, since Marcian seems to have been the 'candidate of the military' an overview of his policy should serve as a proof of that hypothesis. Unfortunately, as it is with many aspects of Marcian's reign, source material is lacking.

The first move in the foreign policy of the newly proclaimed emperor was however quite clear. At some point in late 450 or early 451 the Huns sent an embassy to Marcian, likely to collect the tribute. The emperor must have felt ready for the confrontation, since the answer the envoys received certainly was not to their satisfaction. Marcian refused to pay, and instead adopted a new rhetoric. He demanded of Attila to stop all hostilities, and if he fulfilled that condition, he would consider sending the tribute as a token of peaceful relations. If, however, the ruler of the Huns would continue making demands, Marcian threatened war[56]. It is no wonder that when Attila learned of this he reacted with fury and supposedly considered changing his plans to invade the West in order to enact his wrath on Marcian, but in the end he decided to follow through with his original plan. There are multiple reasons which might explain his choice; he probably considered the West to be a more profitable target[57] and the preparations for the invasion were already underway, but it might just as well have been that he was unsure of a positive result of another campaign in the Balkans, when the bulk of the Roman forces was neither away nor disorganized due to calamities as they were in 447. Cracking a well-organized and intact Roman defence system would have been unprecedented for the Huns[58], and Attila must have known that. It can probably be assumed that Marcian has undertaken precautions in order to strengthen the border, as he had military experience himself and his advisors certainly were professional enough to suggest such course of action. Thus, Edward Thompson's assumption that Marcian avoided a defeat similar to that of 447 only thanks to luck and the fact that Attila had to follow through with his plans is unfounded[59].

---

[56] Priscus, fr. 20. Cf. K. Rosen, *Attila. Der Schrecken der Welt*, München 2016, p. 201.

[57] G. Wirth, *Attila...*, p. 89.

[58] Contrary to the popular belief, the Huns were generally at a disadvantage when facing regular, well organized Imperial troops and most of their successes took place in the absence of sufficient defences on the border, cf. E.A. Thompson, *A History...*, p. 92–93; G. Wirth, *Attila...*, p. 74; 89; R. Lindner, *Nomadism, Horses and Huns*, PP 92, 1981, p. 9.

[59] Cf. E.A. Thompson, *A History...*, p. 135; idem, *The Foreign...*, p. 69.

Considering how quickly after his accession to the throne Marcian made this radical change in the foreign policy indicates that it was likely done in cooperation with the major players, namely Zeno and Aspar, who were instrumental in installing him on the throne and likely interested in the dealings with the Huns. There is a distinct possibility that the person who was responsible for conducting the diplomatic negotiations was none other than Flavius Zeno himself. The evidence is unfortunately thin; however, Flavius Zeno was granted the title of *patricius* during that time and such nominations were often done to give its recipient the right to represent the emperor in negotiations with foreign rulers[60]. The uncompromising tone of the Roman diplomats also seems to indicate that the diplomatic exchange was headed by a staunch opponent of the appeasement policy, and Zeno was indeed one.

Still, some fighting did occur in 451. No details are known beyond what the letters of Marcian to the assembly of Chalcedon inform of. The emperor excused his absence on account of taking part in a military campaign and asked the bishops to pray for victory[61]. In another letter, from 22 September, he informed of his success and that he would soon arrive to take part in the Council[62]. Otto Maenchen-Helfen points out that the bishops from the provinces of Moesia Prima and Dacia Ripensis were absent, which indicates that this was where the fighting occurred[63].

According to Michel Rouche, Attila detached some of his forces to cover his flanks while he was invading Gaul in order to prevent Marcian from sending support to the West[64]. It is doubtful, as it seems that the king of the Huns needed to concentrate all of his forces in his campaign, and it was rather unlikely for Marcian to be even willing to help Valentinian, considering the issues of the legitimacy of his rule and, consequently, tense relations. Furthermore, the evidence suggests the fighting to have occurred in the late summer of 451, thus, after the famous battle of the Catalaunian Plains. The above appears to suggest that the Huns invaded Illyricum when they have been returning from Gaul. After all, Attila's army was not completely destroyed; the battle of the Catalaunian Plains was a strategic victory for the Romans, however, tactically it remained undecided[65]. Because of

---

[60] K. Feld, *Barbarische...*, p. 221. On that practice, cf. R.W. Mathisen, *Patricians as Diplomats in Late Antiquity*, BZ 79, 1986, p. 35–49.

[61] *The Acts...*, p. 107–109.

[62] *The Acts...*, p. 109–110.

[63] O. Maenchen-Helfen, *The World...*, p. 131.

[64] M. Rouche, *Attila. La violence nomade*, Paris 2009, p. 190.

[65] On the campaign and the battle, cf. Jordanes, *Getica*, 190–217; T. Stickler, *Aëtius. Gestaltungsspielräume eines Heermeisters im ausgehenden. Weströmischen Reich*, München 2002, p. 135–145; M. Rouche, *Attila...*, p. 202–210; B. Bachrach, *A History...*, p. 66; P. Heather, *The Fall...*, p. 334–339; K. Rosen, *Attila...*, p. 204–217.

the above, it would have been possible for Attila to attack the Eastern Roman Empire in the year of his Gallic expedition. That being said, such an unprepared move seems rather unlikely for such a capable leader as the king of the Huns. Furthermore, the invasion of Illyricum in 451 is barely recorded in the sources. The only historian who might have mentioned it is John Malalas, and I say he 'might', since he reports some fighting which took place at the Danube in 451, but he links it with Aetius and his struggle against Attila[66]. It is, however, quite likely that the chronicler from the far-away Antioch had mistakenly conflated two distinct events. Considering all of the above, it seems more likely that the fighting in Illyricum in 451 was not a part of some major Hunnic invasion. During the diplomatic talks before the war of 447, Attila intimated that he might not be able to hold his warriors from doing independent raids if he did not receive tribute in gold to appease them. Thus, when Marcian withheld the payments of tribute and the Hunnic warriors were not satisfied with the spoils from Gaul, considering the failure of the campaign, it is likely that some disgruntled warlords tried their luck invading the East. The smaller scope of those raids explains also how those raids were not widely recorded by the sources due to their lesser relevance, why the Eastern forces managed to easily deal with the danger, and why Marcian considered his appearance on the Council more important than continuing the military campaign. It is also possible that the Roman army did not manage to engage the Huns, but only pursued them retreating to their dwellings[67].

The war of 451 leaves many questions unanswered. There is nothing known of the specifics of the military movements of either the Hunnic forces or the Romans. Not one battle is recorded. Who was leading the Roman forces is up to speculation, although with Anatolius present at the Council in Chalcedon, it seems very likely that the commander-in-chief was Apollonius. Ardaburious the Younger, son of Aspar, took part in the fighting and distinguished himself, for which he was awarded the Oriental mastery after the death of Zeno[68]. He would have been either a *comes rei militaris* or *magister militum vacans* at that time[69]. It is possible that Aspar has also been present, perhaps as a *magister militum vacans*, overseeing development of his son's military career. An important detail of this campaign is also the fact that the emperor took part in it in person. It seems likely that he relied on his officers' counsel in regard to strategic and tactical decisions, as it is unknown and rather improbable if he had any experience commanding

[66] Malalas, XIV, 10.

[67] K. Rosen, *Attila...*, p. 217. It is possible, but probably less likely, as it would require the Roman army to operate deep in the enemy territory.

[68] Priscus, fr. 19 = *Suda*, A 3803.

[69] *PLRE*, vol. II, p. 135–137 (s.v. *Ardabur iunior 1*).

large units of the Roman army. That being said, even his appearance at the front is a notable event, an unusual act in the age of the late Roman Empire, when emperors mostly stayed in the confines of their palaces. We can only imagine how much it must have boosted the morale of the troops and affected the popular opinion. Marcian presented himself in stark contrast to his predecessor, as a strong-willed leader who possessed martial virtue, while Theodosius was cowardly and submissive. The campaign of 451, even if of little importance strategically, was a major factor contributing to Marcian's legacy.

The War of 452

The most important achievement of Marcian's foreign policy was yet to come. A year later, in 452 Attila ventured west yet again. The Huns managed to enter the Italian Peninsula, capturing the fortified city of Aquileia that stood in their way, and swarmed into the Po valley, ravaging Mediolanum and Ticinium[70]. According to the main sources for these events, *Getica* of Jordanes and the chronicle of Prosper, Attila was dissuaded from capturing Rome only by the intervention of Pope Leo[71]. The person who once saved the West from the Hunnic menace, Aetius, is either not mentioned at all by Jordanes, or comprehensively criticized for the failure to stop the Huns by Prosper. The chronicler claims that Aetius was surprised by the Huns invading Italy and he failed to defend the mountain passes leading to the Italian Peninsula[72]. It has, however, been observed that there was very little he could have done. Prosper, a layman in terms of military strategy, was unaware that blocking the mountain passes to Italy was not feasible[73]; especially since Aetius lacked troops to organize any serious resistance. His allies from the year prior were unavailable; first, the death of Theodoric I, the king of Visigoths, led to his descendants fighting each other for power, and then, a war between the Goths and the Alans erupted[74]. Even considering these unfortunate circumstances, the critique of Prosper would be somewhat justified if the general did nothing to prevent the fall of Italy to the Huns. However, it does not fit with the character of that capable leader, and luckily, there are some additional sources that seem to expand on the biased accounts of Prosper and Jordanes.

---

[70] Jordanes, *Getica*, 222. Cf. P. Heather, *The Fall...*, p. 339–340.
[71] Jordanes, *Getica*, 223; Prosper, 1367.
[72] Prosper, 1367.
[73] O. Maenchen-Helfen, *The World...*, p. 136; T. Stickler, *Aëtius...*, p. 146–147.
[74] A. Bachrach, *A History...*, p. 68.

Thanks to the Iberian chronicler, Hydatius, there is another version of events that appears to clarify the previously pointed out reservations. According to him, the Huns were forced to retreat from Italy because of two, possibly three, factors. Firstly, the marshes of the Po Valley caused a plague among the Hunic hordes. Secondly, Marcian decided to help the Empire in the West by sending forces to invade the barbarian homeland, and possibly, dispatching auxiliaries to help Aetius[75].

Generally there is an agreement that the plague was a major contributing factor in stopping Attila's advance. It was neither the first, nor the last time when the putrid bogs of the Po Valley caused death among masses of men who invaded the Italian peninsula. In the contemporary Roman history it happened to the Alaric and his hordes 50 years prior to the events related above[76], as well as to the Franks, twice: in 540, when the plague killed a third of their forces[77], and in 553, when they almost lost their whole army[78]. Pestilence spreading among the Hunnic troops was certainly enough of a reason for Attila to retreat with all the collected loot and to not risk a lengthy siege of a fortified city like Rome. It is also far more convincing than the official version of Prosper, who claimed that Pope Leo, incidentally, Prosper's superior, saved Rome from the bloodthirsty Huns like, as Otto Maenchen-Helfen wittily states, '*pontifex ex machina*'. It is plausible that the embassy of Leo only sought to ransom Roman prisoners of war[79].

The other piece of information brought up by Hydatius is more contentious. Some scholars misread the source to claim that it only mentions one force and that the Aetius in question is the Eastern *comes*[80], but Richard Burgess, the editor of the modern translation of the chronicle, points out that Hydatius distinguishes between the *auxillia* that were sent to help Aetius and *exercitum* that attacked the Huns in their own territory[81]. The scholar, however, deems the whole passage untrustworthy. He compares it with a piece of information about later events, a defeat of the Vandals at Corsica in 456, which the Eastern traders, who arrived in Hispalis, falsely attributed to Marcian's military action[82].

---

[75] Hydatius, 146.

[76] Claudian, *De sextu consulate Honorii*, 300–304.

[77] Procopius, *History of the Wars*, VI, 25. 17–18.

[78] Agathias, II, 3.

[79] O. Maenchen-Helfen, *The World*..., p. 140–141; T. Stickler, *Aëtius*..., p. 149–150.

[80] J.B. Bury, *History*..., p. 295–296; E. Stein, *Histoire*..., p. 336; E.A. Thompson, *A History*..., p. 147–148; J.M. O'Flynn, *Generalissimos of the Western Roman Empire*, Edmonton 1983, p. 98–100; *PLRE*, vol. II, p. 29 (s.v. *Aetius 8*).

[81] Similarly, cf. T. Stickler, *Aëtius*..., p. 147–148.

[82] Hydatius, 177. Cf. R.W. Burgess, *A New Reading for Hydatius "Chronicle" 177 and the Defeat of the Huns in Italy*, Phoe, 42, 1988, p. 363.

There are two major counter-arguments to his theory. Firstly, in the letters to the Council of Chalcedon, Marcian claims he has postponed his campaigns to take part in the assembly. It means that continuing the war in the next campaigning season was already in his plans. Secondly, Aetius apparently forced the emperor Valentinian to accept Marcian as a legitimate ruler in March of 452 and it would be unreasonable to think there were no strings attached; likely he understood the sorry state of the Italian defences and wanted to convince Marcian to send help[83]. Thus, contrary to Burgess' claims, there is another source supporting Marcian's military involvement in 452 and there is a plausible justification as to why the emperor would be willing to do it[84].

In addition to the above, Burgess makes a couple of mistakes in his argumentation. He claims that it would have been extremely unlikely for the Eastern Empire to send forces to help the West, since that supposedly did not happen after 425. However, that omits two major and costly operations against the Vandals in 430 and 441[85]. He also argues that the information about Marcian's military campaign in 452 is a claim 'even more fabulous' than that about Marcian's fleet destroying the Vandals. Considering the abundance of sources puzzled by Marcian's passive approach to the Vandal problem or trying to excuse his behaviour, compared to the fragmentary, but still existing sources on Marcian's hard-line policy towards the Huns and actual military involvement, it bears saying that Burgess's evaluation is deeply flawed.

---

[83] *Continuatio Codicis Reichenaviensis*, 21. Cf. T. S t i c k l e r, *Aëtius...*, p. 75–76; 147–148. Considering the chronology and the fact that there was no *détente* in the tense relationship between the East and the West up to this point, this fact must have been connected to the Hunnic invasion. Furthermore, it is evidenced by the words of Valentinian himself, who accused Aetius of forcing him to let go of his rights to the Eastern throne. Cf. P r i s c u s, fr. 30.

[84] In addition, there is an interesting passage in the *Gallic Chronicle of the year 452* (132), where its author criticizes the West for its inaction in the face of the destruction that their Eastern brethren suffered from the Huns in 447. If, as Burgess claims, each part of the Empire had to look after itself and could not reasonably expect any aid, why would it cause such commentary on the anonymous chronicler's part? Considering his work was written around the time of Attila's invasion of Italy, perhaps his critique was informed by the knowledge that the East actually came to the Western Empire's aid in the time of need, contrary to the analogous situation when it was the East which was in grave danger.

[85] It is puzzling how a scholar of this calibre made such a mistake, unless he considered those not 'solely for the purpose of defending the West'. It is however an arbitrary distinction; we could ask ourselves, how often in all of history does it happen that military aid is offered out of sheer goodwill? Alternatively, Burgess could have meant only the situation when military auxiliaries were being sent directly to the Italian peninsula, but it is quite obvious why the Eastern Romans did not send help to Italy between 425 and 452; it was not under direct threat.

This faulty logic seems to stem from Burgess's belief that Marcian was completely unwilling to become involved in the West. Otherwise his argumentation is well presented and his points are strong; however, due to his preconceptions, he is willing to discount the passage altogether instead of seeking nuance. Burgess is entirely right in pointing out that the plague was the most plausible primary reason for Attila's retreat. He is however completely wrong in claiming Marcian's military offensive to be implausible. The evidence points to Marcian's involvement in the war of 452 to be a historical fact[86]; the question that remains is what the course of the events was.

The generals involved in the offensive of 452 were likely the same as those the year before, however, there is again little evidence. Appolonius was named patrician just after the war and conducted diplomatic talks, as was often the case for the commanders-in-chief of the forces engaged in a campaign, which indicates his involvement[87]. The information regarding Ardaburious martial achievements can just as well concern the events of 452; thus, it is possible that he and maybe his father, Aspar, commanded some forces against Hunnic settlements. If Marcian managed to send any auxiliaries to help Aetius directly, we have no means of knowing who could have commanded them. Additionally, there is the possibility that the previously mentioned Eastern official, Aetius, to whom many modern historians attributed the victories of 452, was also involved, despite Burgess's critique. While it is clear that Hydatius meant the famous *magister militum* from the West, there is a possibility that he might have misunderstood the information he was presented with. *Comes* Aetius (the Eastern one) was likely a military official before in 451, and could have taken part in the war of 452 as a *magister militum vacans*. This might have led Hydatius to think that his sources meant that the Eastern soldiers were being led by Aetius, the patrician that he knew well.

Thus, the most likely course of action was that Flavius Aetius, aware of the fact that the Huns are about to invade, asked emperor Marcian for help, offering Valentinian's recognition in exchange. Marcian agreed, and possibly started preparing troops in Illyria. To transport the soldiers across the Adriatic would need considerable time and preparation of ships and supplies, not to mention waiting

---

[86] Cf. M. M e i e r, *Geschichte der Völkerwanderung. Europa, Asien und Afrika vom 3. bis zum 8. Jahrhundert n.Chr*, München 2019, p. 459; O. M a e n c h e n - H e l f e n, *The World...*, p. 137–140; T. S t i c k l e r, *Aëtius...*, p. 147–149; i d e m, *Die Hunnen*, München 2009, p. 87; P. H e a t h e r, *The Fall...*, p. 340–341; K. R o s e n, *Attila...*, p. 225. Interestingly, Hyun Jin K i m (*The Huns...*, p. 83–84) does not question the fact that Marcian sent troops against the Huns in 452, but he claims it was largely inconsequential, and the invasion was overall a success for Attila, regardless of the plague, ignoring the dissent in the Hunnic camp as well as any evidence towards Attila's loss of prestige following the retreat. It is difficult to agree with such reasoning.

[87] P r i s c u s, fr. 23.

for suitable weather conditions. However, the sudden fall of the fortress of Aquileia thwarted Aetius' plans, as it meant that the Huns could advance unimpeded into defenceless Italy. When the realization that there was no longer any time to prepare came, Marcian decided to turn his soldiers northwards, attacking Pannonia, striking at the heart of the Hunnic territory. It is possible that at the same time Aetius was conducting hit-and-run attacks against isolated Hunnic detachments[88]. It could not have saved the northern Italian cities and it brought him no fame, but luckily for the general the amassed forces of Attila were no longer mobile enough due to their being overburdened with wagons carrying the spoils of war, and due to the plague, making their advance further down the Italian Peninsula impossible[89]. At the same time, it is possible that the news of their own settlements being raided and pillaged by the forces of Marcian had arrived, which might have been the reason why the companions of Attila urged their king to retreat[90]. In fact, the arrival of a diplomatic mission of Pope Leo helped Attila save his face and leave Italy while still keeping up the appearance of a victory, dictating harsh terms for the release of captives, and pretending that he was only restraining his wrath and his warriors thanks to the agreement negotiated with Leo. This would also conform very well to the expectations of Prosper, who could then attribute the rescue of Italy to the Pope and Pope only, not even necessarily in bad faith.

The Conclusion of the Hunnic Problem

It seems that the wars of 451 and 452 turned out to be exactly what the prominent members of the military had wanted when they supported Marcian's ascension to the throne. Those victories were small in scale from our perspective, but the Roman territories were never threatened by Attila. Marcian's decisions in the Hunnic policy were careful and involved little risk; they were the opposite of those of Theodosius. Contrary to the common belief in historiography, Marcian did not avoid confrontation; instead, he made sure the conflicts played out on his own terms. Furthermore, those military successes were a source of prestige for

---

[88] They would have been forced to split into smaller squads because of the lack of fodder for the horses, as the state of the pastures at that point of the year in Italy was very bad, cf. R. L i n d- n e r, *Nomadism...*, p. 11–12.

[89] Cf. R. L i n d n e r, *Nomadism...*, p. 11–12; O. M a e n c h e n - H e l f e n, *The World...*, p. 139; T. S t i c k l e r, *Aëtius...*, p. 150.

[90] Cf. K. R o s e n, *Attila...*, p. 225.

the generals: Ardaburious was rewarded with the Oriental mastery, Apollonius became *patricius*, and *comes* Aetius was awarded with consulate, and those are the only honours we are aware of from our scanty sources.

Later this year Attila once again tried to threaten Marcian into submission and demanded for a tribute to be sent. Just as before, the emperor had no intention of appeasing Attila, his aims were quite to the contrary. After preliminary talks with Hunnic envoys in Constantinople, in which Marcian again refused to pay himself off, the Roman embassy was assembled. The envoy to the Huns was the general Apollonius, a freshly appointed patrician. To understand the importance behind this nomination it should be noted that Apollonius was a supporter of Zeno and a brother of Rufus[91]. The same who had been married to a woman promised to Attila's secretary as part of a peace deal. It is up to speculation whether Attila was fully aware of that, but it seems like this nomination was meant as a political insult. And, it appears that it was taken as such. Attila refused to speak with Apollonius at all and was about to confiscate the customary gifts under the threat of killing the general if he opposed it. Apollonius, however, would not be intimidated, which clearly impressed Priscus, who calls the general's behaviour an act of bravery. Thankfully, the Hunnic king did not follow up on his threats and the envoy returned home safely[92].

These events illustrate how tense the relationship between the Eastern Roman Empire and the Huns must have been. The phantom of the war continued to loom over the East for three years after Marcian's accession to the throne. In 453, however, Attila died. The circumstances of his death are often brushed over[93], and much more attention is dedicated to the aftermath which is commonly

---

[91] E.A. T h o m p s o n, *A History...*, p. 148; H. E l t o n, *Illus and the Isaurian Aristocracy under Zeno*, B 70, 2000, p. 396. It should however be recognized that Priscus' passage is not exactly clear, cf. R.C. B l o c k l e y, *The Fragmentary Classicising Historians of the Later Roman Empire. Eunapius, Olympiodorus, Priscus and Malchus*, vol. I, Liverpool 1981, p. 391, n. 114. Some scholars claim Rufus was not the brother of Apolonius, and that Priscus meant some other, otherwise unknown person who was Apollonius' brother and who married the daughter of Saturninus, cf. *PLRE*, vol. II, p. 121 (s.v. *Apollonius 3*). However, as Blockley rightfully points out, Rufus and Apollonius being related makes more sense, because otherwise, why would the historian even bring up the affair of Saturninus' daughter in this passage? In fact, a further conclusion can be made that Priscus wanted to stress how much of a political provocation the nomination of Apollonius was.

[92] P r i s c u s, fr. 23.

[93] Interestingly, this seems to happen because J o r d a n e s (*Getica*, 254) who is generally a reliable source, explicitly says that Attila died of natural causes. However, M a r c e l l i n u s C o m e s (a. 454) claims otherwise, saying that the king was stabbed to death by his newlywed wife. John M a l a l a s (XIV, 10) reports only that Attila's wife was suspected of murdering him, and he supports it by invoking Priscus' authority. He also informs that other sources claimed Attila was murdered by Aetius, who bribed Attila's sword-bearer.

understood as a predetermined fate of Attila's empire in case of the death of its great leader[94]. While its instability and reliance on the powerful authority figure should be recognized, such approach omits the process that could be observed in the years 450–453. In effect, Marcian's policy towards the Huns challenged Attila's authority and resources. After the king's less than successful campaigns in the West, a rift between the Huns and more volatile elements in his empire, primarily the subjugated Germanic tribes, appeared[95]. The death of Attila was not the main reason why the Hunnic Confederacy dissolved, but it seems it was rather one many factors that contributed to it happening, or even possibly, its result[96].

---

[94] Cf. E.A. T h o m p s o n, *A History...*, p. 148–149; J.B. B u r y, *History...*, p. 296; R.C. B l o c k l e y, *East Roman Foreign Policy. Formation and Conduct from Diocletian to Anastasius*, Cairns 1992, p. 68; R.L. H o h l f e l d e r, *Marcian's...*, p. 61; P. H e a t h e r, *The Huns and the End of the Roman Empire in Western Europe*, EHR 60, 1995, p. 29; K. R o s e n, *Attila...*, p. 230.

[95] It should be noted that the lands the Eastern Roman forces attacked in 452 were most likely in Pannonia, which was settled likely settled by Gothic allies of the Huns, cf. P. H e a t h e r, *Goths and Romans 332–489*, Oxford 1991, p. 242. J o r d a n e s (*Getica*, 264) reports that Goths, after breaking from the Hunnic Confederacy, claimed Pannonia since they did not want to fight other tribes for land. Thus, it would mean that is where their settlements were. H. G r a č a n i n and J. Š k r g u l j a (*The Ostrogoths in the Late Antique South Pannonia*, AAC 49, 2014, p. 171) argue, that Goths settled in Pannonia only after the battle of Nedao, when they asked the emperor to grant them these lands. However, Pannonia was previously in the hands of the Huns, and the Imperial claims over it were only *de jure*. Cf. H. G r a č a n i n, *The Huns and the South Pannonia*, Bsl 64, 2006, p. 49–66. Thus, it is likely it was settled by barbarians before that, probably by more tribes than just the Goths: Sarmatians, Huns and Alans as well. Cf. P. M a c G e o r g e, *Late Roman Warlords*, New York 2002, p. 39. A possibility of dissent among Goths, caused by Attila's falling prestige and influence over his allies could have been a serious problem, even to a point of rebellion. Why else did the Hunnic king marry a Gothic princess, Ildico, if not to re-establish the political connections by marriage? Cf. J o r d a n e s, *Getica*, 254. On a more detailed analysis of that problem, cf. Ł. P i g o ń s k i, *Polityka zachodnia cesarzy Marcjana (450–457) i Leona I (457–474)*, Łódź 2019, p. 91–97. Cf. also, M. M e i e r, *Geschichte...*, p. 459–461.

[96] If Attila was in fact murdered. Michael B a b c o c k (*The Night that Attila died. Solving the Murder of Attila the Hun*, Berkeley 2005) presents some convincing arguments why this could have been the case. His hypothetical, however, suspects Western *patricius* Aetius conspiring with Hunnic nobles Edeco and Orestes is much less likely (although, to be fair, there is some fragmentary mention of that in the chronicle of John M a l a l a s (XIV, 10), but the rest of that passage seem to imply that Aetius was involved in it personally and that his deed was recognized as a 'victory' against the Huns. The chronicler is known to confuse many matters regarding the Western history, so those remarks alone do not offer a solid basis for an argument). If I were to speculate, such plot would seem more probable if it was Marcian who ordered it. After all, we know of one attempt to murder Attila that failed due to potential barbarian conspirators choosing loyalty to their king over Eastern Roman gold. After Marcian's diplomacy undermined Attila's position enough, the plotter's dilemma might have had a different conclusion. On the capacity of Roman diplomacy for intrigues, cf. A.D. L e e, *Abduction and Assassination: The Clandestine Face of Roman Diplomacy in Late Antiquity*, IHR 31, 2009, p. 1–23.

This bears posing a question: was Marcian fully aware of how his decisions affected the enemy, and were his actions purposeful and pre-planned? Naturally, as is usually the case with questions of intent, the answer is speculative, but the evidence is convincing. The key to understanding Marcian's policy against the Huns is the fact that he was chosen to become an emperor by Aspar and Zeno, probably to the universal approval of others in the military. The previous chapter answered how important the problem of the Huns was to those commanders and how much they wanted to change the policy directed towards them. Marcian consulted his decisions on the matters of eastern policy and it only makes sense that he did the same when making moves concerning the Huns. The generals fighting Attila, many of them of barbaric origins, might have had a good understanding of the workings of the Hunnic confederacy and its weak spots. It is thus highly probable that the policy towards the Huns was deliberately conceived to undermine the basis of their power and after their collapse, to prevent them from ever regaining it.

The Northern Border and the Career of Procopius Anthemius

After the death of Attila, his sons were not able to stay in power for long. The tribe of Gepids rose up in a rebellion, and soon after, other disgruntled tribes joined in. The culmination of these events was the battle of Nedao, which was lost by the Huns and where Attila's heir, Ellak, met his demise. The Hunnic confederacy collapsed as a result[97]. The Gepids conquered the Hunnic abodes and sent their envoys to Marcian, asking for peace and tribute. Other tribes who supported the rebellion, and even those who remained loyal to the Huns until after the battle of Nedao, also sought arrangements with the Marcian, who allowed them to seek refuge in the territories of the Empire. As such, the Ostrogoths were settled in Pannonia, the Sarmatians and some of the Huns in Scythia and Dacia Ripensis, the Sciri and the Alans in Scythia and Moesia Minor and the Rugians in Thracia[98].

It is likely that all of those tribes were brought into the Roman defence system by arranging alliances with them. The Gepids' plea for a tribute was undoubtedly linked with concluding a *foedus*, it is also known that the Ostrogoths

---

[97] H.U. Wi e m e r, *Theoderich der Große. König der Goten – Herrscher der Römer*, München 2018, p. 120.

[98] J o r d a n e s, *Getica*, 264–266; H.U. W i e m e r, *Theoderich...*, p. 120–121.

received a tribute as well. It can be speculated how expensive was this operation for the Empire; the numerous and powerful tripartite confederacy of the Ostrogoths received no more than 300 pounds of gold[99], but we have no data on other tribes. That being said, considering that the reign of Marcian was a time of prosperity and that he left a full treasury to his successor, it must have been less straining for the budget than paying Attila off.

There was also an added benefit to this policy. Since most of the formerly confederated tribes were now settled on the territories of the Empire and bound to it by alliances, it would have been much more difficult for the sons of Attila to ever rebuild their power. These tribes, no longer being united, even in case of a worsening of relations were too weak alone to seriously threaten the Empire. If, however, the relations stayed amicable, it would have meant that Marcian created a buffer zone on the always porous and notoriously difficult to defend northern border, from then on protected by the federated barbarian tribes. Notably, the lands where the tribes were settled were previously depopulated by the Hunnic raids, thus their settlement did not impact the local populace to the extent it normally would.

The arrangement of the alliance agreements was likely the responsibility of local military commanders. They were the ones overseeing the peaceful resettlement of the tribes into the territories of the Empire and were negotiating with their leaders. It would not be surprising if the whole policy was consulted with them. Unfortunately, this is all up to speculation save for just one example that was luckily recorded due to his later prominence, the future emperor in the West, Procopius Anthemius[100].

Procopius Anthemius was a son of general Procopius, who served under Theodosius, and a grandson of *praefect* Anthemius[101]. His career seems to have quickly developed during the reign of Marcian. Around 453 or 454 he was just a *comes rei militaris* responsible for the defences of the northern border, however, in 455 he was already appointed as *magister militum praesentalis*, *consul*, and *patricius*[102]. He might have received those offices in recognition of his successful efforts at the northern border when dealing with the barbarian settlement, and the rapid growth of his career could indicate how important of a matter it was for the Em-

---

[99] The Ostrogoths were a major power, well organized and cohesive, cf. H. G r a č a n i n, J. Š k r g u l j a, *The Ostrogoths...*, p. 168. The tribute was likely paid in grain, since there are no coin findings in Pannonia from the period of Marcian's reign, (cf. *ibidem*, p. 169), and later, because king Valamer, after the tribute was cancelled, justified starting a war by having the lack of means to live, cf. P r i s c u s, fr. 37.

[100] S i d o n i u s, *Carmina*, II, 199. Cf. P. H e a t h e r, *Goths...*, p. 44.

[101] *PLRE*, vol. II, p. 96–98 (s.v. *Anthemius 3*).

[102] S i d o n i u s, *Carmina*, II, 205–207.

pire. In addition, the title of *patricius* might have been granted to Anthemius to equip him with the proper authority to further arrange the necessary agreements with the barbarian tribes. Anthemius was probably already an influential figure, because of his ties to illustrious members of the Roman elite. While it seemingly looks like an anomaly to have a previously unknown individual rise to the highest offices and to receive so many honours in such short order, it has to be recognized that it might simply be an illusion caused by the fragmentary nature of the sources. Having said that, there is a possibility that there was more to Anthemius' sudden advancements, which I shall explore in the corresponding sub-chapter.

The Problem of the Vandals

After 452 the relationship between both parts of the Empire slowly normalized. Valentinian still apparently held a grudge and did not accept Marcian's consul of 453 in the first months of the year, but later on the issue was resolved, and in 454 the Eastern emperor was allowed to pick both consuls, one of whom was the previously mentioned Eastern official, Aetius[103]. However, the short period of *détente* was about to end soon. The young Valentinian had enough of the control that Flavius Aetius exercised over him; perhaps he grew bolder knowing Attila had died and his empire no longer posed a major threat, or perhaps his actions were simply caused by an emotional breakdown and the long-lasting build-up of hostility and resentment towards the overbearing general. Regardless, in 454, when Aetius came to discuss some state business, Valentinian lashed out in anger and killed the commander on the spot[104]. For the West this was arguably a turning point that initiated the era of turmoil and political instability, which would eventually result in the fall of the Empire in the West. For Marcian, it seems as if Aetius was his primary connection and after the general was murdered, the emperor's policy towards the other part of the Empire became passive and uninvolved. Plausibly, there were other reasons as well, but undoubtedly the lack of a reliable partner in the West was a major factor.

When in 455 Valentinian was in turn murdered by two soldiers connected to Aetius and instigated by a Roman aristocrat, Petronius Maximus[105], Marcian did not react to those events, but neither did he recognize the new emperor.

---

[103] *CLRE*, p. 441.

[104] P r i s c u s, fr. 30. Cf. T. S t i c k l e r, *Aëtius...*, p. 58–79; S. O o s t, *Aetius and Majorian*, CPh 59, 1964, p. 24–25.

[105] *PLRE*, vol. II, p. 749–751 (s.v. *Petronius Maximus 22*).

However, the accession of Petronius Maximus started a chain of events that eventually resulted in the Vandal attack on Rome, which was captured and sacked by the Vandal Fleet in 455. The empress Eudoxia with her daughters was captured by the Vandal king Geiseric along with many other captives and looted treasures[106]. Petronius Maximus was killed while fleeing the endangered city. It would not be an overstatement to say that the West was undergoing the worst crisis in its recent history; however, Marcian appeared seemingly unconcerned by this fact. While it is not true that he was completely passive, his reaction was limited at best. In fact, he only resorted to sending embassies to Geiseric, asking for the return of the women from the Imperial family and the withholding of the Vandal raiders[107].

The Vandal king seems to have ignored the first embassy, since Marcian sent another one. In contrast to Marcian's stalwart attitude towards the Huns, when dealing with the Vandals he clearly sought compromise. This is best illustrated by the choice of the envoy that was sent the second time, Bleda, who was an Arian bishop. This fact underlined by Priscus was probably a gesture of goodwill from Marcian, perhaps the emperor hoped that the Vandal king would be more willing to find common ground when speaking with his brother in faith. This however did not happen. Bleda's demands were, as far as we know, the same as before. Nevertheless, Marcian's accommodating attitude did not make the impression on Geiseric that the emperor was probably hoping for. When the king refused, Bleda assumed a more demanding posture, even threatening war[108]. It did not change the outcome of the negotiations and, in the end, Marcian did not act upon his threats.

The Vandal policy of Marcian warrants an explanation. This aspect of his reign received, alongside his religious policy, much attention in the scholarship. It is arguably the primary reason why it is sometimes described as passive, and the same quality is being incorrectly ascribed to his dealing with the Hunnic problem[109]. The ancients also seemed puzzled by Marcian's inactivity in regard

---

[106] On those events, cf. Ch. C u r t o i s, *Les Vandales et l'Afrique*, Paris 1955, p. 194–197; M. W i l c z y ń s k i, *Gejzeryk...*, p. 145–155; A. M e r r i l l s, R. M i l e s, *The Vandals*, Oxford 2010, p. 115–117; Y. M o d e r a n, *Les Vandales et l'Empire Romain*, Arles 2014, p. 187–189; M.R. S a l z m a n n, *Emperors and Elites in Rome after the Vandal Sack of 455*, AnTard 25, 2017, p. 245–246; R. S t e i n a c h e r, *Die Vandalen. Aufstieg und Fall eines Barbarenreichs*, Stuttgart 2016, p. 196–205.

[107] P r i s c u s, fr. 31.

[108] P r i s c u s, fr. 31.

[109] A notable exception is the overview of Ralph M a t h i s e n (*Avitus, Italy and the East in A.D. 455–456*, B 51, 1981, p. 241), who correctly observes that Marcian could not freely become involved in the West because at that point in time the Danubian provinces still were not fully secured and the emperor was already involved militarily in the east, in Lazica.

to the Vandals. Perhaps this is the reason why the story of Marcian's captivity in Africa and his promise to never take up arms against Geiseric originated in the historical records, either as the authors' own rationalization or him following the propaganda of the regime[110].

That being said, Marcian's policy towards the Vandals is consistent with his decisions in other spheres. The emperor was averse to risk in his policies and the experience of the previous reign of Theodosius had shown that expeditions against the Vandals were very costly endeavours, and despite the resources invested, generally failed to achieve satisfactory results. Marcian was well aware of that as he took part in one of them. In addition, they exposed the Empire to other threats. And finally, the Vandals posed a threat to the Roman Empire as a whole, but the West was much more affected. Considering that Marcian lacked the dynastic interests that his predecessor had, and for the majority of his reign the relationship with the Western government was not amicable, he might not have seen a reason to invest so much to the cause that mattered to him little. From the perspective of the Empire as a whole, it contributed to the crisis in the West and its eventual fall, but for a ruler of the East, it was a pragmatic decision.

Marcian's Vandal policy was likely the result of emperor's own convictions and previous experiences, but it is highly likely that it was an important matter to the main person to whom he owed the throne, Aspar[111]. While there is no direct evidence of Aspar's influence over Marcian during his reign, it would be naïve to assume that the emperor was free to do as he pleased. That being said, there is no evidence of any conflict either. Admittedly, the sources on the reign of Marcian are scarce, however, in case of the reigns of his predecessor and successor, the conflicts between the emperor and the generals were a central piece of the narrative. While there can be no certainty that there were none, the most likely conclusion is that the emperor closely cooperated with his previous superior. Considering that the Vandal policy of Leo was a major part of his falling out with Aspar, Marcian's policy, which was on the other end of the spectrum when compared to Leo's, seems to have been in accordance with Aspar's convictions. This would not have been strange as they shared the experiences of the failed expedition in the 430s. The embassy of Bleda might be an indirect evidence of Aspar's involvement in policy making. The general was an important figure in

---

[110] Some authors claim these stories could have also originated as hearsay, critical of Marcian and Aspar, cf. A. M e r r i l l s, R. M i l e s, *The Vandals*..., p. 119; R. S t e i n a c h e r, *Die Vandalen*..., p. 208.

[111] Many scholars bring up Aspar's Alan origins on that occasion. Cf. G. V e r n a d s k y, *Flavius*..., p. 58–60; B. B a c h r a c h, *The Alans*..., p. 45; E. G a u t i e r, *Genséric. Roi des Vandales*, Paris 1935, p. 253–254; 264; M. W i l c z y ń s k i, *Gejzeryk*..., p. 162.

Arian circles and certainly would be more likely to arrange the mission, as opposed to the devout orthodox Christian that Marcian was. In fact, the whole idea might have come from the general.

As such, Marcian's policy against the Vandals is another aspect of his reign that was influenced by the military elite. There is however a possibility that it might have changed towards the very end of his life, which will be explored in the corresponding sub-chapter.

The Eastern Policy of Marcian

The eastern policy of Marcian is, unfortunately, even more difficult to research, since there is no relative abundance of the sources from the West to sketch the background and the only Eastern accounts are fragmentary in nature, or otherwise lacking in detail.

The exception to that rule is the case of Armenia, where the developed historiographical tradition recorded some of the most notable events related to Marcian's eastern policy. Theodosius II had promised the Armenians his military support, however, his sudden death put a stop to those plans. Both Yeghishe and Ghazar mention that Marcian, when facing this issue, sought counsel on how to best deal with it[112]. They relay, the latter even in quite a lot of detail, an answer that Marcian had gotten, which is the more interesting, considering that one of those who gave it was none other than the general Anatolius[113]. The counsellors argued that helping the Armenians would compromise stability in the relations with Persia and most likely lead to war. The conflict, however, could go either way and the results would be uncertain.

This event shows not only that Marcian relied on his military advisors when deciding his foreign policy, but also gives a unique insight into a military commander's convictions in regard to how it should be conducted, and it is the only known explicit statement on those issues coming from a member of the military. Interestingly, the similar pragmatism to Anatolius' overview of the situation

---

[112] Ghazar Parpets'i, 41; Yeghishe, III.

[113] The other one was some court official, both chroniclers record his Syrian origin; Ghazar records a name P'ghorent while Yeghishe calls him Ephlalios (Eulalios). According to Martindale (*PLRE*, vol. II, p. 478, s.v. *Florentius 7*), Ghazar's version is the correct one and the official in question was Florentius, who already had a long career in the bureaucratic apparatus of the Empire. He was still present at Marcian's court in 451, since he attended the Council of Chalcedon, however, as a representative of the Senate.

in Armenia can be observed in Marcian's dealings on the international scene in general. While we should recognize that attributing such convictions to other members of the military and other situations is just speculation, it seems to align well with all the other evidence.

Regardless, the insurgency that Theodosius had promised to support had already started when Marcian was deliberating whether to follow his predecessors plans. The bitter remarks in the Armenian sources, and accusation of cowardice and impiety (more so of Marcian's advisors than the emperor himself) are understandable in that context. The rebels anticipated they would receive help they had been promised, but the change of the regime in effect doomed their efforts.

The policy towards Armenia in 450 provides direct evidence of Marcian's turn in foreign policy which can be observed in all other areas, and, interestingly, links it directly to advice received from military circles.

The Arab Raids

At some point before 453 the Arab tribes, called by Priscus the Saracens[114], invaded the Roman Syria. Ardaburious, who held the office of the *magister militum per Orientem*, fought against them near Damascus[115]. The historian does not record the outcome of the battle, but at the time he was travelling to Egypt with his superior, Maximinus, general Ardaburious was already negotiating peace with the invaders, which allows us to assume the situation was under control and the general contained the threat one way or another.

Maximinus is called in the passage a *strategos*, which means he had received a military command of some sort. Either he was freshly appointed *dux Thebaidis* and was travelling to take his assignment, or, which is probably more likely, he was a *comes rei militaris* or even *magister militum vacans*. If either of the latter two options was true, it is possible that Maximinus had some soldiers at his disposal and the reason he and Priscus made a detour to Damascus could have been that

---

[114] The name, at that point did not imply a specific tribe and was used as an umbrella term for Arabs, but more likely just for the nomads. For an in-depth overview of the topic, cf. T. W o l i ń s k a, *Arabs, (H)agarenes, Ishmaelites, Saracens – a Few Remarks about Naming*, [in:] *Byzantium and the Arabs. The Encounter of Civilizations from Sixth to Mid-Eight Century*, ed. T. W o l i ń s k a, P. F i l i p c z a k, Łódź 2015, p. 31–36. Roger. B l o c k l e y (*East...*, p. 69) assumes they were part of Salih confederacy, Irfan S h a h i d (*Byzantium and the Arabs in the Fifth Century*, Dumbarton Oaks 2006, p. 56) supposes they could have been Kindites.

[115] P r i s c u s, fr. 26. Cf. I. S h a h i d, *Byzantium...*, p. 57–58.

they were meaning to reinforce Ardaburious, but the general managed to deal with the raiders on his own. The short passage that tells of those events includes, however, no evidence of any of that and due to its brevity, everything else is left to speculation. It is interesting though, since in the book of Suda there is an entry on Ardaburious, according to which his term in office was a time of peace which resulted in the general becoming lax[116]. The information about this war thus stands in contrast with that, or else the critique relates to later developments[117].

The Blemmyes and Nobades

After their Syrian detour, Maximinus and Priscus ended up in the Egyptian provinces. In the south, the tribes of Blemmyes and Nobades invaded the Roman territories and Alexandria was in turmoil after a contentious election of the patriarch. We know that Priscus helped a local praefect of Alexandria, Florus, to quell the unrest in the city[118]. Maximinus, however, was responsible for the diplomatic arrangements after the conflict with the invading tribes.

Unfortunately the details of the war were lost, since as it often happens the author of *excerpta de legationibus* omitted the information pertaining to the conflict itself, so that the eleventh fragment of the embassies of foreign peoples relates in detail the course of diplomatic talks and conditions of the treaty. Of the war, however, it is only known that it was won by the Romans. It can be assumed that the command of the Roman forces was in the hands of Maximinus. The representatives of the tribes seemed to treat him with exceptional respect, at first wanting to keep the treaty for the duration of Maximinus' stay in the province, then, when he disagreed, for the duration of Maximinus' life. In the end a 100-year-long treaty was agreed upon[119]. It might indicate that it was so because Maximinus was the leader of the forces which defeated the tribes. It would explain the special treatment of his person and Maximinus had already lead Roman soldiers before, when a punitive expedition against Flavius Zeno had been dispatched.

---

[116] *Suda*, A 3803.

[117] Alternatively, that information could have originated from anti-Ardaburii propaganda, probably broadcasted by Leo's regime, cf. M.E. S t e w a r t, *The First Byzantine Emperor? Leo I, Aspar and Challenges of Power and Romanitas in Fifth–century Byzantium*, Porph 22, 2014, p. 10.

[118] P r i s c u s, fr. 28 = E v a g r i u s, II, 5. The passage says that Priscus arrived in Alexandria from Thebaid, so the problems in Alexandria must have happened after the first part of the war was over, or he split from his superior, of whom the source says nothing.

[119] P r i s c u s, fr. 27.

The commanding officer in charge of defending the southernmost borders of Egypt was *dux Thebaidis* and it is possible that this was the assignment Maximinus was travelling to take up. However, as noted before, considering his diplomatic experience and the detour in Syria, it seems more likely that he had a more independent command role, such as *comes* or even *magister militum vacans*. That would mean that he must have been sent to deal with the problems at hand in eastern provinces, first in Syria, where the problem had been resolved before his arrival, and then (it is possible he was rerouted, especially if Maximinus had some forces at his disposal) in Thebaid.

There is however some additional evidence that might change this overview. Jordanes in *Romana* claims it was Florus who defeated the invaders[120]. The passage is short but explicit. It is a fact that Florus combined both civil and military prerogatives holding both the title of *comes Aegypti* and of *praefectus augustalis*[121]. He might have received such broad powers to better deal with the unrest in Alexandria, or perhaps the invasion of the Blemmyes and Nobades was the reason. It is possible he took part in the fighting in the first phase of the war; however, it seems more likely that Jordanes' information on Florus adheres to the seconds stage of the war. Soon after the afore-mentioned peace had been concluded, Maximinus died which prompted the tribes to break the treaty and renew hostilities. Priscus does not say what the outcome of this incursion was, but from the general remarks of Jordanes it seems that the barbarians were in the end defeated, possibly by Florus.

The conflict with Blemmyes and Nobades was probably not a major one. Having said that, the tendency in the literature to disregard it as a minor skirmish is unsubstantiated. Of the war itself we know far too little to properly judge the danger. Despite the scale, it was yet another example the success of Marcian's policy in ensuring the security of the Empire's borders.

The Expeditions to Lazica

Another lesser conflict known solely from the description of the diplomatic arrangements following it was the conflict in Lazica. The reason for the hostilities mentioned by Priscus was the fact that the ruler of this land, Gobazes, had decided to rule jointly with his son. It appears that the Romans assumed the rights

---

[120] Jordanes, *Romana*, 333.

[121] *PLRE*, vol. II, p. 461–482 (s.v. *Florus 2*). This would however mean Florus' prerogatives extended to the province of Thebaid.

of investiture of their subject state as a mean of control. Lazica was a strategically important region in the Caucasus and controlling it allowed for potential interventions in the area. Therefore, what Gobazes did must have been recognized as an attempt to shake off, to some extent, the subordination to his suzerain[122].

It seems as if the campaign was moderately successful, however, the Romans must have not achieved all their goals as they were preparing a second one. Priscus mentions that the emperor's advisors were considering whether to attack along the same routes, or to move through Armenia, negotiating it beforehand with the Persians, as the route was apparently close to the Persian border. Perhaps the reason the first campaign was aborted had something to do with the deficiencies of the chosen route of approach. Priscus also writes that the sea route, normally the fastest and the most convenient mode of transport of the time, was out of question due to the ruggedness of the coastline and the lack of harbours. Maybe the route chosen originally was by the coast with the intention of having the army supplied by sea, however, unfavourable conditions made it impossible and the army was forced to retreat[123].

Unfortunately we are almost completely in the dark as to who could have been the commander of the expedition and who took part in the council on how to organize the second expedition. Priscus does not bring up any names. The most likely candidate was probably Ardaburious, a *magister militum* of the east. Any general could have advised the emperor on the matter, but if Anatolius was still in office, then he surely would have, although it would have been unlikely at this point due to his venerable age, if he was still alive at all.

Eventually, the Roman forces were sent to intervene in Lazica for the second time. Gobazes tried to get Persian support for his cause but the Lazi envoys were sent away[124]. Consequently, he sent an embassy to Rome where he was informed that only in the instance he or his son abdicated would the hostilities cease. This proposal came from *magister officiorum* Euphemius, who was one of the closest

---

[122] R.C. Blockley, *East...*, p. 70.

[123] Priscus, fr. 33. Roger Blockley (*East...*, p. 209, n. 22) observes that the sources seem to imply that the first expedition was a naval one. There is an interesting fragment of *Suda* (T 134) that refer to some Roman–Lazi war, which describes Romans getting surprised by concealed spear-pit traps and running away. It is likely that it originates from Priscus and it may refer to that conflict, cf. Ph. Rance, *A Roman-Lazi War in the "Suda": A Fragment of Priscus?*, CQ 65, 2015, p. 852–867. It is, admittedly, impossible to say, whether it describes a major defeat or just a single stratagem taken out of context. It does seem to indicate, however, that the Lazi were quite adept at asymmetric warfare.

[124] Priscus, fr. 33. The historian claims it was mostly due to the Persian king being occupied by the war with the Kidarite Huns and was probably not willing to antagonize the Romans in such a situation.

associates of Marcian at that time, as Priscus informs. Gobazes agreed to it and abdicated, leaving his son on the throne. Thus, the resolution of the conflict was found diplomatically.

In case of the conflict in Lazica it is difficult to judge how successful the Romans were militarily; however, even though they had to retreat, the show of strength was enough to arrive at some kind of political compromise.

The Soldier Emperor

The political record of Marcian's reign was, as evidenced in the chapter so far, a successful one. In general, the lack of appreciation for his achievements in the scholarship comes either from the fact that the dramatic developments in the West (arguably better illuminated by the sources) overshadow what was happening in the East ruled by Marcian, or from limited attention given to the sources combined with certain preconceptions. It can be argued that the conflicts the Eastern Roman Empire had to deal with during Marcian's reign were minor and only of local importance; however, it still speaks volumes to the political pragmatism of Marcian that he was able to avoid entanglement in wars that he potentially would not have the means to conduct with benefit to the Empire.

In any case, Marcian managed to contain every external danger threatening the Empire during his reign. In his less than seven years he had to deal with no fewer than five wars, and in all of them the Romans had the upper hand. The Hunnic confederacy dissolved and the resettlement of some of its constituent tribes within the borders of the Empire prevented its recreation. All this success was achieved with minimal expenditure of resources. When presented in this way, it is no wonder why the ancients considered Marcian a very good emperor and why on the event of the accession of Anastasius, the citizens shouted for him to 'rule like Marcian'[125].

The Emperor of the Soldiers

We know of only two generals who were nominated by Marcian to the highest military office: Ardaburious, who was made the *magister militum* of the east after the death of Zeno, and Anthemius, who became a *magister militum*

---

[125] Constantine Porphyrogennetos, 425 B.

praesentalis. When it comes to most of the conflicts, the information on the make-up of the command is severely limited, which makes it impossible to create a chronology of the various military offices for this period. However, despite all that, the reign of Marcian is fundamental to understanding the military elite in the fifth century.

Marcian was the emperor chosen by the military, and all of the evidence points to his decisions having been informed by the military establishment. He reshuffled his cabinet, letting officials connected with the previous regime go, but he seems to have kept the military positions intact. This appears to be in line with the assumption that Marcian, owing the throne to the generals and coming from martial background, effectively was an executor of the will of the military elite.

The main aspect in which Marcian's decisions affected the generals was his foreign policy. The emperor concentrated on the immediate threats to the Empire, especially the Huns, while avoiding being entangled in the conflicts that affected the West; this was both true in the case of the Vandal menace and the issues of Western Imperial succession[126]. In addition, Marcian's thoughtful administration and tax cuts benefited the elites of the Empire, which obviously included the prominent members of the military as well.

Lack of evidence of conflicts between Marcian and his commanders, while not unambiguously convincing due to over-all scarcity of sources, also implies Marcian's cooperation with the military, especially if we consider that during both his successor's and predecessor's reigns they were prominently displayed in historiography. We can reasonably assume that Marcian cooperated primarily with Anatolius in regard to eastern policy, Apollonius (and probably Zeno, while he was still alive) when dealing with the Huns, and sought Aspar's counsel when deciding on how to deal with the Vandals and the West.

The Puzzling Last Years of Marcian's Reign

Even though it has been argued in this chapter that Marcian consistently followed his vision of pragmatic and safe approach in his foreign policy and internal administration, there is some evidence to the contrary, to which I have previously alluded to. Considering the limitations of available information, it is largely speculative whether that was the case; nevertheless, it is important

---

[126] R.C. B l o c k l e y, *East...*, p. 68, 71.

to consider as it might put Marcian and his relationship with the military in a completely different light.

The main point of interest that seems to indicate the possibility of some change in Marcian's policies late in his reign is his sudden elevation of Procopius Anthemius to both the office of *magister militum* and the rank of the consul. This, in combination with the fact that Marcian married his daughter, Euphemia, to the general seems to indicate that emperor had some far reaching plans, possibly even to establish his own dynasty. Sidonius Apollinaris, who later wrote a panegyric on Anthemius, related that the latter was considered next in the line of succession after Marcian due to his having married the emperor's daughter[127]. Sidonius however is not a very objective source and his claims do not have to necessarily mean Anthemius was formally recognized as Marcian's successor or that the emperor had any dynastic ambitions.

It is however important to consider as that could have put the emperor in a potential conflict with Aspar, who was at that point the only remaining powerful statesman who was responsible for installing Marcian on the throne. It is possible that Marcian was influenced by a certain Euphemius, who was a *magister officiorum* and apparently one of his closest associates, as Priscus records[128]. Due to that passage some scholars consider Euphemius to have been Marcian's right-hand man, however, that seems to be a far reaching conclusion based on inadequate evidence. It is unknown when he took up the office, although it is most likely that he succeeded Vincomalus who was last attested on 13 March 452 and was a consul for the next year. Thus it is possible Euphemius was in office since 453 up until Marcian's death. The name of Marcian's daughter seems to indicate that the emperor and his minister might have been related. Thus, it is possible that Euphemius was influencing Marcian and encroaching on the matters that were dear to Aspar.

One of those might have been the Vandal problem. Marcian's inactivity in that matter was certainly puzzling to his contemporaries. There is however a possibility that Marcian was eventually, when diplomacy failed, willing to act. The envoy to the Vandals, Bleda, threatened war as the representative of Marcian after all. In addition, one source, albeit secondary, claims that Marcian was in fact preparing a military action. The *Church History* of Theodor Lector informs us that the emperor was planning a grand campaign against the barbarians occupying North Africa[129]. It would have been incredibly costly in

---

[127] Sidonius, *Carmina*, II, 216–218.

[128] Priscus, fr. 33; *PLRE*, vol. II, p. 424 (s.v. *Euphemius 1*).

[129] Theodor Lector, *Epitoma*, 367. Cf. R. Mathisen, *Avitus...*, p. 243. Frank Clover (*The Family and Early Career of Anicius Olybrius*, Hi 27, 1978, p. 194) claims that

terms of time needed for preparation and resources, and Marcian managed to accumulate the latter, collecting about 100,000 pounds of gold of surplus in the treasury. It might have been simply due to his efficient administration, but it is not without reason to claim that he was amassing resources with a specific goal in mind.

Another piece of evidence that may support the above argument is Marcian's policy towards the Western part of the Empire and its rulers. Considering the logistical and political realities of a hypothetical expedition to Africa, this was a matter of utmost importance. Even though the emperor at first did not recognize Avitus who came into power after the sack of Rome[130], it seems that he eventually walked back on his decision. Perhaps the prime reason for Marcian's change of heart was the news of the achievements of the new emperor: his successful subjugation of the Goths and the Burgundians and, most importantly, the victories over the Vandals at Agrigentum on Sicily[131] and at Corsica[132]. According to Ralph Mathisen the emperor was willing to recognize Avitus, however, any potential cooperation against the Vandals was cut short by the rebellion against the Western emperor and his subsequent defeat by the plotters, Majorianus and Ricimer, at the battle of Placentia in late 456[133].

It can be argued that Marcian wanted to send the expedition against the Vandals but simply did not manage to in his lifetime. Considering the time and resources it would take to prepare one, the possibility of bad weather conditions and the unstable situation in the West, there are many reasons why it could have been postponed. Thus a following hypothesis could be put forward regarding Marcian's last years in power: with the help of Euphemius, Marcian attempted to break his ties with Aspar to pursue other goals that were at odds with the general's interest, namely changing his policy towards the Vandals and establishing his own dynasty by supporting Anthemius[134]. Curiously enough, this would be almost the same dynamic that could be observed between Aspar and Marcian's successor, Leo; thus, it is certainly possible and would present an interesting historical pattern.

There are, however, also major counter-arguments to that hypothesis, even beyond it being based on very weak evidence. Firstly, the chronology does not

---

those threats were just a response of the emperor to the outcry when the news of the betrothal between Huneric and Eudocia arrived in Constantinople.

[130] R. M a t h i s e n, *Avitus...*, p. 235–237.

[131] S i d o n i u s, *Carmina*, II, 366–367; J.B. B u r y, *A History...*, p. 367.

[132] H y d a t i u s, 170.

[133] R. M a t h i s e n, *Avitus...*, p. 243–244.

[134] R.A. B l e e k e r, *Aspar...*, p. 107–110.

exactly follow the supposed cause and effect: the elevation of Anthemius happened before the Vandals' sacking of Rome and the failure of Marcian's diplomacy. In addition, the idea to send the Arian bishop Bleda to talk with Geiseric appears to have been Aspar's, thus the general did not lose influence to Euphemius before that point, nor did Anthemius' rapid career affect him. To add to those points, Frank Clover offers an explanation to Marcian's supposed war plans. He argues that the emperor threatened war as response to an outcry, when the news of Huneric's and Eudocia's betrothal arrived in Constantinople. This time, however, Geiseric sought compromise and allowed Placidia, who was in his captivity, to marry Olybrius to whom she was engaged[135]. This would mean that Marcian's threats amounted to not much more than a public relations move, that surprisingly had some actual effect.

Marcian's supposed attempts to establish a dynasty can be explained otherwise. Euphemius' influence on the court might have been exaggerated by Priscus, who was his direct subordinate and might have wanted to elevate his superior. He was certainly influential, if anything, due to his office alone, and likely because of his long tenure, but Marcian is known to have sought counsel of many officials at his court on many occasions. Giving Euphemia's hand to Anthemius would not have necessarily meant that Marcian wanted to secure his political legacy. Anthemius was an up-and-coming general of an illustrious lineage, who likely had already distinguished himself when dealing with barbarians on the northern borders. The emperor (and possibly Euphemius as well, if they were related) might have wanted to simply make sure that Euphemia got married to a promising candidate. Finally, even if Marcian wanted to establish his dynasty, would that necessarily cause a conflict with Aspar? This hypothesis is based on the assumption that Aspar always sought Imperial power; yet, curiously, he did not reach for the Imperial diadem when he had a chance. If Marcian's plans would not involve challenging the general's authority and influence it is doubtful that they would have a falling-out.

In conclusion, the lack of sources prevents the clear establishment of the meaning behind certain events in the last years of Marcian's reign. Nevertheless, even if it is simply speculative, it is important to consider, these things as it might completely reframe our understanding of Marcian's relationship with his generals. In my opinion, however, it seems more likely that Marcian was consistent in his policies to the very end, and the alternative interpretation seems to be based on the analogies to Leo's reign, more so than the available evidence.

---

[135] F.M. C l o v e r, *The Family...*, p. 194.

Conclusion

The emperor Marcian stood in stark contrast to his predecessor in many ways, and his relationship with the military was not any different. Marcian was the candidate chosen for the throne by the most prominent members of the military elite and it seems that he fulfilled their expectations. His reign was the pinnacle of the influence of the generals in the matters of the state, which is most vivid in the area of his foreign policy. In such a manner, Marcian was not only a soldier emperor himself, but also, the emperor of the soldiers.

The Military Elite during the Reign of Leo I

On 26 January 457 Marcian took part in a procession, commemorating the victims of the earthquake from ten years ago. During the ceremony the elderly emperor, who suffered from inflammation of his feet, must have overexerted himself and had to retire. On the next day he died in his palace[1]. This event marked the end of an era. Even though Marcian was a mere officer of common descent, his marriage with Pulcheria brought him into the Theodosian dynasty that ruled the Empire for nearly 80 years. Marcian left no male heir, the house of Theodosius in the West had also expired as well in 455 when Valentinian III died. The fact that there was no obvious successor meant that the political forces in Constantinople had to choose their emperor once again.

The Question of Succession

It appears that the most likely successor to the throne was the general Anthemius. One of the sources, Sidonius, goes as far to state that he was considered

---

[1] B. Croke, *The Date and Circumstances of Marcian's Decease, A.D. 457*, B 48, 1978, p. 5–9.

a natural successor to the late emperor[2]. Even though the poet had a clear goal to paint the hero of his work in as positive a light as possible, his claims should not be discounted. Anthemius was related to the emperor by marriage, he served in the highest military office as the *magister militum praesentalis*, and had a prominent place in the Senate as an ex-consul and *patricius*. His ancestry was similarly notable, as he was grandson of the praefect Anthemius and the son of *magister militum* Procopius. Considering such political background and heritage, it poses the question why he did not ascend to the throne. For all intents and purposes Anthemius was the perfect candidate. One possible obstacle could have been his young age[3]; we do not know exactly how old he was, but he appears still to have been in his prime 20 years later when he travelled to the West. It was not uncommon for relatively young people to receive high military offices[4], but it might have been less acceptable for a candidate to the throne[5].

Regardless, it would certainly not have been a problem at all, if Anthemius were to succeed Marcian with the former emperor's blessing. The fact that he did not is perhaps the best evidence that Anthemius was not officially designated as Marcian's successor. In fact, there is no evidence of any problems with the succession. Sidonius claims that Anthemius continuously refused to accept the throne[6], which meant that he must have had the senators' support[7]. The former could have been true, if slightly exaggerated. Anthemius simply must not have tried to secure the power for himself. If he were to do so and had he any support for his claims, he would have been likely to succeed, and if not, the sources would probably record some events related to the attempt.

On the contrary, the transition of 457 seemed smooth given the circumstances. The inter-regnum took only a week and a half, a reasonable timeframe for all the arrangements to be made, from deciding who should receive the diadem to organizing all the ceremonies[8].

---

[2] S i d o n i u s, *Carmina*, II, 212–215.

[3] Cf. Е.П. Г л у ш а н и н, *Военная знать ранней Византии*, Барнаул 1991, p. 119.

[4] Aspar himself comes to mind.

[5] Naturally, much younger emperors ascended to Roman throne, but that tended to happen when they were born to established dynasties (Theodosius II is such an example) or had a strong family backing otherwise. The succession of 457 was much more open, and up to the choice of Constantinople's rich and powerful; it did not simply follow a dynastic process. In that case, the relative youth of Anthemius could have posed a problem.

[6] S i d o n i u s, *Carmina*, II, 210–213.

[7] J.B. B u r y, *History of the Later Roman Empire from the Death of Theodosius I. to the Death of Justinian*, vol. I, London 1958, p. 314.

[8] Brian C r o k e (*Dynasty and Ethnicity. Emperor Leo I and the Eclipse of Aspar*, Chi 35, 2005, p. 149–150) is of the opinion that such inter-regnum was proof of some complications in the succession. While a delay could indicate political trouble, as it has been argued in case of

The Role of Aspar in the Succession

This time, however, most sources quite explicitly point to the person who was behind the decisions; it was Aspar. Interestingly, it is not certain what his function at that time was. It is very likely that he was the second *magister militum praesentalis*; most scholars assume so[9], but there is no direct evidence for that to have been the case. Only the relative power of the general, his influence, and the fact that sources are quiet about any other potential senior officer who could have served in that function at that time make this scenario likely. All that being said, Aspar's power-base at that point extended beyond the army. As Gereon Siebigs accurately observes, Aspar was a senior senator, an ex-consul, possibly second in rank only to Florentius and Valerius[10], if they were still active in politics or alive at all[11]. Aspar's influence and connections among powerful civilian notables was also a factor. While the existence of a specific political body, akin to a 'Roman cabinet', is debatable[12], Gereon Siebigs assumes that there was some kind of 'Crown Council' that had such a function and consisted of dedicated members. Whether it played any part in those events, or if the political arrangements of 457 were being made in a much more fluid and *ad hoc* fashion, is a matter for discussion, but ultimately it does not change the main point. Among the political elite of the Eastern Roman Empire, Aspar was of senior rank and possessed major influence.

Little is known of other powerful generals who served under Marcian. Zeno was recorded to have passed away[13]. Of Anatolius and Apollonius nothing is known; thus, it appears that they must have died as well, or at least retired from active military duty and political life in general. As matters stood, Aspar was the only one who was left of the military elite which assisted the previous emperor

Marcian, since it was important for the throne to be occupied as soon as possible, a week and a half is very little compared to a month. In 450 there is additional evidence for a political crisis which is lacking in 457, thus his argumentation is most likely incorrect. In the eyes of Ronald B l e e k e r (*Aspar and the Struggle for the Eastern Roman Empire, AD 421–71*, London 2022, p. 117) the transition in 457 happened swiftly compared to 450.

    [9] B. C r o k e, *Dynasty...*, p. 150; G. S i e b i g s, *Kaiser Leo I. Das oströmische Reich in den ersten drei Jahren seiner Regierung (457–460 n. Chr.)*, Berlin 2010, p. 195; P. C r a w f o r d, *Roman Emperor Zeno. The Perils of Politics in Fifth-century Constantinople*, Barnsley 2019, p. 42. Interestingly, Evgeniy Glushanin claims otherwise, cf. Е.П. Г л у ш а н и н, *Военная...*, p. 119.

    [10] Brother of empress Eudocia, consul of 432, last mentioned in 455, cf. *PLRE*, vol. II, p. 1145 (s.v. *Valerius 6*).

    [11] G. S i e b i g s, *Kaiser...*, p. 198–199.

    [12] Both the Senate and the *consistorium* were relegated by that time to mostly ceremonial roles, and real political decisions were being made by the emperor and his closest advisors.

    [13] J o r d a n e s, *Romana*, 333.

in the governance. Seven years prior, Aspar took part in seating Marcian on the throne, primarily due to fortunate circumstances, being in the right place at the right time. This time Aspar was undoubtedly the most influential individual in the state[14]. Aside from honorary ranks and offices, he certainly built many political connections, had vast resources at his disposal, and arguably controlled half of the standing forces of the Empire[15].

Gereon Siebigs poses an interesting theory, that the matter of succession in 457 was in fact very contentious. Aspar and his supporters, mostly from the Theodosian era, faced the new elite introduced by Marcian, who in turn had supported Anthemius. However, even if we disregard the unlikelihood of Anthemius' candidacy being actively supported, Siebigs' hypothesis is grounded in the incorrect assumption that Aspar stood in opposition to the late emperor and his will. If we consider that nothing indicates that there was a conflict between those two groups, it appears that Aspar was in fact supported by the majority.

A Dangerous Precedent

There is an interesting source related to the succession of 457 that provides some unique information. Theodoric the Great in his speech on the Roman synod of 501, mentioned to the bishops that the Constantinopolitan senators even offered the purple to Aspar. The general reportedly refused, claiming that it would set a dangerous precedent[16].

What he could have meant has been a topic of speculation. Some scholars claim that he could not ascend to the throne due to his Alano-Germanic roots and his Arian creed[17]. Alexander Demandt posits that Aspar did not think

---

[14] R.A. B l e e k e r, *Aspar...*, p. 107, 117.

[15] One praesental army under his command, the eastern army under his son, and he had the support of the Gothic *foederati* in Thrace as well, cf. A. U r b a n i e c, *Wpływ patrycjusza Aspara na cesarską elekcję Leona*, USS 11, 2011, p. 196.

[16] *Acta Synodorum Habitarum Romae*, 5, 23–26; E. S t e i n, *Histoire du Bas-Empire*, t. I, *De L'état romain à l'état byzantin (284–476)*, Paris 1959, p. 353–354; L. S c o t t, *Aspar and the Burden of Barbarian Heritage*, ByzS 3, 1976, p. 62.

[17] J.B. B u r y, *History...*, p. 315; P. C r a w f o r d, *Roman...*, p. 45. Other authors disregard the heritage as a factor, and concentrate on Arianism, cf. B. C r o k e, *Dynasty...*, p. 150; A. U r - b a n i e c, *Wpływ...*, p. 196. An interesting counter-point has been put forward by Meaghan M c E v o y (*Becoming Roman? The Not-So-Curious Case of Aspar and the Ardaburii*, JLA 9, 2016, p. 498–502) who observed that neither Arianism nor Barbarian heritage were major obstacles to Aspar's claim to power.

his current office allowed him to legitimately assume the throne[18], and that he simply preferred his current position of influence over the senate and the army, playing the part of a Constantinopolitan grey eminence[19].

Alternatively, Evgeniy Glushanin doubts the historicity of that event altogether[20]. It was a part of the king's speech at one of the synods meant to solve a dispute over papal nominations and Theodoric had an agenda to push through. It is probably an exaggeration to consider this account completely made up, but it is very likely that the king distorted it to suit the needs of his political rhetoric, or simply did not know the details[21]. Even if we cannot be certain that the events went exactly as Theodoric reported them, it is yet more evidence of the officials entrusting the responsibility for the choice to Aspar.

Leo, the *comes et tribunus Mattiariorum*

All of the above proves that it was up to Aspar to name the emperor. He decided to choose a very similar candidate in many aspects to the late Marcian, a previously unknown middle rank military officer, Leo. Jordanes and Malalas report him as being of Bessian stock[22]. Candidus claims he was from Dacia[23], however, there is a number of sources which say that he was born in Thrace[24]. Regardless, it is safe to say that he came from the northern, Balkan provinces of the Empire. He had a military career and held the rank of tribune, and, thanks to Candidus, we know that he was stationed in Selymbria[25] as a commander of a regiment of the field army called *Mattiari*, one of the elite units subordinate to one of the *magistri*

---

[18] A. D e m a n d t, *Magister militum*, [in:] *RE*, t. 12 suppl., 1970, p. 770–771.

[19] Another powerful general from a later period, Illus the Isaurian, seem to have arrived precisely at such a conclusion, cf. H. E l t o n, *Illus and the Isaurian Aristocracy under Zeno*, B 70, 2000, p. 393–407; M.J. L e s z k a, *Kilka uwag na temat losów Illusa Izauryjczyka w latach 479–484*, M 62, 2007, p. 106–107.

[20] Е.П. Г л у ш а н и н, *Военная...*, p. 122.

[21] He was present in Constantinople in his youth, possibly under Aspar's care, but he arrived later, in the 460s, and was a child during his stay, so he was probably limited in his capacity to understand political intricacies.

[22] J o r d a n e s, *Romana*, 335; M a l a l a s, XIV, 35.

[23] C a n d i d u s, fr. 1.

[24] T h e o d o r L e c t o r, *Epitoma*, 367; T h e o p h a n e s, AM 5959.

[25] C a n d i d u s, fr. 1. Selymbria, modern Silivri, was located just about 60 km from Constantinople.

militum praesentales, who at that point was likely Aspar himself[26]. Theophanes and Zonaras report that he used to manage the general's estates as a *curator*[27], however, Evgeniy Glushanin discounts that piece of information as a later justification for Aspar's choice, not grounded in historical facts[28]. In 457 Leo was already beyond his prime, being 56 years old at that time[29]. It is curious in how many aspects Leo resembled Marcian. An older soldier from the Balkans, directly connected to Aspar through his service. Aspar's political bet on Marcian must have really paid off, since he was willing to do essentially the same thing yet again.

Leo must have been a trusted subordinate of Aspar, however, we do not know if he took part in any of the general's campaigns. That being said, Aspar's intention in choosing Leo must have been to pick a reliable candidate who would ensure that the general's political influence stayed as strong as it had been and that he could work with the emperor on matters dear to himself[30].

In that regard it is important to note that Leo was even more reliant on Aspar than Marcian ever was. Not only was Aspar probably the only driving force behind Leo's candidacy and he did not have to pay any heed to the interests of other individuals, but the new emperor's legitimacy was also even weaker than that of Marcian. Even though they had a similar status before ascending to the throne, Leo had absolutely no links to the previous dynasty, while Marcian's rule

---

[26] Constantine Porphyrogennetos, 1, 91. The unit in question was probably *Mattiari Seniores*. Cf. B. C r o k e, *Dynasty...*, p. 150, n. 11; *Notitia Dignitatum Orientis*, 6, 42.

[27] T h e o p h a n e s, AM 5961; Z o n a r a s, XIII, 25.

[28] Е.П. Г л у ш а н и н, *Военная...*, p. 123–124. The Russian scholar's reservations are well grounded; however, it is possible Leo could have been privately involved with Aspar much earlier, before he was a tribune. After all, it is likely that *magistri militum* had a say in recommending their candidates for lower officer ranks. Cf. A.H.M. J o n e s, *The Decline of the Ancient World*, London 1966, p. 147.

[29] G. S i e b i g s, *Kaiser...*, p. 221. He was 73 when he died, cf. M a l a l a s, XIV, 46. It is claimed in *Chronicon Paschale* (a. 457) that he was 65, however, it seems like an exaggeration and the version of Malalas is probably the accurate one.

[30] Evgeniy Glushanin claims that Aspar picked a random candidate, and that he knew little if anything of Leo before the crowning. Cf. Е.П. Г л у ш а н и н, *Военная...*, p. 124. While his arguments that Leo was not a curator of Aspar's estates are sound, this going is too far and his line of reasoning is not convincing, It is extremely unlikely that Aspar, who over the years built his political connections and extensive networks in the military, would not have loyal and reliable supporters and clients among the middle ranks. Consequently, why would a politician of his calibre ever pick a random candidate over one that he could trust and rely on? Glushanin seems to be arguing against an established narrative portraying Aspar's choice of Leo as an extraordinary event, and instead compares it with similar instances of the military making the choice when dynastic succession was impossible. While his observation is interesting, in the specific instances of Marcian and Leo the role of Aspar was undeniably paramount. Cf. P. C r a w f o r d, *Roman...*, p. 45.

did get legitimized by his marriage with Pulcheria. Thus, Leo's political position was extremely weak at the beginning of his reign[31].

On 7 February 457 a new emperor was crowned. The ceremonies surrounding the accession are well recorded in *De ceremoniis* of Constantine Porphyrogennetos[32]. Thanks to this account, it is known that Aspar was present during the event as the first patrician, and accompanied Leo in the Imperial carriage. When they arrived at the Forum of Constantine, the new emperor received a golden crown from the head of the senate, who, again, was Aspar.

The Influence of Aspar

Aspar's influence over the new regime was soon apparent. When Pope Leo referenced the emperor and his general in his letters, he used terms that likened Aspar to Aetius[33], which probably meant that for external observer Aspar's position was that of a *de facto* co-ruler of the country[34].

Some of the first laws issued by Leo in 458 also seem to bear Aspar's mark. They are concerned with the defensive capabilities of the Eastern Roman state, forbidding soldiers from turning to private ventures since their necessities were fully provided for by the state, and similarly, prohibiting military officials from using soldiers to their private benefit[35]. The concern there was clearly that the military should remain a professional force, paid for by the state and separate from civilian enterprises. One reason for that was certainly to keep it in fighting shape and ensure the security of the state, a matter that, as we can infer from all of Aspar's involvement thus far, was very dear to him.

Aspar's influence was also apparent in nominations to important state offices. In the first year of his reign, Leo assumed consulship as was customary; however, just after that in 459 Aspar's younger son, Julius Patricius received that honour. Two years later, in 461, the consulship was bestowed on Flavius Dagailaphus, who was the husband of Godisthea, who in turn was the daughter of Ardaburious, and thus Aspar's granddaughter[36]. The *praefectus praetorio* of the east, Flavius Constantinus, was succeeded by certain Vivianus, who was in all likelihood connected

---

[31] G. Ve r n a d s k y, *Flavius Ardabur Aspar*, SF 6, 1941, p. 59.

[32] C o n s t a n t i n e   P o r p h y r o g e n n e t o s, 1, 91.

[33] He is referred as: *Magnificus vir patricius Aspar*. Cf. L e o, *Epistolae*, 149;153.

[34] A. D e m a n d t, *Magister...*, p. 771.

[35] *CJ*, IV, 65, 31; *CJ*, XII, 35, 15.

[36] G. Ve r n a d s k y, *Flavius...*, p. 59.

politically to Aspar[37]. The general secured important offices for his supporters and family, expanding his network of connections. It also meant that the emperor was surrounded by people loyal to Aspar. The general's influence was at its peak. For an ambitious man that Leo was, such a situation must have been hard to swallow, yet he was likely aware that he could not do much about it at that point. It is probable that he decided to dedicate his attention to other matters, namely foreign policy.

Leo's Own Ambitions

The first decision of the new emperor was related to the developments in the West. The emperor recognized the outcome of the power struggle and showed his support to the victors. Ricimer was granted the title of *patricius*, while Majorian received the office of *magister militum*[38]. What happened after is more contentious. Some scholars claim that Majorian proceeded to crown himself a *Caesar* on 1 April, which was recognized by Leo, and then assumed the title of *Augustus* on 28 December[39]. Gereon Siebigs, again analysing these events in great detail, brings up many relevant counter-arguments and discounts the information on the coronation in April[40], however, the most pertinent question remains, namely whether Leo recognized and supported Majorian. According to Siebigs that was simply a literary *topos*[41]. That being said, it is possible that Majorian was elevated by his soldiers on the 1st of April[42]. His holding the office of *magister militum* had Leo's approval, so it is possible the emperor also accepted that fact. The later date of 28 December could correspond to the official coronation in Ravenna[43].

---

[37] B. C r o k e, *Dynasty...*, p. 157; G. S i e b i g s, *Kaiser...*, p. 247.

[38] G. S i e b i g s, *Kaiser...*, p. 257; M. W i l c z y ń s k i, *Germanie w służbie zachodniorzymskiej w V w. n.e.*, Oświęcim 2018, p. 260–261.

[39] *PLRE*, vol. II, p. 702–703 (s.v. *Maiorianus*); G. H a l s a l l, *Barbarian Migrations and the Roman West, 376–568*, New York 2007, p. 263; M. J a n k o w i a k, *Bizancjum a kryzysy sukcesyjne w Cesarstwie Zachodniorzymskim w ostatnich latach jego istnienia (465–474)*, [in:] *Chrześcijaństwo u schyłku starożytności. Studia źródłoznawcze*, t. III, red. T. D e r d a, E. W i p s z y c k a, Warszawa 2000, p. 195–196.

[40] G. S i e b i g s, *Kaiser...*, p. 794–801.

[41] *Ibidem*, p. 262, 793.

[42] G.E. M a x, *Political Intrigue during the Reigns of the Western Roman Emperors Avitus and Majorian*, Hi 28, 1979, p. 234; J. P r o s t k o-P r o s t y ń s k i, *Roma – solium imperii. Elekcja, koronacja i uznanie cesarza w Rzymie w IV–VIII wieku*, Poznań 2014, p. 56.

[43] Such delay before conducting the official ceremony could be explained by the fact that Majorian was involved in military campaigns thus far.

The reign of Marcian shows that the generals were interested in the Empire's foreign policy, and the western policy was of particular concern to Aspar. Thus, Leo's ambitions to get involved in the West could have potentially faced obstruction from the powerful general. In fact, all evidence points to Leo's being relatively reluctant in his western policy at first. As long as he did not dedicate any actual resources to help Majorian, it was unlikely that Aspar would take an issue, and nothing evidences that he did[44]. That being said, simply recognizing the new emperor in the West could have set the stage for political cooperation in the future. Judging by Leo's later policies, the efforts of Majorian in defending the country[45] and his expedition to put an end to the Vandal threat[46] were tacitly approved by him. However, he could not, and probably did not, want to dedicate any resources at this point either.

The Ostrogoths and Marcellinus of Dalmatia

Soon after Leo's accession the situation in the Balkans deteriorated. The tribe of the Ostrogoths, settled in the regions of Pannonia by Marcian[47], stopped

---

[44] Gereon S i e b i g s (*Kaiser...*, p. 257) claims Leo's recognition of Majorian as *magister militum* and Ricimer as *patricius* was due to Aspar's initiative.

[45] He and Ricimer managed to catch and destroy the Vandal raid on Campania in 458. Cf. H. C a s t r i t i u s, *Die Vandalen. Etappen einer Spurensuche*, Berlin 2006, p. 113; F. A n d e r s, *Flavius Ricimer. Macht und Ohnmacht des weströmischen Heermeisters in der zweiten Hälfte des 5. Jahrhunderts*, Berlin 2010, p. 161; K. V ö s s i n g, *Das Königreich der Vandalen. Geiserichs Herrschaft und das Imperium Romanum*, Darmstadt 2014, p. 60; M. W i l c z y ń s k i, *Gejzeryk i „czwarta wojna punicka"*, Oświęcim 2016, p. 165–166.

[46] Majorian managed to gather a massive army and fleet numbering 300 ships (cf. P r i s c u s, fr. 36; S i d o n i u s, *Carmina*, V, 474–483). However, Geiseric managed to trick the emperor into negotiations to delay the offensive (cf. H y d a t i u s, 204; M. W i l c z y ń s k i, *Królestwo Swebów – Regnum in extremitate mundi*, Kraków 2011, p. 180), while he himself rallied his forces, bribed some of the Roman captains, and destroyed the rest of the vessels, cf. K. V ö s s i n g, *Königreich...*, p. 60; R. S t e i n a c h e r, *Die Vandalen. Aufstieg und Fall eines Barbarenreichs*, Stuttgart 2016, p. 214–215; A. M e r r i l l s, R. M i l e s, *The Vandals*, Oxford 2010, p. 119–120; M. W i l c z y ń s k i, *Gejzeryk...*, p. 170.

[47] J o r d a n e s, *Getica*, 265; 268. They settled the territories between Sirmium and Vindobona: the provinces of Pannonia prima, Pannonia secunda, and fragments of Pannonia Savia and Pannonia Valeria. Cf. H. W o l f r a m, *Die Goten. Von den Anfängen bis zur Mitte des schsten Jahrhunderts*, München 2001, p. 261–262. In this specific case, however, it is likely that Marcian simply accepted the fact of Gothic settlement in Pannonia, since it appears the tribe came to live there when those territories were under the Hunnic control, cf. H. G r a č a n i n, J. Š k r g u l j a, *The Ostrogoths in the Late Antique South Pannonia*, AAC 49, 2014, p. 168–169,

receiving tribute. One of the its leaders[48], Valamer, sent envoys to Constantinople, however, he achieved nothing. Instead, he learned about the preferential treatment of the other group of Goths that was settled in Thrace, who were the subjects of Theodoric Strabo. Consequently, Valamer, irritated by this perceived injustice, decided to open hostilities and raided the territories of Illyricum and Epirus. At least this is how those events are being relayed by Jordanes[49].

On the subject of the war itself not much is known, but it appears that the commander of the Roman forces in the conflict was Anthemius. According to Sidonius, Illyricum was completely defenceless since it was left abandoned by the local commander. Thus, Anthemius saved the day, destroying the invading force. However, Sidonius' claims are probably a little exaggerated because the conditions of the treaty of 461 that followed the war were quite lenient towards the Goths. The *foedus* alliance was renewed and a tribute of 300 pounds of gold a year was agreed upon again[50]. As a guarantee, the son of Thiudimer, Theodoric, later to be known as the 'Great', was sent as a hostage to Constantinople[51].

It is likely that the reason for the expiration of the tribute was Marcian's death[52]. Treaties with barbarian tribes were usually signed not between the tribe and the state, but the leaders of the parties involved. It still leaves an important question as to why Leo did not renew the treaty. It is possible he sought to change the system of the treaties with the barbarians, although it is puzzling why had he not prepared for an attack that obviously had to come given the circumstances.

Friedrich Lotter provides an interesting theory. He assumes that Majorian set out on a campaign in Pannonia where he was gathering soldiers for his grand expedition against the Vandals in 461. As a result the Ostrogoths were to be included in the Western Roman sphere of influence, and the Western Empire would have been responsible for paying the tribute, thus easing the tributary obligations of Leo[53].

171–173; H.U. W i e m e r, *Theoderich der Große. König der Goten – Herrscher der Römer*, München 2018, p. 123–124; Cf. P. C r a w f o r d, *Roman...*, p. 37.

   [48] The Ostrogoths were divided into three groups ruled by Valamer, Thiudimer, and Vidimer.

   [49] J o r d a n e s, *Getica*, 270–271. Cf. H.U. W i e m e r, *Theoderich...*, p. 125–126.

   [50] P r i s c u s, fr. 37; H. G r a č a n i n, J. Š k r g u l j a, *The Ostrogoths...*, p. 174; O. M a e n c h e n-H e l f e n, *The World of Huns. Studies in Their History and Culture*, London 1973, p. 164; H.J. K i m, *The Huns, Romans and the Birth of Europe*, Cambridge 2013, p. 114.

   [51] H.U. W i e m e r, *Theoderich...*, p. 126–127; H. W o l f r a m, *Die Goten...*, p. 263; *PLRE*, vol. II, p. 1077–1084 (s.v. *Fl. Theodericus 7*).

   [52] Peter C r a w f o r d (*Roman...*, p. 39) claims there was no tribute agreed upon with Marcian, and that the Goths invaded Illyricum only due to the famine they were suffering from. He does not however elaborate why he disregards Jordanes' account in this case.

   [53] F. L o t t e r, *Völkerverschiebungen im Ostalpen–Mitteldonau–Raum zwischen Antike und Mittelalter*, Berlin 2003, p. 108.

This would however indicate a much closer cooperation between Leo and Majorian than the sources suggest.

Another interesting hypothesis was put forward by Gerald Max, who proposed that Leo cut the payments to the Ostrogoths in order to manipulate them into attacking Marcellinus, a local warlord who ruled Dalmatia since the mid-450s[54], which in turn would force him into cooperation[55]. However, this theory is, as Penny MacGeorge observes, not built on strong evidence[56]. After all, Leo could not control the direction of the barbarians' attack, so even if it appears to make sense on paper, one cannot imagine how such a plot could have worked in practice.

That being said, Max's observations of causality between the Ostrogothic raids and a later alliance between Marcellinus and Leo are a lead worth following. The lands controlled by Marcellinus lay just next to Pannonia. This created an opportunity for the general to recruit the barbarians into his armies, and it is likely that they constituted a major part of his forces. It is possible that the Ostrogoths did not have a treaty with Majorian or Leo, but rather with Marcellinus.

Around that time Marcellinus was on Sicily and found himself in a conflict with Ricimer[57]. Priscus informs us that the Western Roman commander bribed the Scythian companions of Marcellinus. Under this anachronistic term the historian probably meant the Ostrogoths[58]. Thus, many scholars consider that Ricimer paid off Marcellinus' soldiers on Sicily, which forced their leader, now lacking the troops to continue his campaign, to retreat.

There is however a problem with this interpretation. Priscus explicitly states that Marcellinus retreated from Sicily fearing a plot[59]. If Ricimer had bribed his army on Sicily, it would have meant that the plot already succeeded; its 'success' would have been the reason for his retreat, not the 'fear' of it. What could have the historian meant, then?

By using the term 'companions' Priscus seems to suggest that he meant the soldiers accompanying the general to Sicily. However, this term could just as well mean

---

[54] On Marcellinus, cf. P. M a c G e o r g e, *Late Roman Warlords*, New York 2002, p. 15–67; M. K u l i k o w s k i, *Marcellinus 'of Dalmatia' and the Dissolution of the Fifth-Century Empire*, B 72, 2002, p. 177–191.

[55] G.E. M a x, *Political...*, p. 235–236.

[56] P. M a c G e o r g e, *Late Roman...*, p. 50–51.

[57] E. K i s l i n g e r, *Sizilien zwischen Vandalen und Römischem Reich im 5. Jahrhundert: Eine Insel in zentraler Randlage*, Mil 11, 2014, p. 246–247.

[58] R.C. B l o c k l e y, *Fragmentary Classicising Historians of the Later Roman Empire*, t. II, Liverpool 1983, p. 394–395, n. 147; Frank W o z n i a k (*East Rome, Ravenna and Illyricum 454–536 AD*, Hi 30, p. 357) claims they were the Huns. See also: E. K i s l i n g e r, *Sizilien...*, p. 246–247.

[59] P i s c u s, fr. 38: εὐλαβηθέντα ἐπιβουλήν.

bodyguards, *bucellari*[60]. Those did not have to be with Marcellinus on Sicily, but could have just as well been guarding his estates in Dalmatia. Bribed by Ricimer, they joined forces with their kinsmen in the Ostrogothic tribe, in which there was already some unrest directed against the Romans. It could be that Ricimer used that to his advantage in his intrigue. As a result of Ricimer's plot, the Goths invaded the lands of Marcellinus' in Dalmatia. Fearing that, Marcellinus retreated to defend his domain.

This interpretation puts the decision of Leo to send Anthemius against Valamer in a different light[61]. Defending Marcellinus' land and normalizing the relations with the Goths afterwards, would have set the stage for an alliance between Leo and the general in Dalmatia, who were yet to become an important asset in the policies of the emperor.

Timothy Ailuros and the Religious Unrest in Alexandria

Just after Marcian's death, the Monophysites in Alexandria consecrated certain Timothy, nicknamed Ailuros, 'the Weasel', as their bishop. However, the Orthodox bishop Proterius was still residing in the city, which meant that Alexandria became divided between two religious factions claiming their candidate's right to the episcopal seat. This crisis was allowed to happen during the absence of the commander of the local forces, the *dux Aegypti* Dionysius, who, upon learning of the developments in Alexandria, hurried to the city and forced Timothy away. The latter's popularity among the city folk, however, resulted in a revolt, which Dionysius failed to bring under control. Thus, to appease the rioters, he agreed to Timothy's return. To make matters worse, in the meantime Proterius was murdered, either by some soldier[62] or by the angry mob of Alexandrian Monophysites[63]. Following that, the Orthodox clergy of the city petitioned the emperor to intervene. Leo decided to write to many important religious figures for advice, asking about Timothy and the dogmas of Chalcedon. After he received assurance of the righteousness of the Orthodox creed and a universal condemnation of the Monophysite bishop of Alexandria, he ordered to punish those responsible for the murder of Proterius and sentenced Timothy to exile[64].

---

[60] Priscus uses the term παρεπόμενοι (παρέπομαι – to follow), which is used three times more in his *History*, meaning 'retainers' in each instance, cf. P r i s c u s, fr. 11.

[61] It also explains who the 'absent commander' was and why he was not present.

[62] P s e u d o - Z a c h a r i a c h, IV, 1–2.

[63] E v a g r i u s, II, 8.

[64] T h e o p h a n e s, AM 5952.

Among those advising the emperor, Theodor Lector mentions the patriarch of Constantinople, Gennadius. After mentioning his stance, he also informs us that Aspar opposed the patriarch in that matter[65]. Gereon Siebigs sees in this an important example of Aspar's religious policy[66]; however, it can just as well be explained pragmatically by positing that the general did not want Leo to adopt a hard-line stance on Timothy considering his popularity[67]. Nevertheless, with an overwhelming support from Orthodox clergy, Leo could ignore the general. This was likely an important moment in the relations between Aspar and the emperor, as Leo must have realized that with the support of the Church he could counteract Aspar's influence to a limited degree.

It does not have to mean, however, that these events were what sparked the conflict between the two. No source states that Leo and Aspar had a falling out over that issue. After all, while the seed of discord might have been planted, the emperor had no reason to openly antagonize the person to whom he owed the throne.

463: the Birth of Leo's Dynastic Ambitions?

According to Brian Croke, the year 463 was a turning point in Aspar's and Leo's relations, since the heir was born to the Imperial couple[68]. The scholar claims that it was an unexpected event which deeply affected the political scene. Aspar chose older Leo, since he believed his wife, Verina, was above the age fit for bearing children. The reason why it was important was that the general had plans of his own in that regard. Even if he had shown humility when approached by the Senate, it does not mean that he was not interested in expanding his power. Aspar either did not want to, or could not become emperor himself, but he likely could, as Brian Croke puts it, be the father of one[69]. Some scholars assume, following the information related by Zonaras[70], that Aspar demanded of Leo to promise to make his son, Patricius, a *Caesar* and the designated successor[71].

---

[65] Theodor Lector, *Epitoma*, 378; Theophanes, AM 5952.
[66] G. Siebigs, *Kaiser...*, p. 700.
[67] L. Scott, *Aspar...*, p. 69.
[68] *Vita St. Danielis Stylitae*, 38; B. Croke, *Dynasty...*, p. 158.
[69] B. Croke, *Dynasty...*, p. 157.
[70] Zonaras, XIV, 1.
[71] J.B. Bury, *A History...*, p. 317–318; E. Stein, *Histoire...*, p. 356.

Nevertheless, this would have placed Patricius as the natural successor, if only he had sufficient political support. Effectively, there was little difference beyond technicalities, because with Aspar's network of connections he would likely have received the Imperial diadem, if only that was what the general had wanted. However, with Leo's son in the picture, those plans would have been put in jeopardy. Having a male heir could allow Leo to pursue his dynastic plans and establish a dynasty regardless of his promises to marry off his daughter.

This interpretation of events laid out by Croke is very convincing. I certainly would not fault anyone for following his ideas, as I did so myself, in the past. One variable however, on which this whole theory hangs upon is the assumption that the birth of Leo's son in 463 was an unexpected event. And that does not seem to be the case, since Verina was still fit to bear children[72]. Ariadne, Leo's daughter was born ca. 455, just two years before his Imperial election. Aspar must have known that and he certainly would not have chosen Leo, if he really wanted to avoid his candidate to ever produce an heir. In fact, second daughter of the emperor, Leontia, was born around 458, so just after his accession to the throne. Moreover, there is evidence that Leo was looking forward to having a male child, in fact, he prayed for it to St. Daniel the Stylite[73].

It is likely that Aspar had plans to have his family married into that of the emperor's. There seems to be sufficient evidence in the sources for that. But it does not necessarily follow that he planned to put his sons on the throne, at least not initially. Gereon Siebigs points out that Zonaras' account is faulty and that it is much more likely that Leo just promised Aspar that Patricius would be allowed to marry his daughter[74]. It appears the general simply sought to establish his family at the very top of the Imperial aristocracy through beneficial marriages.

It does not seem he cared if Leo had an heir or not, and it does put a nail in the coffin of the claim that the general planned from the very beginning to make his son the next emperor. It would have been obvious that Leo's offspring would have a much stronger claim than Aspar's, even if Patricius was married into the emperor's family. The image of Aspar as this powerful schemer, who relentlessly plans generations ahead, only to finally put his grasp on the Imperial throne, seems more like a modern invention than actual reality. It does not mean that he lacked capacity to do so, but his hunger for power might have not been overstated.

---

[72] Cf. P. C r a w f o r d, *Roman...*, p. 47. I would like to express my sincere thanks to prof. Rafał Kosiński for pointing that out in the review of my Ph.D.

[73] *Vita St. Danielis Stylitae*, 38. Admittedly it is possible that the author just claimed so, to show the miraculous power of the saint.

[74] G. S i e b i g s, *Kaiser...*, p. 772–773.

Behind Every Great Man... The Role of Verina

While the birth of Leo's son was probably not an issue for Aspar at first, it likely turned into one. Considering, admittedly, the limited evidence at our disposal, it appears that the emperor became interested to establish a political position for his family. Verina's influence and power rose immensely after the birth of Leo's son. From then on, she was no longer just the wife of Leo, but also the mother of a potential successor. Her image appeared on Imperial coinage, and she herself received the title of *Augusta*[75]. It is interesting, how all what transpired might have affected her, considering the context of the period after Leo's reign, when her political abilities and ambitions became apparent[76]. Nevertheless, it is very likely that she was instrumental in the developments of 463. The nomination of Basiliscus, her brother, to the office of *magister militum per Thracias* also took place around that time. He succeeded general Rusticius, who was rewarded with the consulate for the next year[77], and it is not implausible that Verina was involved in steering the emperor's decision. Unfortunately, the sources do not allow for anything beyond speculation, yet perhaps it is true that Aspar was mistaken in his judgement of Verina; the subject of it was not her fertility, but rather political ambition and ability to influence her husband[78].

It also seems that around the same time the emperor tried to become more independent and removed some people connected to Aspar from his immediate circle. Vivianus, a close supporter of the general, was likely replaced as *praefectus praetorio Orientis* in 463[79]. He received the consulate for that year[80], which could have been a way to defuse potential conflict. Vivianus was later the subject of a quarrel between Aspar and Leo, however, perhaps such a thing might have happened on more than one occasion, as the sources do not give clear information on the matter[81].

---

[75] B. C r o k e, *Dynasty...*, p. 158.

[76] Cf. M.J. L e s z k a, *Empress-Widow Verina's Political Activity during the Reign of Emperor Zeno*, [in:] *Mélanges d'histoire byzantine offerts à Oktawiusz Jurewicz à l'occasion de son soixante-dixième anniversaire*, red. W. C e r a n, Łódź 1998, p. 128–133; i d e m, *The role of Empress Verina in the events of 475/476 – revisited*, Bsl 75, 2017, p. 30–42.

[77] M a l c h u s, fr. 7; A. D e m a n d t, *Magister...*, p. 766–767; Е.П. Г л у ш а н и н, *Военная...*, p. 126.

[78] P. C r a w f o r d, *Roman...*, p. 47.

[79] He is directly attested in 459–460, but it is likely that he could have served until 462 or 463, cf. G. S i e b i g s, *Kaiser...*, p. 558, n. 3. His successor was likely Pusaeus, first attested in 465. Cf. *PLRE*, vol. II, p. 930 (s.v. *Pusaeus*).

[80] *CLRE*, p. 461.

[81] C a n d i d u s, fr. 1; B. C r o k e, *Dynasty...*, p. 162–163; *PLRE*, vol. II, p. 1179–1180, (s.v. *Vivianus 2*). George C e d r e n u s (607D–608A) gives the information that the subject of

Leo might have also started thinking about getting openly involved in the Western politics. The evidence for that is only fragmentary, but it is known that Marcellinus was preparing an expedition against Ricimer and his puppet emperor, Libius Severus. At this time, the Dalmatian warlord seems to have been allied with Leo, so it would have been unlikely for the general to make such a decision without the emperor's approval. It does not mean that Leo was already planning to dedicate the Empire's resources to pursue a more active foreign policy towards the West, but it seems that his interest in those matters was growing.

It might be that the birth of Leo's son affected the political scene, just how Croke claims, but in a different, indirect way: sparking Verina's ambitions and making her steer her husband towards the conflict with Aspar. However, when the sickly baby died after five months, it seems that Leo came around again to choose a compromise, in order to appease the general in the area of foreign policy. When an embassy from the West came to ask Leo to prevent Marcellinus from attacking Italy, he agreed to lend his help, and sent an envoy named Phylarchus to the general, who convinced him to call off the offensive[82].

The envoy then continued on to Africa, to negotiate a new settlement with Geiseric. The king refused to stop raiding Italy, however, it seems that he decided to finally release Eudoxia and Placidia, who were held captive since 455. In addition, Leo nominated Flavius Olybrius, who was for a long time supported by Geiseric as a candidate for the Western throne, as the consul for the year 464[83]. It is possible that Leo was considering supporting Olybrius' claims and, by extension, pursuing his own ambitions of gaining influence over the Western part of the Empire by reaching a compromise with the Vandals. It was certainly not an

---

the quarrel was the nomination of the city praefect, however, neither Vivianus, nor the other official mentioned by Candidus, Tatianus, were ever named as city praefects during the reign of Leo (Tatianus served in that office in 450–452). Perhaps the data is distorted, (which is likely, considering the brevity of Candidus' fragments and the chronological gap to Cedrenus' and Zonaras' accounts) and there were more points of contention as far as personal policies went. It would not be unlikely for a later Byzantine scholar to mistake different praefects the of fifth-century administrative system, so perhaps the events relayed by Cedrenus could be attributed to some quarrel over the nomination of *praefectus praetorio Orientis*. That being said, this is speculation based on the assumption that Leo tried to seek independence already in 463, and it might as well not have been the case.

[82] P r i s c u s, fr. 39.

[83] Brian C r o k e (*Dynasty...*, p. 159) claims that Leo simply sought the political support of Olybrius, considering the precarious position he found himself in. Marek J a n k o w i a k (*Bizancjum...*, p. 211) links those events with the foreign policy, and posits that Leo wanted to pressure Ricimer. Both of these could have been factors which Leo took into consideration, however, nominating Olybrius was primarily an apparent political statement of *détente* in relations with the Vandals.

ideal choice[84], but likely one that Aspar could accept. It also seemed more realistic at that point in time, considering that Flavius Ricimer held power over the Western Roman Empire with a firm grip.

It appears that up until mid-460s there was not one event that would irreversibly cause a falling out between Aspar and Leo. The emperor might have grown tired of the overwhelming influence the general had on the matters of the state, and he might have been was progressively looking for new ways to challenge it and realize his own plans. It is very likely that his wife played no small part in it. However, there is no evidence that their relations ever reached an open conflict; if there was one already brewing, Leo's conciliatory stance after 463 must have eased any tensions.

That being said, the emperor certainly advanced his position since his accession; he could count on the alliance with Marcellinus in Dalmatia and some control over elements of the army, thanks to the nomination of Basiliscus, as well as the continued support of the Church and important Orthodox figures. In case Aspar's influence were to be challenged, Leo had the means to independently pursue his goals, but it appears he did not want to do it at that point. That, however, was soon to change.

The Turn to the West

In the mean while the Western part of the Empire led by Ricimer was struggling with external and internal enemies. Aside from the previously mentioned opposition from Marcellinus, a certain Aegidius rose up in Gaul in an open revolt[85]. To make matters worse, the constant Vandal raids were a menace to the coastline. Although the pressure from Marcellinus was eventually relieved through diplomatic arrangements with Leo, and the pressure from the usurper in Gaul ended being a threat due to Aegidius' death[86]; the Vandals were a problem Ricimer could barely deal with. Their raiders struck and pillaged the Roman coasts, usually successfully avoiding engagements with regular Roman forces[87].

---

[84] Leo appears to have played that card once again later, when similarly he could not dedicate resources to the intervention in the West.

[85] *PLRE*, vol. II, p. 12–13 (s.v. *Aegidius*); P. M a c G e o r g e, *Late...*, p. 82–110.

[86] Cf. H y d a t i u s, 228; P. M a c G e o r g e, *Late...*, p. 108. He might have been killed on Ricimer's orders, cf. M. W i l c z y ń s k i, *Germanie...*, p. 270. It is however possible he might have died in the plague, cf. D. Z o ł o t e ń k i, *Galia u schyłku panowania rzymskiego*, Kraków 2011, p. 207.

[87] P r i s c u s, fr. 39.

Ricimer's problems ended up being a boon for Leo, since the Western Romans decided to send an embassy to Constantinople pleading for help. The details of the negotiations are unknown, but it can be safely assumed that the they signalled a willingness to compromise on Ricimer's part. Given the fact that the general disposed of his puppet on the throne, Libius Severus, earlier in the year, Leo seems to have been receptive to the overture and nominated Tatianus to head the embassy, likely giving him the title of *patricius* at that point. His mission must have been pretty clear: to establish some basis for the involvement of Leo in the West. For Aspar that must have been unacceptable, and the sources state that he quarrelled with the emperor over the nomination[88]. It seems, however, that Leo dismissed the general.

It seems that Tatianus has arrived in the West, where he then made arrangements for the Eastern Roman intervention[89]. There is some evidence of him being nominated as a consul in the West, which might have been in recognition of Leo's answer to the Western pleas of help[90]. Later on, he seems to have sailed to Carthage; however, he did not even receive an audience from Geiseric[91]. Unfortunately, Priscus did not record what Tatianus' demands were; however, this event clearly showed to Leo that it was not possible to find a common ground with the Vandals if he was going to pursue a more active western policy.

So far the said policy was rather reserved. Leo had certainly shown more interest in it than his predecessor, but he was mindful not to overreach in his involvement, and ready to take a step back to seek compromises. In essence, being observant of the developments and conducting diplomacy was all that it entailed. However, when an opportunity to become more engaged came up in 465, he decided to act on it, much to Aspar's discontent. Leo might also have been behind Marcelinus' intervention on Sicily in the same year[92]. All of that was likely to worry the powerful general, and could have done permanent damage to the relationship between himself and the emperor. Tracking whether the above events were the reason for the falling out is difficult, however, because of what was to happen shortly after.

---

[88] C a n d i d u s, fr. 1. For alternative interpretation as to why the nomination of Tatianus caused issues between Aspar and Leo, cf. P. C r a w f o r d, *Roman...*, p. 51–52.

[89] Cf. M. J a n k o w i a k, *Bizancjum...*, p. 212. There is no direct evidence of Tatianus' arrival in Italy, however, it is perfectly plausible considering the distances. It is, however, possible that someone else conducted the talks with the Western Romans, but there is no information whatsoever who it might have been.

[90] *CLRE*, p. 466–467. The situation with the consular nominations for 466 is very difficult to ascertain. It has also been argued that Tatianus was nominated for consulate in the East, which however, was suppressed through Aspar's influence, cf. *PLRE*, vol. II, p. 1053–1054, (s.v. *Tatianus 1*); B. C r o k e, *Dynasty...*, p. 162.

[91] P r i s c u s, fr. 41.

[92] H y d a t i u s, 227; G. M a x, *Political...*, p. 236; P. M a c G e o r g e, *Late...*, p. 50.

The Arrival of Tarasikodissa and the Situation in the East

In 466 a certain Isaurian commander named Tarasikodissa[93] arrived at the court of Leo. He brought letters that informed the emperor of treason committed by Ardaburious, the general of the east and son of Aspar, who according to the presented evidence conspired with the Persian monarch. As a result, Ardaburious was dismissed and his office was given to Jordanes, son of John the Vandal. Aspar, in spite of his influence, accepted the emperor's judgement in this matter and did not try to excuse or defend the actions of his son[94].

The question remains what did Ardaburious' betrayal amount to. The source states that he was inciting the Persian king to attack the Empire, and offered to support him if he did so[95]. If that were the case, Ardaburious received a surprisingly mild punishment. The emperor followed there the counsel of Aspar, who claimed his son acted against his advice, asked the emperor to strip his son of his command and come home to make his defence[96]. How did it go, we do not know, but it does not seem as if Ardaburious was punished further or absolved. It would, however, be difficult to believe the emperor would let it slide if he indeed was found guilty of high treason. Furthermore, it is difficult to say how Ardaburious would have benefited if that supposed plan of his came into fruition[97].

Coincidentally, around that time the relations with Persia were tense. Around 465 an embassy from the king Perozes arrived in Constantinople, complaining about the mistreatment of Zoroastrians in the Roman territories, the

---

[93] On the name, cf. R. K o s i ń s k i, *The Emperor Zeno: Religion and Politics*, Cracow 2010, p. 59–60; P. C r a w f o r d, *Roman...*, p. 29; on early career, cf. R. K o s i ń s k i, *Początki kariery Tarasikodissy–Zenona*, [in:] *Byzantina Europaea. Księga jubileuszowa ofiarowana Profesorowi Waldemarowi Ceranowi*, red. M. K o k o s z k o, M.J. L e s z k a, Łódź 2007, p. 289–304; P. C r a w f o r d, *Roman...*, p. 28–32.

[94] *Vita St. Danielis Stylitae*, 55; B. C r o k e, *Dynasty...*, p. 160. Peter C r a w f o r d (*Roman...*, p. 49) entertains the idea that the letters could have been fabricated by Leo to discredit Aspar.

[95] *Vita St. Danielis Stylitae*, 55. There is also another plot conceived by Ardaburious in the sources, related by Candidus (fr. 1) and involving the Isaurians. Rafał K o s i ń s k i (*The Emperor...*, p. 64, n. 47) claims that either account speaks of the same event and only one version is true. However, the sequence of events reported by Candidus appear to place the plot after Zeno already arrived in Constantinople, thus it must be a different event altogether.

[96] *Vita St. Danielis Stylitae*, 55.

[97] Peter C r a w f o r d (*Roman...*, p. 50) assumes Ardaburious could have wanted war to break out, to then easily defeat the invaders and, as a result, gain prestige and fame. It is not impossible, but it would be a very risky plan in a situation when the status of Aspar and his son probably did not even need to be improved.

Romans accepting refugees from Persia, and demanding that that Leo bear some of the expenses of manning the fortresses of the Caspian Gates and of the wars against Kidarite Huns that the Persians were conducting. Leo rejected the complaints and refused to help, however, he sent an embassy under the leadership of Constantine to discuss all the matters raised. Perozes must have been very disgruntled with the Roman stance, since he delayed the talks with Constantine up to a point when he made him travel all the way to the border with the Kidarites, and after that, he dismissed the envoy without reaching any kind of agreement[98]. The Persians asked again for the financial contributions after the invasion of the Saraguri and again were dismissed[99]. Another embassy was sent by Perozes after the Persians had managed to defeat Kidarites, and in addition to the usual demands, the envoys indirectly threatened Leo by boasting about the forces they had at the ready, but were again dismissed since Leo was preoccupied with his western policies at that point[100].

Another flashpoint was in Lazica where a local conflict erupted between the Lazi and Iberians, the latter being Persian subjects. Such a situation could have easily forced intervention of either great power and resulted in a war, but it seems that the Persians were more preoccupied with other issues, most likely the ongoing war with the Kidarites[101].

The takeaway from the Romano–Persian relations in these years is that they were growing tense, possibly even to the brink of an armed conflict[102]. It does not appear that Leo wished to reach any kind of compromise with Perozes. The fact that a war did not break out should be attributed to the coincidence that both sides happened to be engaged somewhere else, rather than any diplomatic efforts from the Roman side.

If Ardaburious had indeed committed treason which involved him contacting the Persian monarch, it is more likely that it concerned some kind of agreement to avoid an outright war. The *Life of St. Daniel the Stylite* claims that Ardaburious urged Perozes to intervene militarily and offered his support, but perhaps its author mistakenly (or consciously) claimed the intervention was supposed to concern the Roman Empire, while in fact it could have involved Lazica, which was a Roman puppet state[103]. Ardaburious might have wanted to organize

---

[98]   Priscus, fr. 41.

[99]   Priscus, fr. 47.

[100]   Priscus, fr. 51; R.C. Blockley, *East Roman Foreign Policy. Formation and Conduct from Diocletian to Anastasius*, Cairns 1992, p. 73–75.

[101]   Priscus, fr. 51.

[102]   R.C. Blockley, *East Roman...*, p. 74.

[103]   Evgeniy Glushanin also links these events with the eastern policy, but focuses more on the issue of the defence of Caspian Gates against the Huns. Cf. Е.П. Глушанин, *Военная...*,

a joint operation to stabilize the region, which was torn by the war between the Lazi and the Iberians. This course of events, even if highly speculative, seems to be the most likely considering the sources at our disposal. If that was indeed the case, Ardaburious might have overreached his competence and thus bring emperor's wrath on himself; however, it is also plausible that Leo used this event as a convenient pretext to further limit the power of the Ardaburii[104].

The Conflict between the Goths and the Sciri

An important event that contributed to the growing conflict between Aspar and Leo was the war between the Goths and the Sciri. The tribes broke off their alliance[105] and sent envoys seeking help against one another. According to Priscus, when deciding on how to approach the problem, the general advised the emperor to leave the matter alone and to remain neutral, however, Leo disregarded that, and decided to intervene on the side of the Sciri[106].

Unfortunately, the sources that inform of that war are limited to a short fragment in Priscus and Jordanes' *Getica*. Even though the latter is seemingly a very detailed account of the whole history of the Goths, the events in Pannonia of 460s seem to be less accurate. All evidence points to Jordanes omitting certain inconvenient details[107]. Thus, the primary source for the chronology of the events should be Priscus. The fragment in question was placed just after the one reporting on the visit of the ruler of Lazica, Gobazes, in Constantinople. Luckily, it is easily datable, since the visit took place after a great fire, that ravaged the city in 465[108].

---

p. 128. This is also highly possible, although, not directly based on sources. Additionally, it would make more sense for Ardaburious to become so involved if the issues at hand were much closer to the Roman territories, as Lazica was compared to the Caucasian mountain passes.

[104] If we assumed that Leo possessed sufficiently Machiavellian character, it not outside of the realms of possibility that the documents brought by Tarasikodissa could have been fabricated.

[105] Both J o r d a n e s (*Getica*, 275) and P r i s c u s (fr. 45) mention this. It is the only event that can link both accounts, which proves how confused the chronology of Jordanes is.

[106] P r i s c u s, fr. 45.

[107] Any mention of a Gothic defeat or of the second subjugation of their tribe by the Huns of Dengizich evidenced by Priscus, is absent from the narrative. It appears that those parts of the *Getica* resemble the legendary story of the heroic deeds of the Amal clan, rather than being a veritable historical account.

[108] M a r c e l l i n u s   C o m e s, a. 465. The exact date was most likely 2 September 465, cf. M.B. L e s z k a, M.J. L e s z k a, *Zarys dziejów Konstantynopola w latach 337–602*, [in:] *Konstantynopol – Nowy Rzym. Miasto i ludzie w okresie wczesnobizantyńskim*, red. M.J. L e s z k a, T. W o l i ń s k a, Warszawa 2011, p. 75.

Thus, the intervention in the war between the Goths and the Sciri should be placed around 465 or 466. Unfortunately, the fragment from Priscus does not contain much information. The more extensive passage of Jordanes completely omits any Roman intervention and only speaks of the despicable treason of the Sciri, who were agitated by the king of the Suebi, Hunimund, and joined arms with him against the Goths. Despite the element of surprise, the Goths won a great victory[109]. The king of the Goths, Valamer, died fighting valiantly in the battle, but the Sciri were completely obliterated, or so would Jordanes want us to believe. Following those events, the enemies of the Goths gathered in a huge coalition, comprised of the Sciri, Suebi, Gepids, Rugii, and Sarmatians, but they were yet again defeated by the Goths, and Jordanes does not spare graphic descriptions of the slaughter[110]. With that one sided account, which completely omits some events reported by the reputable *History* of Priscus, it is difficult to say what is true and what are exaggerated war stories that were circulating in the Amal court, written down by Cassiodorus and abridged by Jordanes.

Priscus, on the other hand, mentions that Leo sent letters to the commander in Illyria to send forces against the Goths. As no record of it can be found in the *Getica*, the course of the campaign or its aftermath can only be a matter of speculation. Similarly, it is unknown who exactly the said general was. The scholarship usually claims that it was a *magister militum per Illyricum*[111], however, it is debatable whether this title existed at this point in time. Furthermore, Priscus speaks of a commander 'in' Illyria, which could mean anyone who was positioned there at the time[112]. The disagreement with Aspar excludes the general from consideration, however, both Anthemius, who was still a *magister militum praesentalis*, and Basiliscus, a *magister militum per Thracias*, could have been in the region. Both were relatively independent of Aspar, so Leo could trust them to execute the order.

Another possibility could be that the commander in question was Marcellinus. If Leo's intent was to weaken the Goths, then those plans benefited the ruler of Dalmatia. The Pannonian Goths once raided his lands and they certainly still posed a threat, considering their continuous successes (even if exaggerated by Jordanes)[113]. If that was the case, it could explain Aspar's opposition. Perhaps the Alan general was wary of Leo and Marcellinus tightening their cooperation which could potentially threaten his position.

---

[109] J o r d a n e s, *Getica*, 275–276.
[110] J o r d a n e s, *Getica*, 277–279.
[111] H. G r a č a n i n, J. Š k r g u l j a, *The Ostrogoths...*, p. 176. They also claim the operation was limited to reinforcing border fortifications.
[112] P r i s c u s, fr. 45: γράμματα πρὸς τὸν ἐν Ἰλλυριοῖς στρατηγὸν ἔπεμπεν.
[113] Peter H e a t h e r (*The Fall...*, p. 369) calls them 'the closest thing to a new superpower'.

Although, the situation is often presented as if the general wanted to preserve the Goths due to them being his political asset, the Goths whose support Aspar had were the Thracian part of the tribe, unrelated to these events. Thus, it could not have been the reason for the disagreement, however, it is possible that the general feared that weakening of the Ostrogoths might be the first step in reorganizing Marcian's system of alliances in the Balkans, and the subsequent ones could then affect his allies. Alternatively, Aspar could have been an opponent of upsetting the delicate balance of power by involving the Romans in tribal conflicts between barbarians, or maybe he wanted both sides to bleed each other out, without risking the lives of Imperial soldiers.

Of the aftermath of the conflict even less is known than of its course. The pro-Gothic propaganda of Jordanes only mentions more victories, while the fragment of Priscus provides nothing on the matter. That being said, in the next passage in which the Goths appear, they have already been subjugated by the Huns[114]. The Sciri might have been allied with the Huns, who were regaining power under the rule of Dengizich. Jordanes mentions a tribe of Angisciri who were Hunnic subjects, and on another occasion he mentions that the Sciri were led by Edeco, who was probably one of the Hunnic noblemen mentioned by Priscus[115]. Perhaps the intervention of the Romans on behalf of the Sciri allowed their Hunnic allies to once again forcefully incorporate the Goths. Even though there is little evidence to support this hypothesis, it is the most likely course of events that explains how later the Romans had to face a rebuilt force of the Hunnic confederacy.

The War with Dengizich

Despite the fact that after the battle of Nedao the empire of the Huns gradually declined, it did not mean that the nomads suddenly disappeared from the map or that they lost all of their influence. The sources are scarce, but all the evidence seems to indicate that two sons of Attila, Dengizich and Ernach, inherited

---

[114] Priscus, fr. 48. Peter Heather (*The Fall...*, p. 363) claims the tribes subjugated by Dengizich were a different, unrelated group of Goths, cf. P. Crawford, *Roman...*, p. 33. Heather argues there were seven different groups of Goths (*The Fall...*, p. 352–353), and while it can be agreed that Jordanes' focus on Amals may be omitting some, it is also unlikely that all these groups were separate and unrelated to each other.

[115] Jordanes, *Getica*, 277. Cf. Jordanes, *Romana and Getica*, ed. P. van Nuffelen, L. van Hoof, Liverpool 2020, p. 351, n. 859.

the remnants of his legacy. Undoubtedly, the years following the defeat passed as they tried to establish themselves and counteract the attempts of various parts of the confederacy to break off. Furthermore, in the sixties the Eurasian Steppe became an arena for other dramatic events.

The tribe of Avars migrated west and attacked the Sabirs. This caused a domino effect, since the Sabirs, banished from their lands, were forced to invade the Saraguri, Onoguri, and Urogi tribes, who in turn attacked the Akatziri Huns. The last tribe was a part of the Hunnic confederacy, and likely was still under Ernach and Dengizich's rule[116]. In this context, it is interesting that the Saraguri sent an embassy to Leo, however, nothing binding was agreed upon. Perhaps they wanted to settle on Roman soil[117], seek alliance, or the emperor unsuccessfully tried to use the Saraguri and incite them to continue fighting the Huns. It is possible, that this contributed to the worsening of the relations between the Huns and the Romans, as Priscus vaguely informs of some unresolved disputes between them[118].

In the middle of 460s, Dengizich and Ernach sent an embassy to Leo, demanding that the markets on the Danube be set up. The emperor refused on the basis that the Huns caused too much harm to the Romans to be allowed access again. Given the failure of diplomacy, Dengizich wanted to declare war and force their demands, while Ernach disagreed since he was troubled by fighting on his own territories, which probably means that he was defending himself against Saraguri raids[119].

In spite of that, Dengizich decided to set out against the Romans himself. It is likely that he could have felt empowered by his recent successes in subjugating the Ostrogoths, weakened by their recent clashes against the Sciri. It follows that his army must have been strong in numbers. The campaign itself can be dated quite accurately thanks to a remark by Evagrius, who mentions that it coincided with the great earthquake that affected Thrace and Ionia[120], which most likely took place in 467[121]. Thus the barbarians must have attacked in the winter of 466–467[122]. A local *comes rei militaris*, Anagastes, who happened to be a son of Arnegisclus, sent envoys to the Huns when they approached the Dan-

---

[116] It was previously ruled by Ellak, cf. H.J. K i m, *The Huns...*, p. 132. Thus it is likely that after his death at Nedao, it was included in the rebuilt empire of Dengizich and Ernach.

[117] K. R o s e n, *Attila. Der Schrecken der Welt*, München 2016, p. 236.

[118] P r i s c u s, fr. 46.

[119] O. M a e n c h e n - H e l f e n, *The World...*, p. 166.

[120] E v a g r i u s, II, 14.

[121] R.C. B l o c k l e y, *Fragmentary Classicising Historians of the Later Roman Empire*, t. I, Liverpool 1981, p. 170.

[122] They are reported to have crossed frozen Danube.

ube. Dengizich, however, refused to parley and sent his embassy straight to the emperor. The Huns demanded land for settlement and a tribute. Interestingly, this time Leo replied favourably, only demanding that the barbarians obey him, which most likely meant introducing the Huns into the *foederati* system[123]. This decision stands in stark contrast with the previous one. It is possible that Leo sought compromise because of problems caused by the earthquake, and his attention was turned towards the preparations for the expedition against the Vandals[124]. However, Otto Maenchen-Helfen presents another interesting interpretation, suggesting that Leo might have wanted to settle the Huns on Roman territories, so that they would act as a counter-balance to the Thracian Goths, who were loyal to Aspar and served as one of the bases of his political power[125].

Unfortunately, this is where the passage ends, and the sources return to these events when the both sides were already at war. It is impossible to ascertain whether something happened in the interim period leading up to the conflict, but it is likely that it took some time for the envoys to travel both ways, and Dengizich did not wait for an answer and simply crossed the border. It is possible that he meant to pressure the emperor, or could not keep his warriors, who wanted to loot and pillage, at bay.

As a result, the Romans gathered an impressive force, led by Basiliscus, Aspar, and Ostrys[126], likely supported by the previously mentioned detachment under the command of Anagastes, and also the army of Anthemius[127].

The Romans managed to encircle the barbarian forces in a ravine. Despite their advantageous position, they did not decide to attack, as apparently the numerous barbarian forces must have been considered a formidable foe even then. Alternatively, the Romans were ordered not to do it by the emperor, who still sought to reach an agreement. However, the forces of Dengizich started to run out of supplies. Fearing starvation, their leader sent the envoys offering that he would submit to the emperor if his people were allowed to settle in the Roman territories. The besieging commanders promised to relay the issue to Constantinople and help feed the encircled barbarians, while they awaited a response. To make that feasible logistically, they were split up into several camps.

---

[123] P r i s c u s, fr. 48.

[124] C.D. G o r d o n, *The Age of Attila. Fifth–Century Byzantium and the Barbarians*, Michigan 1961, p. 160.

[125] O. M a e n c h e n-H e l f e n, *The World…*, p. 166.

[126] P r i s c u s, fr. 49.

[127] Peter C r a w f o r d (*Roman…*, p. 57) claims Zeno took part in this campaign as well, but that seems unlikely.

At least that is how it was presented to them, because Aspar, who was likely the senior commander, did not wish to parley at all. His subordinate, Chelchal, who was of Hunnic origin, was sent to one of the camps that was occupied by the Goths. He appeared in front of the council of the elders and began to incite them against Dengizich. He claimed that the emperor had agreed to give them land for settlement, however, he continued that it would not solve their problems, as they would remain Hunnic slaves, and would have to pay tribute in their crops to their masters. He also accused them of staining their honour, since their ancestors had sworn to shake off the Hunnic yoke. One has to be impressed by the rhetoric skills of Chelchal. His speech must have really resonated with the Goths, since, as a result, they decided to attack the Huns[128].

However, this was all a ploy orchestrated by Aspar. As soon as the fighting had started, the Roman forces formed up to strike the barbarians. When they realized what was happening, the barbarians joined forces to fend off the attack. Despite their favourable position, the Roman forces had a hard time defeating the barbarians, since according to Priscus, only Aspar's contingent managed to destroy their enemies. The forces of the other commanders were apparently less prepared, and, as a result, many barbarians managed to escape the encirclement, including the leader of the army, Dengizich[129]. It is not recorded what exactly happened to him or to the remnants of his army afterwards. As far as the Roman forces were concerned, it appears that a portion returned to continue their preparations for the Vandal expedition. In the meantime, Anagastes was designated *magister militum per Thracias* in place of Basiliscus. The latter received command over the praesental army, which had been under the command of Anthemius up to this point. Anthemius was left with no office, but Leo had already planned to send him to the West to assume the throne in Ravenna. The forces of Thrace commanded by Anagastes continued to hunt for Dengizich and managed to finally defeat him around 468 or 469[130].

An additional source providing more detail on those events is the panegyric on Anthemius by Sidonius Appolinaris. The poet mentions that his hero defeated a group of Huns at Serdica under the command of a certain Hormidac. It is the only source containing such information and the only place where the name of the Hunnic chieftain appears. However, in the description of the battle the

---

[128] P r i s c u s, fr. 49; P. R o u c h e, *Attila. La violence nomade*, Paris 2009, p. 302–304; H.J. K i m, *The Huns...*, p. 86.

[129] P r i s c u s, fr. 49; T. B u r n s, *A History of the Ostrogoths*, Bloomington 1984, p. 54.

[130] M a r c e l l i n u s   C o m e s, a. 469. Cf. H.J. K i m, *The Huns...*, p. 86; I. B ó n a, *Das Hunnenreich*, Stuttgart 1991, p. 209; T. S t i c k l e r, *Die Hunnen*, München 2007, p. 105–106; K. R o s e n, *Attila...*, p. 237–238.

same elements appear as in the fragments of Priscus referenced above: the logistical problems[131] and the siege of a camp[132]. Although it is possible that Sidonius mistakenly twisted the name of Dengizich, the two names are not all that similar, and Sidonius was generally well informed on the details of the events in the Balkans[133]. It seems more likely that Hormidac was a lesser Hunnic commander, a subordinate of Dengizich, most likely in command of the specific camp that the forces of Anthemius guarded after the barbarians were split into different camps. Sidonius also mentions that Anthemius' allies failed him, which further supports linking the poet's and Priscus' passages together, as the historian also reported that many of the barbarians escaped the encirclement. Sidonius omits other names, especially the most important in these events, those of Aspar and Dengizich, but that is completely understandable. The poet wished to show the glory of his hero, and mentioning the military success of Aspar and the escape of Dengizich would only detract from Anthemius' achievements. Nevertheless, the passage of Sidonius proves that Anthemius and his forces were also present in the battle against Dengizich, and locates it close to the city of Serdica[134].

The invasion of Dengizich shows that the dissolution of the Hunnic confederacy after the death of Attila and the battle of Nedao was neither full nor final. The crisis which it experienced in the fifties was relatively soon alleviated, and just ten years later the Huns ruled by Ernach and Dengizich returned as active players on the political scene.

It is crucial to understand this context when analysing the afore-mentioned events. It seems very likely that Aspar made the decision to attack on his own. The sources state explicitly that Leo was willing to come to an agreement, yet the general forced a battle. Priscus states that the other generals did worse in the battle, since contrary to Aspar's men, they might have not been prepared, which may indicate that Aspar put his plan of antagonizing the Goths and Huns into motion without anyone's approval or knowledge. This would be understandable in the context of Aspar's attitude towards the Huns, and, even more so, if the hypothesis that Leo was planning to use the warriors of Dengizich to counter-balance Aspar's supporters is correct. It would also indicate that the tensions between Aspar and Leo already reached a boiling point, and either looked to the ways in which he could undermine the other.

---

[131] Sidonius, *Carmina*, II, 228.

[132] Sidonius, *Carmina*, II, 225.

[133] For example he knows of Valamer, the king of Goths, and records his name correctly. Cf. Sidonius, *Carmina*, II, 223–226.

[134] Assumedly, the forces of Dengizich were advancing along *Via Militaris* and were surrounded in some ravine close to Serdica; the general characteristics of the terrain seem to support such hypothesis.

There is, in fact, some evidence for the tightening of co-operation between Leo and Marcellinus. It is possible that Leo tried to reinstate the long-non-existent office of *magister militum per Illyricum* to give it to Marcellinus, and, perhaps, introduce the general's forces, with him as a commander, in to the Eastern Roman military system[135]. Not only would that have bound Marcellinus closer to Leo, but it would also have meant that the emperor could use his loyal ally as a direct counter-weight to Aspar.

After securing his immediate alliances, Leo decided to send Anthemius to the West, in order to occupy the throne in Ravenna. A common assertion in the literature is that Leo, thanks to that move, dismissed Anthemius, who was his potential rival[136]. There is probably some truth to that, however, it is more likely that Anthemius was a party of uncertain allegiance to Leo, and by giving him such a boon, he secured his support and made sure he would not have worked with Aspar. Those plans had to be postponed because of the barbarian incursions in the Balkans, however, in 467, Anthemius was dispatched to Italy supported by the forces of Marcellinus.

In the same year Leo sent Phylarchus to bring the ultimatum to the Vandals, which was naturally turned down[137]. The emperor probably hoped to send his troops to Africa already in 467, however, the expedition had to be postponed one year due to bad weather[138]. In the meantime, Geiseric reacted by sending raiders to Illyria and Greece, especially brutal was the plunder of Zakynthos, where apparently 500 citizens were captured and cut to pieces. Perhaps the Vandal king tried to intimidate the Eastern Romans[139], however, Leo seemed to have been adamant in his plans.

---

[135] There is a law in the *Codex Iustinianus* (*CJ*, XII, 59, 8) issued by Leo, dated to 467–470, which mentions the prerogatives of territorial *magistri militum*, including the one of *Illyricum* alongside generals of the east and Thrace. This is probably the first unequivocal evidence for the existence of this office since 395. Frank W o z n i a k (*East Rome...*, p. 359) assumes that Marcellinus received the title of *magister militum* from Leo in 461, however, he claims it was a mastery of Dalmatia, cf. P. M a c G e o r g e, *Late...*, p. 40–41. J.B. B u r y, *History...*, p. 333. There is some merit to that claim, since there was a similar case of Julius Nepos, who held the title of *magister militum Dalmatiae* in 473, cf. *CJ*, VI, 61, 5. It was, however, an anomalous position, only mentioned in the sources this one time, cf. M. K u l i k o w s k i, *Marcellinus...*, p. 186, n. 29. It is possible that the commands of Dalmatia and Illyricum largely were the same office that underwent a change of name.

[136] F.M. C l o v e r, *The Family and Early Career of Anicius Olybrius*, Hi 27, 1978, p. 195; J.M. O' F l y n n, *A Greek on the Roman Throne: The Fate of Anthemius*, Hi 40, 1991, p. 124.

[137] P r i s c u s, fr. 52.

[138] H y d a t i u s, 232.

[139] Geiseric also pursued alliances against the Romans, possibly with king Rechimund of the Suebi and Euric, the king of the Visigoths. Cf. H.J. D i e s n e r, *Das Vandalenreich. Aufstieg und Untergang*, Stuttgart 1966, p. 68.

At the same time, Leo further tightened his connection with Tarasikodissa-Zeno, giving the Isaurian general the hand of his daughter, Ariadne[140]. Since she was likely promised to Patricius, this was a direct blow to Aspar and the status of his family. It is telling how the change in the direction of the emperor's foreign policy coincided with his distancing himself further from the Alan general in other respects[141].

Aspar's Opposition

There are several reasons why Aspar was so adamant in his opposition to Leo's plans. Procopius mentioned that the general supposedly feared that such a great victory would bring Leo political prestige, which could in turn lead to the emperor becoming completely independent. Considering how tense their relationship was, and how many instances of conflict can be traced from the sources, Aspar could have reasonably feared that Leo would continue to limit his influence.

By 467 Leo managed to considerably improve his standing; however, Aspar still had power within the army and civil administration. Winning a great victory and being recognized as a senior *Augustus* in the West would have built a stable foundations for Leo's dynastic plans. After all, the greater the success in the West, and the more recognition he received there, the less the internal power structures, in which Aspar was so firmly embedded, would matter in the grand scheme of things.

There are, however, other reasons related to foreign policy. It has been argued multiple times in the present work that the military elite cared deeply about how it was conducted, and this was no exception. In fact, Aspar's interests, as far as it is possible to ascertain, seemed to concern primarily the western policy and the relations with the Vandals. This should be of no surprise, since he had personally experienced the outcome of Theodosian policies when leading troops on the campaigns that were a result of them. In the literature, the problem of foreign policy is recognized, however, it is often presented in a wholly different light. Aspar's opposition to the war with the Vandals is commonly explained by the general's feeling some sort of loyalty towards Geiseric, either because of a supposed ethnic brotherhood between the two, or because of an oath that he swore according to some scholars[142].

---

[140] The date of the marriage is a subject of discussion, however, the arguments of Rafał K o s i ń s k i (*The Emperor...*, p. 65–66) placing it in 468 are convincing.

[141] In addition, Leo issued a law in August 468, forbidding the possession of private retinues, cf. *CJ*, IX, 12, 10. It seems to have been aimed against Aspar.

[142] E. G a u t i e r, *Genséric. Roi des Vandales*, Paris 1935, p. 240; G. V e r n a d s k y, *Flavius...*, p. 48–49; B. B a c h r a c h, *A History of the Alans in the West. From Their First Appearance in the Sources of Classical Antiquity through the Early Middle Ages*, Minneapolis 1973, p. 47–48.

There is however a more reasonable explanation. The situation the Empire was in at that point almost mirrored the one when Theodosius was in power. The barbarians at the northern border suffered a major defeat, but it is likely it was so only because of Aspar's own decision and, essentially, insubordination. After all, Leo wanted to let the Huns settle in Roman lands. Furthermore, Dengizich and his forces were still at large and the operations against him would continue until 469.

In the east, however, the situation was still unstable. As mentioned before, the Persians managed to deal with the Kidarites and indirectly threatened the Romans, boasting about their military might. Priscus observes that despite Persian's threats, Leo dismissed their envoys because he was more concerned about the developments in the Sicily concerning the Vandals and the West. Due to fragmented sources, the Persian response is not known; in the end the peace was not broken, perhaps because Leo finally paid up. Roger Blockley, however, assumes Perozes simply intervened in Lazica expanding his sphere of influence, which the Romans could not have contested due to their problems elsewhere[143].

From the perspective of 468, however, no one knew that the threat of a destructive war, either from the north or the east, would in the end not materialize. It did during the reign of Theodosius, and considering what can be assumed of Aspar's convictions, he must have feared that Leo's policies would bring the same misfortunes to the Empire.

The Expedition of Basiliscus

In the year 468 all plans of Leo were finally set in motion to deal with the Vandal problem once and for all. With the threat from Dengizich mostly contained, Anthemius seated on the Western throne, and an alliance with Marcellinus firmly secured, a huge army and fleet gathered with the emperor's brother-in-law, Basiliscus, at the helm was finally ready to set out.

The army counted about 100,000 men on 1,100 ships according to Procopius[144]. Some scholars put those numbers in question[145], however, it is likely that in this exceptional case they are reliable. Procopius, thanks to his military experience, was less likely to inflate numbers to unreasonable proportions. Furthermore,

---

[143] R.C. B l o c k l e y, *East Roman...*, p. 75.
[144] P r o c o p i u s, *History of the Wars*, III, 6. 1.
[145] M. W i l c z y ń s k i, *Gejzeryk...*, p. 176; K. V ö s s i n g, *Königreich...*, p. 67–68.

a detailed description of the order of battle of the forces of Belisarius can serve as a frame of reference for the expedition of Basiliscus. Belisarius was sent with an army that was select, but only adequate in number, counting 15,000 soldiers. However, they were accompanied by around 33,000 sailors and 2,000 marines who manned 500 transport ships and 92 warships[146]. Thus, the total number of men was about 50,000, that is around half of the forces that Basiliscus had at his disposal. Considering that this campaign was probably the greatest of the ones ever launched against the Vandals, the number of 100,000 seem plausible, if it includes both sailors and soldiers. Thus, following the pattern of Belisarius' expedition, there should have been around 30,000 soldiers at Basiliscus' disposal[147], which amounted to one praesental army with supporting forces.

The amount of resources that it took to equip and send the expedition was substantial. John the Lydian reports 65,000 pounds of gold and 700,000 pounds of silver[148], Candidus a similar amount of 60,000 pounds of gold, 700,000 pounds of silver and some undisclosed sums gathered by Anthemius[149]. Procopius claims 130,000 pounds of gold, which at first glance looks different from the others, but if we were to take into account the conversion of value between gold and silver it may amount to a very similar sum[150]. Regardless, it was clear that it was a great effort in economic and military terms.

The fleet probably sailed along the coast for as long as it was possible for ease of navigation and safety, and for a similar reason it is likely that it made a stop on Sicily[151]. Theophanes and Jordanes report several clashes with Vandal ships, victorious for the Roman side, unfortunately with no further details[152]. Whether these were major engagements that crippled a part of Vandal fleet or just minor skirmishes is unknown, although the latter seem more likely. Thus, the expedition arrived in Africa and anchored near *Promunturium Mercurii*, a northernmost point of the peninsula that encloses the Gulf of Tunis from the east. This location was just 280 stadia from Carthage, as Procopius informs, which translates to about 60 km to the north-east[153].

---

[146] P r o c o p i u s, *History of the Wars*, III, 9. 1–23; P. K r u p c z y ń s k i, *Trudności zachodnich wypraw Belizariusza*, Łódź 1984, p. 95.

[147] Y. M o d é r a n, *Les Vandales et l'Empire Romain*, Arles 2014, p. 194–195.

[148] J o h n   L y d u s, III, 43.

[149] C a n d i d u s, fr. 2.

[150] P r o c o p i u s, *History of the Wars*, III, 6, 2.

[151] Due to the strategic value of the island, it can be assumed that any major expedition to Africa had to take Sicily into account. Cf. T. W o l i ń s k a, *Rola Sycylii w wojnach wandalskich i gockich Justyniana*, PH 41, 2000, p. 321–322.

[152] T h e o p h a n e s, AM 5961; J o r d a n e s, *Romana*, 337.

[153] Cf. K. V ö s s i n g, *Königreich...*, p. 68; H. D i e s n e r, *Das Vandalenreich...*, p. 69.

Apparently, the wind favoured the Romans, and, if we are to believe the judgement of Procopius, had Basiliscus attacked right away he would have easily won the victory[154]. However, despite the advantage, the general was tardy and did not strike. To many ancient historians, as well as modern scholars, that was a surprising and inconceivable development. Procopius himself presents as many as three possible interpretations of the events, in an attempt to make sense of the general's decision.

The first one, which is also confirmed by a number of other sources, is that Basiliscus decided to postpone his attack, having been bribed by Geiseric. Procopius said that the general, due to his greed, thought that a couple of days of armistice that the Vandal king had asked for would do no harm[155].

The second one is predicated on Aspar's influence and Basiliscus' Imperial ambition. Procopius supposes that Basiliscus willingly sabotaged the expedition as a favour to Aspar, who had promised the general that he would be elevated to the throne in return. The existence of such a deal is rather dubious. Nevertheless, two other sources mention that besides Procopius, that is Theophanes and Hydatius[156].

The third one is simply that it was a mistake on Basiliscus' part. It would no doubt be the most prosaic reason for the defeat. It does not assume ill will on the general's part or any conspiracy. Interestingly, Procopius is the only source that takes such a possibility into account. It might be due to him being one of a few historians who had actual military experience, and who truly understood the unpredictability inherent in warfare. For others, a defeat despite favourable conditions and force superiority would have been proof of the general's wrongdoing; Procopius, however, could have understood that it did not need to be the case.

The scholarship tends to agree with the last interpretation. The claims of Basiliscus' betrayal caused either by greed or lust for power are seen simply as a way to excuse such a disastrous defeat. Arguing against these points is difficult. The tendency of ancient authors to explain events by invoking individual virtues or vices of those who took part in them is a common trope. Furthermore, mistakes, bad decisions, and random occurrences can often dictate the outcome of many events and can never be truly discounted. Our knowledge of Basiliscus' previous conduct and his military experience seem to contradict the claim that he could have made such an obvious mistake; however, not enough is known of his orders, the condition of his forces, the intelligence he possessed on the enemy, and other crucial tactical and strategic considerations. It is no less possible that

---

[154] Procopius, *History of the Wars*, III, 6. 10.

[155] Procopius, *History of the Wars*, III, 6. 16. It is commonly repeated in other sources, cf. Jordanes, *Romana*, 337; Theophanes, AM 5961; Malalas, XIV, 44.

[156] Theophanes, AM 5961; Hydatius, 241.

the claims he could have won easily are misguided and do not take into account the specific situation that the general was in.

Discounting sources and their interpretation of events altogether is a risky proposition and requires justification. The information on the conspiracy involving Aspar and Basiliscus can be explained by the existing conflict between Leo and the Alan general. It is possible that the rumours of his betrayal were spread to paint Aspar as a villain, responsible for the failure of the expedition against the Vandals. The way in which these events are portrayed by Hydatius seems to confirm that, as he points to Aspar's supposed connection to the Vandals as the reason for his later execution[157].

Thus, it appears that the correct course of action is to consider whether there could be a grain of truth in the information about Basiliscus taking the bribe. What is referred to as a 'bribe' could have been the gifts that customarily accompanied diplomatic talks. Procopius reports that Geiseric sent envoys asking for the armistice and that was probably the true nature of the events[158]. The narrative of Priscus survived only through the lens of other historians, much less informed in diplomatic matters. The sending of gifts would have been a natural occurrence for the experienced envoy, but that could have been wrongly understood by those who used him as a source afterwards, and likely seen as suspicious. In addition, the common soldiers could have heard of said gifts, and after having to cope with the defeat, the rumour could have spread that it was Basiliscus' greed that damned them.

When all that is taken into account, it appears much more likely that Basiliscus did not get bribed with money, but decided to parley with the Vandals. This was common practice when a show of force was enough to contain the threat[159]. It is also widely repeated by later Byzantine military manuals[160]. Even though the ancient authors want us to believe the victory was certain, for an experienced commander such as Basiliscus accepting what seemed like an offer of surrender could have appeared preferable to taking any risks inherent to combat.

---

[157] Hydatius, 241.

[158] K. Vössing, *Königreich...*, p. 70. Ronald A. Bleeker (*Aspar...*, p. 107) argues that Basiliscus might have acted on Aspar's advice. Such interpretation binds what probably happened to the accusations of treason, however, it assumes incredible cunning, manipulativeness, and predictive abilities of Aspar. Afterall, how could the general predict exactly that Vandals would want to negotiate, and that Basiliscus would follow what Aspar had said to the note?

[159] Yves Modéran (*Les Vandales...*, p. 196–197) argues that the concept of total war had not yet been developed in those times, so it is likely that Basiliscus' orders would account for a possibility of seeking an arrangement with Geiseric.

[160] Mauricius, *Strategikon*, VIII, 2, 4; *Peri strategias*, 33. See also: W. Kaegi, *Some Thoughts on Byzantine Military Strategy*, Brookline 1983.

Unfortunately for the general, he did not realize how cunning a foe he was facing. All evidence seems to point to Geiseric playing for time. The wind was favourable for the Romans and he needed to wait long enough for it to change, so he could take advantage of it. This was not the first time the Vandal king faked his willingness to offer a diplomatic solution in order to find a right opportunity to strike at unsuspecting enemies. In 461, the Western emperor Majorian gathered a great army and marched to Spain to meet with his fleet, which was waiting to transport his troops to Africa, to deal with the Vandal threat. In response, Geiseric sent envoys to parley with the Romans, however, at the same time he put precautions in place. In case the Romans went ahead with their plan, he poisoned the wells in Mauretania along the way of suspected approach of Majorian's army[161]. Furthermore, he bribed captains of several ships and sent his own forces to capture the remaining vessels that were anchored in the Spanish ports[162]. Thanks to that display of subterfuge, the danger to the Vandal kingdom in Africa was averted. The events of 461 are the best example of Geiseric's cunning, but there is also some evidence of him doing the same in 441.

If Basiliscus was to be criticized, it would have mostly to do not with his greed or hunger for power, but rather naivety. And interestingly, this is how one of the preserved fragments in *Liber Suda* portrays the general[163]. It is possible that in the original source that judgement was related to his conduct in Africa.

The details of the negotiations between Geiseric and Basiliscus are unknown, but it is clear that the king only wanted to stall. At the same time the Vandal fleet stationed in Carthage was getting ready to sail out. Some of the vessels were kept unmanned, in order to be used as fire ships in the attack[164].

When the wind changed, the Vandals sallied out and set loose the fire ships. The attack was a complete surprise, and the Romans were unable to react in time. The fire ships crashed into the Roman vessels anchored by *Promunturium Mercurii*, setting them ablaze. Due to how close they were to each other, the fire spread from ship to ship, causing chaos among Roman ranks. The sailors desperately tried to push away the burning ships with poles to save their own vessels. To make matters worse, the main part of the Vandal fleet arrived soon after the fire ships made contact, ramming and boarding the disorganized Roman ships. In all this chaos there were some pockets of Roman resistance. Procopius recounts

---

[161] Priscus, fr. 36.

[162] Hydatius, 200. On the campaign see: K. Vössing, *Königreich...*, p. 60–63; A. Merrills, R. Miles, *The Vandals...*, p. 119–120; M. Wilczyński, *Gejzeryk...*, p. 170.

[163] *Suda*, B 163.

[164] J.H. Pryor, E.M. Jeffreys, *The Age of Dromon. The Byzantine Navy ca. 500–1204*, Leiden 2006, p. 9.

the story of John, who was most likely one of *magistri militum vacantes* who took part in the expedition[165]. The historian acquits him of any responsibility for Basiliscus' betrayal and explains how bravely he fought while surrounded on all sides by the enemies. Apparently, the son of Geiseric, Gento, in awe of John's valiant resistance, offered him to surrender honourably, in response to which the general threw himself into the water in with his armaments, screaming obscenities at his enemies as he was going down. This was likely the fate of many Roman soldiers, and only some of them managed to escape the fiery doom, death by Vandal sword, drowning, or captivity[166].

The Aftermath of the Defeat

The defeat at Cap Bon was a catastrophe for Leo. It turned out that all of the resources invested in that great endeavour had been wasted, not to mention the loss of trained soldiers, sailors, and all the warships and transport vessels, now lying on the sea floor by the Tunisian shores. Only a fraction of the forces managed to escape. Basiliscus was among them; however, the set-back soon took its toll in other areas. The expedition of Basiliscus was in many ways the cornerstone to Leo's achieving his goals, both in internal and foreign policies. Its failure meant his aims were not going to get realized anytime soon.

Soon after the retreat, Marcellinus was killed on Sicily[167]. The person responsible for that deed was likely Ricimer, who took the opportunity to help improve his own standing in the face of Leo's defeat[168]. The death of the Dalmatian general benefited him greatly, as Marcellinus was a loyal ally to Leo and was of great help in establishing Anthemius on the throne. He also had considerable forces at his disposal. With Marcellinus out of the picture, the emperor Anthemius had nowhere to look for to counter-balance the influential general Ricimer anymore.

Leo also lost Basiliscus as his ally, at least for the time being. The only information on what happened to the general can be found in the *History of the Wars* by Procopius, who claims he sought refuge in the Church Hagia Sophia, and only the intervention of Verina saved him from Leo's wrath. There is no disputing that Leo must have been furious about the outcome of the expedition.

---

[165] Е.П. Глушанин, *Военная...*, p. 130.

[166] Procopius, *History of the Wars*, III, 6. 22–24.

[167] P. MacGeorge, *Late...*, p. 59; M. Kulikowski, *Marcellinus...*, p. 188–189.

[168] Marcellinus Comes (a. 468) mentioned that he died at the hands of people for whom he was fighting.

However, it does not seem as if Basiliscus had lost his office[169]. This was largely inconsequential, since there were barely any soldiers from his praesental army left, however, probably the bigger problem was not that Leo denounced Basiliscus in his anger, but that the general, due to his monumental failure and widely repeated rumours of his betrayal, was politically compromised.

Thus, because of the defeat in 468, Leo lost most of his allies on whom his policies had hinged. In the meantime, the Vandals remained a constant threat; thus, if Leo wanted to salvage his western policy, he had to find a new way to deal with that problem. The only person close to the emperor who had not been compromised in some way was Zeno.

In 469 Jordanes stepped down from his office of *magister militum per Orientem*. Interestingly, he served for just 3 years and there is absolutely no evidence of him falling out of emperor's favour or suffering any major set-back that would justify him getting demoted. On the contrary, he was announced as the consul for the year 470[170]. Similarly, no evidence can be found for Jordanes' achieving extraordinary results that would explain him getting such an honour. Naturally, consular nominations for officials stepping down from office were not an uncommon thing, however, in this case there might have been more to it. The nomination itself was a very controversial one. It seems that the obvious candidate for this year was *magister militum per Thracias* Anagastes, who had just delivered the proof of his victory over Dengizich in the form of the Hun's head[171]. Anagastes took the decision of the emperor very badly. The justification was that the general was epileptic; however, it seems to have been just an excuse and a bad one at that. If such condition did not prevent him from leading the army in the field, how could it make him ineligible for an honorary civic office?

It seems that the emperor wanted to free one of the military commands, specifically to place his son-in-law and a loyal subordinate, Zeno, as Jordanes' successor. It is likely that after Basiliscus' disgrace, Leo sought to re-establish his influence over the army, and having someone he could trust as a leader of the eastern forces certainly served to further that goal[172]. Dismissing Jordanes so abruptly ensured that Zeno could assume the office immediately. The consulship might have been a means to appease the general and convince him to accept losing a prestigious office and all the advantages that came with it. Interestingly, by doing that, Leo irreparably damaged his relations with Anagastes.

---

[169] *PLRE*, vol. II, p. 212–214 (s.v. *Fl. Basiliscus 2*).

[170] *CLRE*, p. 475.

[171] Marcellinus Comes, a. 469.

[172] There are no sources on Jordanes' loyalties, but it is safe to assume that he was not as close to the emperor as Zeno, who had family ties with Leo at that point.

One of the reasons for such a hasty appointment of Zeno could have been an intention to resume the emperor's foreign policy to try to salvage the situation after the failure of Basiliscus. The praesental army that he commanded was almost completely destroyed[173], and the other one had been under the command of Aspar for almost twenty years by then. It is not unlikely that those forces were more loyal to the general at this point than to the Empire. Knowing the convictions of the general, expecting him and his forces to embark on the campaign against the kingdom of Geiseric would be foolish on Leo's behalf.

If the emperor had wanted to make war on the Vandals again, only transferring the soldiers from the east could have provided him with sufficient forces. Zeno becoming a *magister militum per Orientem* meant the eastern army was under the command of Leo's most loyal associate and it meant that the emperor could use those forces as he wished. In 470 an army, presumably comprised of the elements from the eastern provinces, was formed in Egypt under the commanders Heraclius and Marsus. Interestingly, Zeno was not going to be the commander-in-chief of the expedition.

There is a reasonable explanation of why it happened. After the failure of Basiliscus, which destroyed the general's prestige and forced him into hiding in disgrace, Leo essentially lost one of his associates. It is possible that this time he specifically chose commanders who were loyal to him, but who at the same time, were of much lower profile than his own son-in-law. Leo could not risk Zeno suffering the same defeat as Basiliscus, as this would have alienated the emperor completely, and, in turn, left him politically at Aspar's mercy.

The Campaign of Heraclius and Marsus

The campaign of Heraclius and Marsus is one of the most misunderstood events of the reign of Leo. Most of the scholarship does not recognize it as a separate endeavour, but as a part of the expedition of Basiliscus. It is arguably a misinterpretation, nevertheless, it is crucial to revisit the evidence and explain how the chronology was established in the present work.

---

[173] It was naturally in Leo's interest to immediately restore that army to full capacity, however, it is doubtful whether he would be able to do so in such a short order. Finding recruits, getting them trained, and having Imperial workshops provide weaponry for 20,000 men would certainly take time, and that does not even take into account the fact the treasury was emptied by the failed campaign of 468. Thus, it is most plausible that the second army *in praesentis* was not reformed yet.

The fiasco of the expedition of Basiliscus was a major set-back for the emperor in multiple ways. Not only a great amount of resources had been wasted, but also the alliances that the emperor had built over the years were either lost or put in jeopardy. For that reason the views of Procopius, who presents the battle of Cap Bon not only as a turning point, but even a point of no return in the Vandal–Roman relations[174], are very believable. Thus, most of the scholarship accepts the course of events as presented by the Byzantine historian[175]. There is however an alternative source that relays these events differently, namely the chronicle of Theophanes[176]. While the chronicler is usually not as reliable and his accounts are often confused, especially chronologically, he most likely did have access to and used Priscus in this instance[177]. Consequently, a case could be made that his version is the one which is closer to the truth.

In the *History of the Wars* by Procopius the historical excurses serve a specific purpose, which is to paint a background to the story of the campaigns of Belisarius and put them in context intended by the author. This is no different in case of the description of the expedition of Basiliscus. The themes of virtue and fate are central to Procopius' work, and the failure of Basiliscus is presented in such a way as to mirror and contrast with the victory of Belisarius nearly eighty years later. The historian's point seems to be that the lack of virtue of Basiliscus, his greed and lust for power, made him blind to the smiles of fate, the favourable wind for instance. On the other hand, Fortuna smiles on Belisarius due to his superior character. The more similarities between the two campaigns could he present, the clearer his point would become[178]. In 533 the fighting took place in three theatres of war: the rebellion on Corsica and Sardinia, the pro-Roman revolt in Tripolitania, and the main operation of Belisarius; thus, to liken both campaign to each other, the historian seems to have

---

[174] At least until the times of Justinian, which, incidentally, were central to Procopius' narrative.

[175] R. S t e i n a c h e r, *Die Vandalen...*, p. 221–222; A. M e r r i l l s, R. M i l e s, *The Vandals...*, p. 121–122; Y. M o d é r a n, *Les Vandales...*, p. 197–198; H. E l t o n, *Illus and the Isaurian Aristocracy under Zeno*, B 70, 2000, p. 397; A. G o l t z, *Sizillien und die Germanen in der Spätantike*, Kok 53/54, 1997/98, p. 224. Notable exceptions are: Ch. C u r t o i s, *Les Vandales et l'Afrique*, Paris 1955, p. 202–203; H. C a s t r i t i u s, *Die Vandalen...*, p. 119–120.

[176] Theophanes, AM 5963.

[177] R.C. B l o c k l e y, *Fragmentary...*, p. 117.

[178] Christian C u r t o i s, (*Les Vandales...*, p. 202–203) offers a very similar point, he however argues that the reason for what Procopius did was rather the wish to exaggerate the scale of Basiliscus' campaign, to elevate Justinian's successful reconquest even more. That is criticized by Yves M o d é r a n (*Les Vandales...*, p. 197–198), who points out that Procopius' attitude towards Justinian was far more complicated and the historian probably would not want to pander to the emperor. It is a fair point, but if the historian's aim was to elevate Belisarius' achievements instead, to whom Procopius had much warmer feelings, Curtois' arguments would remain agreeable.

condensed the events from several years and put them all under the date of 468, so that it better suits his narrative[179].

Naturally, assumptions about the motivations of historical figures are always speculative in nature. Regardless of whether that was the goal Procopius had in mind, there are more reasons to believe Theophanes over him. The chronicler, despite writing much later after these events, records them in greater detail. This may indicate that he was following his source more closely, and it appears that would be the very reliable *History* of Priscus. Aside from historiographical considerations, there are also practical ones. Splitting forces unnecessarily would not have helped the Roman efforts, and there was little reason to securing Tripolitania when the heart of the Vandal kingdom was already under attack.

Some scholars attempted to find a middle ground between the accounts of Procopius and Theophanes, and claim that while the expedition of Heraclius and Marsus was dispatched in 468, they held Tripolitania until 470 or 471[180]. From a practical perspective, however, this would not have been feasible. Supplying a large body of men in Africa for several years would have been a logistical nightmare, especially since most of the Roman fleet had been sunk and the seas were under Vandal control. Furthermore, considering how difficult Leo's situation after 468 was, it is unlikely that he would just allow these forces to station in far-away lands for such a long time and accomplishing nothing. Due to internal problems, first with Anagastes, and then, as he learned of the plot of Ardaburii, he likely needed every loyal soldier he could get.

All the evidence indicates that the expedition of Heraclius and Marsus took place in 470 or early 471. The primary consequence of such an interpretation is that the failure of Basiliscus, even if of catastrophic proportions, did not make Leo's situation unsalvageable. The emperor was still able to pursue his ambitions and challenge the Vandals, albeit in a limited scope.

The expedition set out from Egypt on land using a coastal route to Tripolitania. The commanders of the expedition were Heraclius of Edessa[181] and Marsus the Isaurian[182]. The choice of the commanders was not a coincidence, as it seems they were loyal to the emperor and independent of the Ardaburi. In fact, considering the ethnicity of Marsus, it is likely that he was connected to Zeno.

---

[179] The capture of Sardinia likely happened before the main invasion, possibly in 466, cf. A. M e r r i l l s, R. M i l e s, *The Vandals...*, p. 121; Ch. C u r t o i s, *Les Vandales...*, p. 200; R. S t e i n a c h e r, *Die Vandalen...*, p. 219; or between 467 and early 468, cf. Y. M o d é r a n, *Les Vandales...*, p. 197.

[180] A. M e r r i l l s, R. M i l e s, *The Vandals...*, p. 122; Y. M o d é r a n, *Les Vandales...*, p. 198; R. S t e i n a c h e r, *Die Vandalen...*, p. 222; M. W i l c z y ń s k i, *Gejzeryk...*, p. 176–178.

[181] *PLRE*, vol. II, p. 541–542 (s.v. *Heraclius 4*).

[182] *PLRE*, vol. II, p. 728–729 (s.v. *Marsus 2*).

Heraclius and Marsus seem to have achieved some success; according to Theophanes, their efforts had greater impact than a much larger and costlier expedition of Basiliscus. Tripoli was captured alongside many other Libyan cities; however, there is no record of any major military engagements[183]; perhaps, originally the intent was to press on further in a joint military action with the Western troops, since Anthemius was reportedly also gathering soldiers for an expedition against the Vandals. However, all the plans turned to nought when the emperor started quarrelling with Ricimer, and the latter rebelled with the afore-said forces at his command[184]. The conflict was resolved for a time due to the intervention of bishop Epiphanius of Pavia, but it was probably too late to turn these forces against the Vandals, especially since it was apparent that the resolution was only temporary for both Anthemius and Ricimer, and, as a result, the Vandal problem has receded into the background.

Nevertheless, Geiseric must have felt threatened since he appealed for peace, which Leo happily accepted. Possibly he could not have expected a better result, especially if it had turned out that he would not be getting any support from the West. Theophanes also informs that Leo needed these commanders and their forces to oppose Aspar. It had been so, because a dangerous plot was incited by the general and his son back in the homeland, and Leo needed every reliable asset for the final resolution of the conflict.

The Revolt of Anagastes

The background to the escalation of the conflict between Leo and Aspar was the revolt of Anagastes. The reason for his open rebellion was the fact that he did not receive the consulate, and instead, it was granted to Jordanes. Not only the official justification for such action, Anagastes' health condition, epilepsy, appears nonsensical, but the general took it as a personal slight. Anagastes and Jordanes were feuding since Anagastes' father, Arnegisclus, had killed John the Vandal, the father of Jordanes.

To solve the crisis, Leo sent an envoy to the general[185]. It seems that the person responsible for this task was none other than Zeno, since the author of the *Life of St. Daniel the Stylite* reports that the general has been dispatched to

---

[183] Theophanes, AM 5963.
[184] Priscus, fr. 62.
[185] Priscus, fr. 56.

Thrace in order to prevent war, which appears to refer to these events[186]. Additionally, Theophanes mentions that he had been sent there for some military purpose, and he was reinforced by the emperor's own soldiers, which likely refers to the units of the Imperial guard, *schola palatina*[187].

Thus, Zeno arrived in force, however, it does not seem that any hostilities between him and Anagastes broke out. In fact, everything points to Zeno being successful in appeasing the disgruntled general. It is not known what arguments the Isaurian used, however, in the end, Anagastes admitted that he had been incited by Ardaburious, Aspar's son, and provided Zeno with documents that proved it[188].

It bears asking what Ardaburious sought to achieve through instigating Anagastes to revolt. Brian Croke, who was the first to link Zeno's involvement in Thrace with those events[189], assumes it was all part of Aspar's master plan. The general and his son, who harboured an obvious grievance against Zeno, sought to get him out of the capital to make it easier to dispose of him[190].

It is true that when Zeno was in Thrace, an attempt was made on his life by his retainers, the same ones who were provided to him by Leo. Theophanes blames Aspar to be directly responsible; the general must have been aware his son's intrigues, and perhaps directly involved in them as well. As mentioned before, the troops that Zeno was reinforced with were likely the elite soldiers of *schola palatina*, and Aspar, due to his extensive network in the military, undoubtedly had connections in there too. Therefore, he certainly had the means to enact the plot.

That being said, Croke's interpretation seems quite convoluted. Aspar might have led the emperor to make Zeno responsible for dealing with Anagastes, and he was likely responsible for inciting the revolt. However, there were probably easier ways to make Zeno leave the safety of Constantinople that did not involve causing an all-out civil war. Thus, the reasons why the Ardaburii needed Anagastes' to rebel must have been different.

An interesting fact is that the only military force that Leo had at his immediate disposal during that time was under command of Aspar. Basiliscus was still in hiding, his army had been destroyed and probably was not reorganized yet. The eastern forces led by Heraclius and Marsus were involved in a campaign against the Vandals, while the Thracian army was under the command of the rebellious Anagastes. The outbreak of the revolt would have meant that the only

---

[186] *Vita st. Danielis Stylitae*, 65.
[187] Theophanes, AM 5962.
[188] Priscus, fr. 56.
[189] B. Croke, *Dynasty...*, p. 185–186.
[190] *Ibidem*, p. 187.

way Leo could have quelled the uprising would require Aspar's help. By making himself indispensable, the general might have hoped he could force the emperor to compromise. Perhaps he incited the revolt having already a contingency plan to appease Anagastes. Thus, he would not only have put the emperor in a precarious position, who would have to plead for Aspar's help, but he would also have 'solved' the problem and received universal acclaim for the success. That appears to have been a much more likely plan for Aspar, as it explains how the revolt would directly help the general's cause.

Leo, however, likely realized that ordering Aspar's army to intervene would have meant him having to give way to general's demands. If Aspar's plan had one failing it was apparently the underestimation of Leo's stubbornness. To deal with the problem the emperor sent for Zeno instead. Whatever forces he had at his disposal were probably not enough to challenge the Thracian army of Anagastes, so the emperor provided him with the troops. Nevertheless, it is probably more likely that his orders were to appease Anagastes. In fact, considering how readily the general abandoned the plot, it seems to suggest he felt misled and lied to. Perhaps, Zeno's (and by extension, Leo's) willingness to make amends contrasted with how the situation was presented to him by Ardaburious.

At that point, however, Zeno came into possession of evidence incriminating Ardaburious. After his previous plot had been discovered in 466 he was effectively side-lined politically, and undoubtedly, this second, much more insolent attempt would result in the gravest consequences. The general must have somehow learned of Anagastes handing over the evidence of his betrayal. If we take into account the fact that Zeno was surrounded by the Imperial guard, it is likely that someone, perhaps connected to Aspar, caught wind of that happening, and sent a courier to inform the Ardaburii. In that situation, murder might have seemed to be the only way out. Thus, the assassination attempt was likely not pre-planned[191], but rather, it might have been a desperate attempt of Ardaburious to save his skin.

Zeno, however, managed to elude the assassins and escaped either to Pylai[192] or Serdica[193]. From there he somehow ended up in Chalcedon, and then he travelled to Isauria, likely to seek refuge[194]. Interestingly, the sources report on Zeno's

---

[191] Rafał K o s i ń s k i (*The Emperor...*, p. 68) argues it was the birth of Zeno's son that prompted Aspar and Ardaburious to order an attempt on his life. Certainly, it was a factor that made disposing of Zeno even more beneficial to the Ardaburii, however, it raises a question why Aspar needed to incite an open revolt. The scholar does not wage in on that.

[192] *Vita st. Danielis Stylitae*, 65.

[193] T h e o p h a n e s, AM 5962.

[194] John M a l a l a s (XV, 12) informs on the occasion of Zeno's return after the revolt of Basiliscus in 475, that this was the second time. Considering he could have the support of his

fighting against a bandit leader Indacus who made his lair on the hill Papirius and has been raiding the region[195]. This isolated account provides little context and could be unrelated to the grand scale politics, since Isauria often had issues with banditry, however, a passage in the fragment of Candidus mentions that Aspar tried to win over Isaurian troops to his side[196]. Perhaps, when the assassination attempt had failed, the general tried another plot, and he incited some Isaurians to cause trouble for Zeno. Unfortunately, the sources do not allow for a definite answer; however, Zeno being tied up with the problems in his homeland was certainly to Aspar's benefit[197].

Aspar's Return to Power

Those events probably took place when the bulk of the Roman forces loyal to the emperor was engaged in Africa. According to Theophanes, Leo learned of Aspar's plot, and because of that, he realized that the general was openly scheming against him. Nevertheless, regardless of Leo's suspicions, the emperor was mostly at Aspar's mercy, as he was completely isolated from his allies.

Even despite the obvious set-backs, the plot of the Ardaburii seemed successful in the end. Leo was forced into a position in which he had to accept their demands. As Croke rightfully observes, it was probably then, when the emperor almost suffered a mental breakdown reported by John the Lydian[198]. This passage offers a rare glimpse at a very personal angle of the events under discussion and should serve as a reminder that aside from the grand politics, the players involved were also human. Leo must have felt defeated. He gave in to Aspar's demands and made Patricius, Aspar's son, *Caesar* and his designated successor.

---

compatriots there, it seems reasonable that this was the course of Zeno's action in 469 or 470 as well. Incidentally, Flavius Zeno did the same in 449, when he was suspected of preparing a revolt, cf. p. 84 of the present work

[195] P r i s c u s, fr. 57.

[196] C a n d i d u s, fr. 1; George V e r n a d s k y (*Flavius...*, p. 69) places those events just before the fall of Aspar. Hugh E l t o n (*Illus...*, p. 397) argues that those events directly led to Leo ordering the assassination. However, Rafał K o s i ń s k i (*The Emperor...*, p. 64) assumes that if Aspar tried to secure support among the Isaurians it was when they arrived with Tarasikodissa in Constantinople.

[197] That being said, putting those events in a chronological order is tricky. Rafał K o s i ń-s k i (*The Emperor...*, p. 66–67) places the operation against Indacus before the revolt of Anagastes. This is entirely possible, and could still mean that Aspar incited the revolt.

[198] J o h n L y d u s, III, 44, 3.

Even though I have spoken before against the idea that Aspar harboured ambition to secure the throne for his family, the situation in 470 has been markedly different. The elder general had arguably little time left to secure his legacy. Due to the way things were progressing, he must have felt worried for his family, his supporters and clients, and all of the things he built over the course of his nearly fifty-year-long involvement in Eastern Roman politics. The conflict with Leo must have made him ultimately realize how fragile was his legacy, if the emperor set his mind to challenge it. There was only one solution to this problem: make sure that the emperor is a part of his legacy.

Thus, Patricius became a co-emperor. Since Ariadne was already married to Zeno, he offered him the hand of his second daughter, Leontia. It appeared that the Alan general was, in the end, triumphant[199].

However, soon the tides turned again. As the nomination of Patricius became publicly known, many renowned Church officials and devout Christians became worried that the emperor, already elderly, would leave the fate of the Empire in the hands of a heretic. Many citizens, with the patriarch Gennadius and the monk Marcellus, marched from Hagia Sophia to the hippodrome to protest the decision. After hours of chanting, the emperor addressed the crowd and informed that Patricius had abandoned his Arian creed[200]. This information is corroborated by Theophanes, who informs that Patricius was made *Caesar* because he converted to Orthodoxy[201]. Most importantly, it seems that the massive popular opposition to the projects of Aspar reinvigorated the emperor. He put in motion a plan to deal with the powerful general once and for all.

Perhaps this was when he decided to completely reorganize the palace guard of *excubitores*. This warrants a further explanation, as that event is commonly misinterpreted in the historiography. Many scholars assume that Leo created a new guard, often linking it with the arrival of Tarasikodissa-Zeno[202] and Leo's supposed attempts to counteract the Aspar led Germanic domination over the armed forces by employing Isaurian soldiers[203]. However, a comprehensive analysis by Brian Croke debunks those arguments[204]. The only source on Leo's deci-

---

[199] B. C r o k e, *Dynasty*..., p. 191–192.

[200] *Vita Marcelli*, 34. Cf. A.C. К о з л о в, *Народные массы в конфликте Аспара и Льва*, АДСВ 10, 1973, p. 263–265.

[201] T h e o p h a n e s, AM 5961.

[202] E. S t e i n, *Histoire*..., p. 361; A. D e m a n d t, *Geschichte der Spätantike*, München 2008, p. 185–187; A. C a m e r o n, *Mediterranean*..., p. 30; W. T r e a d g o l d, *Byzantium*..., p. 13.

[203] A. J o n e s, *The Later*..., p. 222; W. K a e g i, *Byzantine Military Unrest, 471–843: An Interpretation*, Amsterdam 1981, p. 27; H. E l t o n, *Warfare in Roman Europe, AD 350–425*, New York 1996, p. 101.

[204] B. C r o k e, *Leo I and the Palace Guard*, B 75, 2005, p. 140–141.

sions involving *excubitores*, John the Lydian, mentions the reorganization of the existing unit and setting it up to be responsible for guarding the palace entrances[205]. As Brian Croke observes, there is absolutely no evidence that *excubitores* were predominantly Isaurian, or that the arrival of Tarasikodissa had anything to do with the formation. Thus, the guard could have been reorganized at any point between Leo's accession and 471[206]. However, the obvious failure of the palace troops given to Zeno on his mission in the Balkans would have been the most obvious and direct reason for this decision of the emperor, especially since he anticipated a violent resolution to his conflict with Aspar; In that case, having loyal troops at his disposal was paramount.

Eventually, Leo sent for the forces of Heraclius and Marsus, probably contacted Zeno and Basiliscus, and maybe also Anagastes. In addition, the emperor might have spread the rumours of Aspar scheming with the Vandals and being responsible for the failure of the expedition of 468. This would have undermined the support for Aspar among the general populace of Constantinople and the senators.

Leo the Butcher

In 471 Leo invited Aspar, Ardaburious, and Patricius for a *conventus*, a routine meeting of senators. Little did the general and his sons know that it was a trap. Suspecting nothing, they were surrounded by the eunuchs and cut down with swords; their bodies were hacked to pieces and thrown out of the balcony. According to some sources, Patricius managed to escape or was allowed to live[207], but either died later of his wounds or otherwise faded into obscurity, since he is not referenced after that time[208]. The youngest son of Aspar, Hermanaric, was at the time of the plot lured outside the city on Zeno's orders, and later set up to marry into Zeno's illegitimate son's family. After the death of Leo he returned to Constantinople, but no sources inform of his political involvements, so it is safe to assume that he led a private life[209].

---

[205] John Lydus, I, 16, 3.

[206] B. Croke, *Leo...*, p. 144.

[207] Candidus, fr. 1.

[208] His marriage with Leontia was also terminated, as she married Marcian, son of emperor Anthemius. Cf. *Vita St. Danielis Stylitae*, 69. Theophanes (AM 5964) claims, however, that Patricius was also killed at the palace in 471.

[209] Theophanes, AM 5964.

Soon, the news of the murder spread around Constantinople. When various groups of Aspar's followers and supporters learned of this, they started a riot in the city. Among them was Ostrys, *comes rei militaris*, who gathered some soldiers and stormed the palace. A fight broke out between them and the *excubitores* who were defending the building. The clash resulted in many casualties, however, in the end the assaulters were overwhelmed. Ostrys managed to escape, taking Aspar's concubine with him, and headed to Thrace[210]. Thanks to the intervention of Zeno, who came back from Chalcedon, the riot was brought under control[211]. The imminent danger had ceased, however, it was not where the consequences of the murder of Aspar would end.

Ostrys went to Thrace to Theodoric Strabo, a leader of Thracian Goths and a nephew of Aspar's wife. It is possible that with Theodoric's followers they attempted attacking Constantinople itself, but were beaten off by Zeno and Basiliscus, however, the passage in Theophanes that informs of that could imprecisely refer to the riots in the city. Regardless, they raided the Thracian countryside.

Eventually Leo decided to send envoys to Theodoric to seek peace. The Goth was willing to compromise, and in a reply he demanded that he should receive the inheritance left to him by Aspar, his people be allowed to remain settled in Thrace, and that he be granted the office of *magister militum praesentalis*. Leo dismissed the first two conditions and agreed to the third one as long as Theodoric would remain loyal. When the king received the envoys, he decided to continue the military operations. Some details of the campaign are known thanks to surviving fragment of the *History* of Malchus[212]. Part of the Gothic army was sent to siege Philippopolis[213]. The defenders held as long as they could, but starvation forced them to surrender.

The course of the war might shine a little light on the crisis that the Empire underwent in the years 471–473. The Imperial forces clearly were not strong enough to challenge the Goths in the field. No serious relief attempt was undertaken to help the defenders of Philippopolis; instead, Malchus informs that the Roman forces used scorched earth tactics[214]. In fact, the war seems to have brought much brutality, a newly appointed commander of the Thracian forces, nephew of Verina, Armatus, cut off the hands of the Gothic prisoners of war[215]. In the end, the Goths were worn down by starvation as well; however, Leo

---

[210] M a l a l a s, XIV, 40.
[211] T h e o p h a n e s, AM 5964.
[212] M a l c h u s, fr. 2.
[213] Called 'Philippi' in the source itself, most likely erroneously.
[214] M a l c h u s, fr. 2.
[215] M a l c h u s, fr. 15.

agreed to most of the demands of Theodoric, except for his claim to Aspar's inheritance. The king was recognized as the sole ruler of the Goths, the barbarians received 2,000 pounds of gold in tribute, and Theodoric was appointed to the office of *magister militum* left vacant by Aspar[216]. Interestingly, Malchus writes that Theodoric refused to ever fight against the Vandals. The only demand that was not met, the one respecting Aspar's inheritance, likely was so because Leo had confiscated it, which was a part of his retaliation against the Arians mentioned by Malalas[217].

A Pyrrhic Victory

The internal problems that the Empire was going through deeply affected the emperor's plans in regard to foreign policy. The retreat from an otherwise successful expedition against Geiseric was already discussed, however, its ultimate outcome was probably agreeable, all things considered. Much worse was the situation in the Western part of the Empire.

With Marcellinus gone, Anthemius feared Ricimer's power. Soon, the conflict escalated when Anthemius ordered the execution of one Ricimer of supporters, to which the general responded by gathering the army, which was originally meant to be sent against the Vandals (perhaps jointly with the forces of Heraclius and Marsus). The conflict found a temporary resolution thanks to the intervention of Epiphanius, the bishop of Pavia. However, in the same year, after a failed campaign against the Goths in which Anthemius' son, Anthemiolus, died in battle, Ricimer took the opportunity to set out against the emperor again. Supported by the Sciri commanded by Odoacer and loyal barbarian soldiers, he overwhelmed the Imperial forces in a battle on Tiber. Anthemius was forced to flee to Rome, where he was besieged.

It is up to discussion whether Leo abandoned his ally at that point. According to Malalas, the emperor sent Olybrius as an envoy, to inform Anthemius of his crack-down on Aspar's family, and he advised him to do the same against Ricimer[218]. The chronicler then reports that Leo also secretly ordered Anthemius to execute the bearer of the news. However, Theophanes offers a different view,

---

[216] H.U. W i e m e r, *Theoderich...*, p. 134–135; H. W o l f r a m, *Die Goten...*, p. 268.

[217] M a l a l a s, XIV, 41.

[218] M a l a l a s, XIV, 45. Cf. M.E. S t e w a r t, *The First Byzantine Emperor? Leo I, Aspar and Challenges of Power and Romanitas in Fifth–century Byzantium*, Porph 22, 2014, p. 13.

according to which Leo sent Olybrius to the West to assume the throne[219]. It seems that the latter is more probable, considering that Olybrius had the support of the Vandal king, Geiseric, it could have been Leo's attempt at keeping at least some control over the situation in the West, while he was unable to dedicate any forces to help Anthemius due to the civil war in the Balkans. After Ricimer dethroned Anthemius, the general allied himself with Olybrius who became the emperor, however, he fell ill and died soon after[220].

Leo tried once again to salvage the situation in the West. The Dalmatian territories, after the death of Marcellinus, came under control of Julius Nepos. Despite the fact that the successor to the Western throne, Glycerius, made attempts to obtain Leo's recognition, the emperor decided to support the claims of the Dalmatian ruler[221]. In June 473 he gave to Julius Nepos the permission to crown himself as a *Caesar*, and granted him the title of *patricius*[222]. He did not manage however to see the outcome of the following struggle for power in Italy.

In October 473, an already ailing Leo nominated as his co-ruler the 6-year-old child of Ariadne and Zeno as Leo II[223]. Shortly thereafter, on 18 January 474 he died.

Conclusion

In many ways, the subject of the military elite under the reign of Leo is completely overshadowed by his conflict with Aspar. Even though Leo came from a similar background as his predecessor, his relations with the person he owed the throne to developed entirely differently. It is difficult to pinpoint why Leo and Aspar ended up in a quarrel that escalated to such a tragic end. Undoubtedly, the animosity kept growing over the years, and there were many singular events that compounded each other. Aspar's overbearing influence, Leo's ambitions related to foreign policy, and his dynastic plans could simply not be accommodated. An important aspect was also the Church's support for Leo, which made the emperor realize that he had ways to challenge the power of Aspar.

---

[219] T h e o p h a n e s, AM 5964.

[220] For the reconstruction of those events, cf. Ł. P i g o ń s k i, *Polityka zachodnia cesarzy Marcjana (450–457) i Leona I (457–474)*, Łódź 2019, p. 167–173.

[221] M. J a n k o w i a k, *Bizancjum...*, p. 235–237. The ambitions of Julius Nepos were also actively supported by empress Verina, cf. M.J. L e s z k a, *Empress...*, p. 129.

[222] J o r d a n e s, *Romana*, 338.

[223] B. C r o k e, *The Imperial Reigns of Leo II*, BZ 92, 2003, p. 570.

A factor that should not be underestimated, is that the conflict between Aspar and Leo could be boiled down to the personalities of the two, both ambitious and stubborn men[224]. It is also highly possible that Leo was influenced by his wife, Verina, also an ambitious woman, who later would show her political aptitude. Although it is impossible to present unambiguous sources for all of the above to have been the case, it would explain why neither side was willing to compromise at any point and why their relationship deteriorated to the point of escalation in 471.

Even though Leo managed to walk away victorious from the conflict, it was for all intents and purposes a Pyrrhic victory. His ambitious western policy had failed, and the Roman Empire in the West was already nearing its end. He secured his legacy the way he wanted, but the reign of his successor, Zeno, would show extensively, that the problem of military commanders reaching for power and influence did not end with Aspar's death in 471[225].

---

[224] Cf. R.A. B l e e k e r, *Aspar...*, p. 203–207.
[225] Interestingly, as Meaghan M c E v o y (*Becoming...*, p. 502–506) observes, extended branches of the family of Aspar were so deeply embedded in the Eastern Roman elite that even Leo's butchery did not manage to undermine their prominence.

Conclusion

The recounting of the story of the military elite during the reigns of Theodosius II, Marcian, and Leo has thus concluded, however, while the events paint their own picture, there have been years of research which attempted to frame them in different interpretations. The various efforts to explain what took place in that period certainly warrant an analysis. The factors most commonly brought up can be grouped into three primary categories: ethnic, dynastic, and religious.

Ethnicity: Solidarity and Division

The problems of ethnicity are probably the aspect of the Eastern Roman military elite in the fifth century, which garners the most attention from historians. Contrary to a popular belief, the barbarians did not constitute an overwhelming majority in the Eastern Roman high command. In fact, if we look at the representatives of various ethnic groups among the *magistri militum*: Plintha, Areobindus, Arnegisclus, and Anagastes were Goths, while John the Vandal and Jordanes were Vandals. The famous clan of Ardaburii was reportedly Alans, although it should be noted that they intermarried with the Goths. Its members who served as *magistri militum* were Ardaburious the Elder, Aspar, and

Ardaburious the Younger. The Isaurians were represented by Flavius Zeno and Tarasikodissa-Zeno. The known Romans were Macedonius, Procopius, Dionysius, Apollonius, Rusticius, Theodulus, Basiliscus, Anthemius, Marcian, and Armatus. Thus, the barbarian element constituted a major, but not overwhelming part of the Eastern Roman military command.

Nevertheless, it has been argued that the Eastern Roman Empire was undergoing a political conflict in which the division followed ethnic lines, with the Romans on one side and the Barbarians on the other[1]. There have been two primary instances in which the scholarship on the subject claimed ethnic factors to have been the driving force behind those events. Interestingly, they nearly constitute the chronological boundaries of the time-period which is the focus of the present work: the revolt of Gainas and its aftermath and the conflict between Aspar and Leo.

In the direct aftermath of Gainas' rebellion there were some calls for anti-barbarian action, namely the works of Synesius of Cyrene, who in the pages of *De providentia* and *De regno* attacked Gainas himself and opposed the inclusion of barbarians in the Roman system, both in the army and in civilian administration. The fact that the population of Constantinople came together and slaughtered the Goths trapped in the city who served the barbarian general, should also be a reminder that prejudices against different ethnic groups did exist at that time. Then, there is the notion that after the murder of Fravitta, there was a period when there were no attested high-ranking military commanders of Germanic origin in Eastern Roman service. The idea of an anti-Germanic reaction taking place within the Eastern Roman Empire thus had some support in historiography, especially in older works[2].

There are, however, numerous arguments against those claims. To begin with, there is little evidence of any policy having been implemented which would have targeted Germanic commanders. Considering the general scarcity of sources, the view that the Germans were not allowed to serve cannot be based on the fact that none was recorded up until 419. For the years 404–419 there are only six commanders mentioned in total, most of them only in passing[3]. Furthermore, when Germanic commanders are finally starting to be

---

[1] Such a view has appeared in many foundational works, such as: J.B. B u r y, *History of the Later Roman Empire Empire from the Death of Theodosius I. to the Death of Justinian*, vol. I, London 1958; E. S t e i n, *Histoire du Bas-Empire*, t. I, *De L'état romain à l'état byzantin (284–476)*, Paris 1959; A.H.M. J o n e s, *The Later Roman Empire 284–602. A Social, Economic and Administrative Survey*, vol. I–III, Oxford 1964.

[2] J.B. B u r y, *History...*, p. 132; E. S t e i n, *Histoire...*, p. 235; A.H.M. J o n e s, *The Later...*, p. 181.

[3] If we assume that each office was occupied by a different individual in each tenure, that would potentially make for twenty different commanders; thus, there is a possibility that there could have been some Germanic officers who were just not recorded.

attested in the sources, they are already recorded in the highest offices of *magistri militum*. Their careers were likely swift and successful, but they still must have been promoted through a number of ranks, which doubtlessly took time. It means that among the *comites*, Germanic officers must have been relatively common even in the years in which they were supposedly barred from attaining high offices[4].

The conflict between Leo and Aspar has long been interpreted as a reaction of the emperor to the Germanic dominance over the army. It has been argued that this was the reason why he invited the Isaurians to the capital, to counter Aspar and his Germanic allies[5]. This interpretation, however, is based on entirely wrong assumptions[6].

This argument was usually associated with the reorganization of the *excubitores*, however, there is no evidence for its members to have been recruited solely, or even primarily, from among the Isaurians. Similarly, the fact that the emperor decided to support Tarasikodissa was not due to his ethnic origins, but because he was not a friend of Aspar or otherwise connected to the clan of Ardaburii. The first time he appears in the sources is in relation to the plot of Ardaburious and the fact he decided to inform the emperor of it, thus proving his loyalty (and burning bridges with the powerful general). Likely, it has been mostly an alliance out of an opportunity. All appears to indicate that until 465 or 466 the grievances of Leo towards Aspar were slowly mounting. The fact that Leo learned of Ardaburious' plot was probably both a factor that further antagonized the emperor and Aspar, but also a first real opportunity for Leo to combat the influence of the all-powerful general. The fact that Tarasikodissa was an Isaurian had no bearing on those events, at least not

---

[4] Е.П. Глушанин, *Военная знать ранней Византии*, Барнаул 1991, p. 102–103.

[5] Cf. E.W. Brooks, *The Emperor Zenon and the Isaurians*, Her 8, 1893, p. 212; J.B. Bury, *History...*, p. 320; R.W. Burgess, *Isaurian Factions in the Reign of Zeno the Isaurian*, L 51, 1992, p. 874; A. Cameron, *The Mediterranean World in Late Antiquity AD 395–600*, New York 1993, p. 30; W. Treadgold, *A History of Byzantine State and Society*, Stanford 1997, p. 150–156. This idea was perhaps most explicitly formulated by Edward Thompson (*The Isaurians under Theodosius II*, Her 68, 1948, p. 31). It has been challenged by Hugh Elton (*Illus and the Isaurian Aristocracy under Zeno*, B 70, 2000, p. 396–397) and then a more comprehensive critique of this view has been put forward by Brian Croke (*Dynasty and Ethnicity. Emperor Leo I and the Eclipse of Aspar*, Chi 35, 2005, p. 147–203). Cf. P. Crawford, *Roman Emperor Zeno. The Perils of Politics in Fifth-century Constantinople*, Barnsley 2019, p. 54–55. Interestingly, there were studies, largely unnoticed in the West, which challenged this view much earlier, cf. А.С. Козлов, *Народные массы в конфликте Аспара и Льва*, АДСВ 10, 1973, p. 263–265.

[6] Cf. p. 170–171 of the present work.

directly. Not to mention the fact, that in place of demoted Ardaburious, Leo appointed another *magister militum* of Germanic ancestry, Jordanes.

Jordanes' alignment is almost impossible to ascertain, and likely he was just on the side-lines of the conflict between the emperor and Aspar. Most importantly, however, he did not seem to be a supporter of the latter and that was enough for Leo. This is additional evidence that the emperor was concerned about loyalty and did not consider ethnicity to be an important factor.

Subsequently, as the contest developed, Leo tried to rely on Basiliscus who was a Roman. While it may appear as though the emperor was again looking for support of non-Germanic commanders, the explanation here is obvious. Basiliscus was Leo's brother-in-law, and the emperor assuredly expected loyalty from a member of his own family. Nevertheless, if Procopius is to be believed, it is possible that Aspar still attempted to drag Basiliscus to his side[7].

It is clear from the above that ethnicity played at most a minor role in the various socio-political developments surrounding the military elite in the fifth-century Eastern Roman Empire. What was observed by various scholars and attributed to some kind of conflict along ethnic lines, was, when subjected to closer scrutiny, mostly a coincidence.

Kinship and Family Matters

There was, however, one aspect in which ethnicity was of some importance. The generals were willing to use their position within the communities from which they originated to their advantage. While this usually intersected with ethnicity, it was not so much a question of an identity of such an order, but of family ties and extended relationships between clans. For example, it was common for the military elite to enter marriages between their families and establish their networks of blood connections that way[8].

This phenomenon was essential to the formation of the military elite as a distinct group, as after all, the Roman generals were made by appointment. However, the practice described above meant that the emperor could choose from a pool of military professionals, largely limited to people who were related to each other. It can also be observed that many of the generals had their sons reach the highest military offices. The most famous example

---

[7] Procopius, *History of the Wars*, III, 6. 2.

[8] Cf. A. Demandt, *Magister militum*, [in:] *RE*, t. XII suppl., 1970, p. 622–628.

are of course the members of the Ardaburii clan, whose careers span three generations, from Ardaburious the Elder through Aspar to Ardaburious the Younger. Furthermore, Aspar himself was related by marriage to Plintha. Other examples include Jordanes, the son of John the Vandal, and Anagastes, the son of Arnegisclus. These are only the known cases, but there is no telling how deep such networks of connections went among the lower officer ranks. Even though this phenomenon was most common among the Germanic commanders, it is known that Basiliscus, who came from a Thracian family with military traditions[9], was related to Marcian, the general of Thrace in 473, and, more importantly, to emperor Leo, whose earlier military career should not be forgotten either.

In some cases, those connections extended very far, giving an illusory appearance of solidarity along ethnic lines. The relationship between Aspar and the tribe of the Thracian Goths is one such example. It is known that one of Aspar's wives was a sister-in-law of Theodoric Strabo, the leader of the Goths. Arguably, this gave Aspar the ability to consider this federated tribe as his asset, however, this was again due to Aspar's marital connections and not because of some kinds of common interests shared by all of those who had Germanic ancestry. The only instance in which that seems to have been partially the case is with the Isaurian commanders. Both Flavius Zeno and Tarasikodissa-Zeno escaped to Isauria when facing political backlash in the capital. Obviously, they must have felt the safest among their compatriots, however, it is impossible to say if this was because they were relying on Isaurian solidarity, or simply the fact that they had many clients and supporters there due to having positions of influence in their homeland.

Family matters were an important aspect of the conflict between the emperor Leo and Aspar. The former's ambition to establish his dynastic legacy could have been one of the factors which put him on a collision course with his general. When Aspar was faced with the perspective of losing power and influence, he concocted a plan to make his son, Patricius, the successor of Leo.

It seems that securing the position of the family, creating beneficial relationships with other notable clans, and establishing a legacy were the ambitions of most members of the military elite, which is no different to most groups that could be classified as aristocracy. It was one of the primary reasons which established this group's cohesion despite its diversity and the fact that its claim to status and power, its members' military careers, were dependent on Imperial nominations.

---

[9] M. S a l a m o n, *Basiliscus cum romanis suis*, [in:] *Studia Moesiaca*, red. L. M r o z e w i c z, K. I l s k i, Poznań 1994, p. 179–196.

Faith and Religious Policy

One of the aspects which exemplify the Eastern Roman military elite's diversity is religion. Religious beliefs of the generals sometimes tended to follow along ethnic lines, however, there were exceptions. Most of the generals of Germanic background are assumed to have been Arians, and that was probably the most defining factor of that group. The majority of the Romans in military offices were orthodox Christians, and some were involved in religious matters and Church politics. For example, at the Council of Ephesus, general Dionysius was reported to have been interfering in some Church affairs in Cyprus[10]. In addition, Anatolius was chosen as Marcian's representative for the Council.

Interestingly, paganism seems to have been relatively common among the military elite, regardless of anti-pagan legislation of the period. The most notable examples are *magistri militum* Flavius Zeno and Apollonius[11]. The latter, however, converted to Christianity in the late 440s.

It has been argued, especially in more modern works, that religion was an important factor in at least some of the events discussed in the present work. Prominently, the Arianism of Aspar has been brought up as the primary reason why the general could never assume the throne, and why he had such problems in promoting his son as Leo's successor. Gereon Siebigs assumes that religious differences were a major cause of the conflict between the emperor and Aspar[12]. Those arguments are not without merit. It should be recognised that Aspar did support the side of Timothy Ailuros during the religious unrest in Alexandria, against the counsel of the Orthodox patriarch Gennadius. Moreover, the personal piety of Leo, particularly as exhibited by his close reliance on the counsel of St. Daniel the Stylite, is beyond question[13].

Disputing all of the above would be difficult, because it is a matter of fact that religion and personal faith were major driving forces behind people's action in late antiquity. Thus, the burden proof is on the one making a claim to the contrary.

---

[10] *PLRE*, vol. II, p. 365–366 (s.v. *Fl. Dionysius 13*).

[11] There was also the case of a pagan commander Lucius recorded in *Philosophical History* of Damascius who wanted to make an attempt on the emperor's life, however, he was prevented by an apparition. Cf. D a m a s c i u s, 115A; *PLRE*, vol. II, p. 692 (s.v. *Lucius*). However, nothing close to such an event was recorded elsewhere and this Lucius is otherwise unknown, thus the historicity of the account is doubtful.

[12] He highlights as many as fourteen instances of Aspar's involvement with religious policy. Cf. G. S i e b i g s, *Kaiser...*, p. 699–706.

[13] Cf. R. K o s i ń s k i, *Holiness and Power. Constantinopolitan Holy Men and Authority in the 5th Century*, Berlin 2016, p. 129–147.

That having been said, while the capacity for sincere belief of those people should never be doubted, there is evidence to suggest that religious matters did not influence the dynamic of the events involving the military elite in the East as much as it is commonly assumed. To give an example, Aspar was able to co-operate with emperor Marcian, who was a pious orthodox Christian. A major part in choosing that same emperor was played by a pagan, Zeno. Anatolius, who was religious enough to have been chosen to represent Marcian at the Council of Chalcedon, argued against helping his fellow Christians in Armenia against the Zoroastrian Persians. Son of Aspar, Ardaburious, sent his retainers to guard the body of St. Symeon the Stylite against relic-hunters and escort it to Antioch. There are many instances in which the religious beliefs of the generals involved did not play any part.

It appears that religion was not something which guided the development of the military elites in any considerable way. Most evidence of its being of any significance refers to singular, specific events of an individual nature. In the case of Aspar, it appears that the general was a sincere follower of the Arian doctrine, as he never abandoned it despite the fact that it undoubtedly created problems for him[14]. Perhaps he saw himself as a protector of the Arians in the increasingly intolerant Empire. However, there is little evidence which would indicate that his attitude towards religious politics extended beyond that. His support for Timothy was likely nothing more than a pragmatic consideration, his aim being to advocate for not interfering in the developing religious conflict which was taking place in Alexandria.

Ultimately, the assertions that religious considerations defined many aspects related to the problem of the military elite in the Eastern Roman Empire seem exaggerated. In fact, the opposite claim could be made: the military elite as a whole tended to consider religious factors as secondary compared to the military, political, or dynastic ones.

The Question of Identity: Becoming Byzantine?

The above break-down shows clearly what the focal point of much of the up-to-date research on the military elites and their membership has been: identity. However, the discussion whether the generals could be defined by their ethnicity,

---

[14] It never was enough of an issue to prevent him from gaining a position of power and influence. Cf. M. M c E v o y, *Becoming Roman? The Not-So-Curious Case of Aspar and the Ardaburii*, JLA 9, 2016, p. 498–502. Nevertheless, it was the support of the Church that allowed Leo to eventually challenge Aspar. If the general were an orthodox Christian, it is likely that the emperor would not have succeeded in rallying the opposition against him.

religious creed, or family ties cannot have a simple answer. To some extent, all of those perspectives are correct and wrong at the same time. This is because there was never one uniform military elite, rather, it was always a collection of individuals, each of whom had different priorities, and the answer for each one is different.

The limited character of the sources do not allow for a deep analysis of every single aspect of their activity; we can only catch a glimpse, being granted a closer insight into just one powerful family and select individuals. In fact, in the recently written biography of Aspar, Ronald A. Bleeker makes a very valuable observation on the individuality of the people involved in historical events, and how it affected their outcomes[15]. The present work can only echo his claims; after all, to what extent was the conflict between Aspar and Leo predicated on their incompatible personalities? What role was played by the ambitious and ruthless woman that was Verina? And also, to what degree was Flavius Zeno's fierce opposition to appeasing the Huns a result of his grief and desire to avenge dead brother. Undoubtedly, if we had more sources on our disposal we could find many more examples; it should serve as a reminder to any historian to never lose sight of the humanity of the people involved in the events he seeks to reconstruct.

There is, however, one observable factor which seems to have been common among this diverse assembly of characters. It is, in my view, the primary reason why it is even possible to talk about the military elite as a group. This common factor was the cause under which a political movement was formed which sought to address the main concern of the generals: the security of the Empire[16]. It was the sticking-point between Theodosius II and many of his generals, and later on, Leo I and Aspar; not because those emperors did not care about the protection of their domain, but because the generals seem to have understood the Empire differently. Both Theodosius and Leo appear to have considered themselves the rulers of the one Roman Empire, in which the power was divided between the East and the West. The members of the military elite, however, were only concerned about the well-being of the country they served directly, and for them, the Eastern Roman Empire seems to have already been a separate entity. It looks as if they were unmoved by the Vandal raids on the Italian coasts, but a looming Hun menace to the north of the Balkan provinces very much concerned them, even if the former was an existential threat to the integrity of the Roman Empire, while the latter was largely a local one.

---

[15] R.A. Bleeker, *Aspar and the Struggle for the Eastern Roman Empire, AD 421–71*, London 2022, p. 203.

[16] Obviously, there was also the component of caring about their personal interest and well-being. Avoiding risky expeditions preserved power and prestige (and, potentially, the lives) of the commanders and allowed them to augment their wealth and influence.

This is where we come full circle to the question of identity, but it is not whether the members of the Eastern Roman military elite felt themselves Roman or 'barbarian'; rather, what it meant for them to be Roman. The generals were thoroughly immersed in Roman culture, but it was the one which radiated from Constantinople. Their Rome was located not on the seven hills around Tiber, but by the Golden Horn and Propontis, in the easternmost part of Thrace.

Closing Thoughts

It is interesting how from the beginning of the fifth century up until the death of Leo, the historical narrative of the military elite makes almost a full circle. Initially, the crisis caused by the revolt of Gainas illustrated to the Eastern Roman emperor and civil elites the danger posed by commanders who could use their influence within the army to assume control of the state. What followed was a period during which no exemplary military careers can be traced and little is known of the Eastern Roman commanders altogether, most likely because the central government tried its best to suppress them and prevent them from growing ever more powerful and influential. It is difficult even to speak of the military elite as a group at that point, as it seems that generals were being appointed and relieved of their positions on a regular basis and thus remained politically insignificant. This was possible in the early reign of Theodosius, however, as soon as the country begun to face wars from the 420s onwards, the situation changed. Thanks to their successes, a few commanders made names for themselves, notably Plintha, Ardaburious, and Areobindus.

Theodosius tried to counteract the influence of the generals by rotating them in and out of their offices, as well as making extensive use of the *magistri militum vacantes*. It appears that his attempts did not prevent the members of the military from achieving positions of significance, however, they were a factor contributing to their dissatisfaction with the emperor's rule. In addition to that, the generals opposed Theodosius and his minister Chrysaphius, especially in the area of foreign policy. Having common grievances and enemies brought the generals closer together, creating unlikely alliances towards the end of Theodosius' reign. The military elite finally emerged as a cohesive group at that point, its members pursuing a common goal despite their diversity.

The death of Theodosius and the following dynastic crisis was finally a chance for the generals to assume control. Aspar, who happened to be the only commander of the highest rank present in Constantinople at that time, chose the next emperor, an officer under his command, Marcian. Even though this lucky coincidence allowed Aspar to make the decision, it appears that the other influential commanders rallied behind the candidate. In addition, the generals entered into a political alliance with Pulcheria, who legitimized Marcian through marriage.

The reign of Marcian represented the pinnacle of military influence over affairs of the state. The emperor addressed most of the issues on which the generals opposed Theodosius. He refrained from conducting costly and bloody campaigns in far-away lands and focused on the Empire's security. He cancelled all payments of tribute to the Huns and when opportunity came, he launched offensive campaigns against them, at times personally commanding the troops. Marcian was for all intents and purposes not only a soldier-emperor, but also an emperor of the soldiers. He appears to have sought the counsel of his generals in most matters of foreign policy, as well as guaranteeing the stability and advancement of their careers. However, despite the latter, at the end of Marcian's reign, one general and his family emerged as the most powerful: Aspar with his son Ardaburious. It was again a coincidence, as most of the other influential generals died or retired during the emperor's reign, specifically Flavius Zeno, Anatolius, and Apollonius (or shortly before it, in case of Areobindus). Towards the end of his reign, Marcian promoted the young Anthemius to consulate and high military offices, and even married his daughter to him. It has been argued that he was trying to secure a legacy for his dynasty with that move, and at the same time, pursue a more proactive foreign policy; however, there is little evidence which suggests that this was really the case.

Thus, when Marcian died, the question of succession was unresolved. The decision on the matter fell to Aspar yet again, however, this time due to his influence and seniority among the Constantinopolitan aristocracy. The general decided to do what he had done seven years before and chose another officer of medium rank who served under his command, Leo. This time, however, Aspar was unequivocally the most powerful person in the whole country. Not only was the whole military elite which emerged in the latter part of Theodosius' rule centred around Aspar and his family and followers, but his status and influence extended even into the civil administration and aristocratic circles. In effect, Leo was constrained by his general in his policy-making and nominations. Even though, as the later events show, the emperor was a highly ambitious individual, he seems to have accepted his position of dependence at first, even if begrudgingly. It appears, however, that their relationship slowly but progressively deteriorated. During the religious crisis in Alexandria involving Timothy Ailuros, the emperor realized that he could, in some cases, find an ally in the Church, and with its help, make decisions independently of his general. His dynastic ambitions were revitalized in 463 because a son was born to the Imperial couple, and thus a potential successor appeared. Although the sickly child died, the event had long-lasting consequences. Around 466 the emperor finally had a falling out with Aspar. One of the points of contention was the disagreement over the policy towards the war between the Sciri and the Goths; but more importantly, a certain Isaurian, Tarasikodissa, later known as Zeno, brought to Constantinople letters proving the betrayal of Aspar's son, Ardaburious. Ardaburious was relieved of command and from then on Aspar was side-lined, while Leo started to realize his own plans. Against his general's advice, he commenced engagement in the West, installing Anthemius as the emperor in Ravenna, and sending a great expedition under the command of Basiliscus, his brother-in-law, against the Vandals in 468. An important role in those events was also played by the sovereign of Dalmatia, Marcellinus, who was allied with Leo. In essence, the emperor was creating a counter-weight to Aspar's power base by placing his allies in positions of influence, not omitting high military offices, as was the case with Basiliscus. The failure of the expedition, however, revitalized Aspar's opposition. His plots, including inciting an open rebellion and an attempt on the life of Zeno, led to a political isolation of the emperor. Leo agreed to Aspar's demand of designating the general's son, Patricius, as his successor. However, the opposition from the Church to this development and the public unrest which followed, convinced Leo that he had enough support to win the confrontation. He ordered the murder of Aspar and his sons in 471. However, the death of the powerful general had serious ramifications in the form of a riot of his followers in Constantinople and a civil war with Theodoric Strabo, which ultimately ended with Leo' accepting a compromise.

The time period between 408 to 474 turned out to be a very tumultuous one for the whole of the Mediterranean. In that time of strife, the ability for the Empire to defend itself was of the utmost importance and a capable core of military professionals commanding the armies was its necessary condition. However, this need eventually led to a growth in the influence and status of the said commanders. With their newly-acquired power, the generals wanted to take part in the decision-making how the Empire would be defended, especially if they felt that the Imperial government, as was the case with that of Theodosius, did it ineptly. That was not acceptable to the court, as the army was meant to be its instrument in pursuing its goals, and in the case of Theodosius, those were irreconcilable with what the military elite wanted. Thus, as that emperor tried to limit the generals' influence and maintain his control, the opposition from the generals grew. This led to their choosing an emperor whose goals would align with theirs: Marcian. His reign was truly the closest one to what could be seen as a realization of the political programme of the military elite. When he died, Aspar, who at that point was the central figure of the group, tried to continue the practice by selecting an analogous candidate. Leo, however, turned out to be a leader driven by his own ambition and someone unwilling to accept Aspar's control. When he realized that he could challenge it, he did so, provoking a conflict which resulted in a violent resolution. However, the only way he could do it was by essentially supplanting Aspar's power over the military elite through the promotion of his own men.

In the end, the source of all conflict was a difference of points of view. Emperors Leo and Theodosius considered themselves responsible for the whole, undivided Roman Empire. That is why they decided to mount expensive and risky expeditions to try and eliminate the greatest threat to the Empire which was the Vandal Kingdom ruled by Geiseric. For many of the members of the military elite this must have seemed like a waste of precious resources needed for protection of the borders of the Eastern part of the Empire. After all, it was the country for which they were directly responsible. This irreconcilable situation inevitably led to conflicts over how to utilize the military capabilities of the Eastern Roman Empire. Ultimately, it is difficult to say which side was right, and it appears that the answer may be that both were. Theodosius and Leo were indisputably correct in their evaluation of the Vandal threat, and the failure to address it was a major factor which brought about the downfall of the Roman Empire in the West. However, the insistence of the military elite to focus on protecting the borders of the Empire in the East might have been one of the reasons why it weathered the storms of the fifth century and survived for another millennium.

Appendix 1

Whe researching certain topics from the history of late antiquity, the frustrating reality of the situation is that not every aspect of it can directly be inferred from the available data. In such a situation a scholar needs to make a call whether to follow a strict methodology and admit his inability to determine one way or the other, or try and make an informed assumption regardless. I, admittedly, have always been drawn to the latter. However, when the Ph.D. thesis which served as the basis for this monograph was reviewed by established and experienced scholars, professors Marek Wilczyński and Rafał Kosiński, some of those assumptions were questioned. While their invaluable and constructive critique certainly helped to iron out many deficiencies which this work contained, some differences of opinion remained. This, however, indicated to me that perhaps some of the more controversial points in the thesis were not elaborated upon enough. It probably would not be possible to include those extended arguments in the first chapter without detracting from the reading experience of the average reader, who might not find some of the minutia all that relevant to the over-all narrative. Thus, I have decided to move those arguments to this appendix.

The following paragraphs seek therefore better to explain the thought process behind some of the author's assumptions, namely, the fact that for the majority of the discussed period there existed only four, and not five, territorial offices of *magister militum*, or that serving as a general of the Eastern Roman army had term limits.

The Question of the Illyrian Command

Almost every single overview of the late Roman military directly follows the exact list of offices mentioned by *Notitia Dignitatum* and assumes that this specific system remained unchanged over the course of the whole fifth century and on, up until emperor Justinian restructured it. However, when subjected to close scrutiny, it does not seem to be the case.

The office which very likely underwent some changes was the Thracian mastery of arms. Some scholars have argued that it was created years before the events pertinent to the present dissertation[1]. However, it must have been a temporary measur, or the office was disbanded, since there is no evidence for its existence under the reign of Arcadius[2]. Alexander Demandt assumes that the office was created, or rather transformed from the *comitiva Thraciae*, in the reign of Arcadius or just shortly after his death[3]. Evgeniy Glushanin links it to praefect Anthemius and his attempts to strengthen the borders of the Empire. It is very much possible that the Thracian mastery was recreated *ad hoc* to counteract the invasion of Uldin in 408 or 409[4], but afterwards remained a stable part of the system.

The example of *magister militum* of Thrace goes to show that there were changes to the organization of the Eastern Roman military command structure

---

[1] Ernst S t e i n (*Histoire du Bas-Empire*, t. I, *De L'état romain à l'état byzantin (284–476)*, Paris 1959, p. 123, n. 149) posits that the Thracian mastery was created around 380. He infers that from Z o s i m u s (IV, 27), who claims that Theodosius I increased the number of generals from two to five. This piece of information, however, must be approached very carefully. Firstly, the historian mentions it only to criticize the emperor Theodosius I and says that it only caused unnecessary expenses for the state. Secondly, it should be noted that the number of *magistri militum* at that point was changing according to military needs, therefore those remarks cannot be taken as proof of the exact number. Irrespectively of Stein's position, Arnold J o n e s (*The Later Roman Empire 284–602. A Social, Economic and Administrative Survey*, vol. I, Oxford 1964, p. 158) acknowledges a *magister militum per Thracias* in 386, a certain Flavius Promotus, who was dispatched against an Ostrogoth named Odotheus. However, according to the original passage in Z o s i m u s (IV, 35), he could have been a commander of infantry (most likely *magister peditum*) in Thrace, meaning the location where he and his forces were stationed, and not necessarily the office of Thracian territorial command.

[2] Е.П. Г л у ш а н и н, *Военная знать ранней Византии*, Барнаул 1991, p. 96; A. D e m a n d t, *Magister militum*, [in:] *RE*, t. 12 suppl., 1970, p. 737.

[3] A. D e m a n d t, *Magister...*, p. 744.

[4] It would also explain why resorting to military action was not deemed the best option and subterfuge was preferred instead. The newly created command was just too weak to counter the Hunnic forces.

during the period with which the present work is concerned. Considering how early the Thracian mastery was established, this realization does not impact the narrative, even if it stands in contrast with some of the established scholarship, as it existed for the greater part of the discussed period. There is, however, a similar question, which appears to be more contentious.

The Illyrian mastery of arms is the fifth one named in *Notitia Dignitatum*. Thus, it must have existed at the time of the writing of the document, and the established position in the literature is that it was a regular part of the Eastern Roman military system.

However, the existence of the office later in the fifth century is almost untraceable in the sources[5]. Martindale counts four Illyrian *magistri militum* in that period[6], but three of them could have just as well served in different offices, and the only 'certain' one, Arintheos, attested in the sources in 449, is not specifically assigned to this post and only named as a commander of the forces which were present in Illyria at the time[7]. This means that the individual in question could have served in almost any other territorial mastery, could have been a *magister militum vacans*, or even just a *comes rei militaris*. The diocese of Illyricum was transferred to the Western Roman Empire after the death of Theodosius I; however, it was returned later in 437 as part of an agreement after the Eastern intervention against the usurper John. Moreover, the province often fell victim to barbarian raids, and much of the Illyrian territory was captured and settled by the Huns and their allies. In the 450s the lands territories of Illyricum achieved a *de facto* independence, being ruled by the local warlord, Marcellinus of Dalmatia. Some scholars assume he has received the mostly honorary title of *magister militum* of Dalmatia or Illyria[8]. However, he made use of his own troops and was largely independent politically[9].

Considering the political instability of that region, as well as the silence of the sources, it appears that the title of *magister militum* of Illyria did not exist as part of the Eastern Roman chain of command for the most of the described

---

[5] An interesting point is brought up by J.H.W.G. L i e b e s c h u e t z (*Barbarians and Bishops. Army, Church, and State in the Age of Arcadius and Chrysostom*, Oxford 1991, p. 41–42), who observes that according to Notitia, the substantial forces in Illyricum offered very little resistance to Alaric in 396. The scholar's conclusion is that the document is misleading in this regard.

[6] *PLRE*, vol. II, p. 1291.

[7] P r i s c u s, fr. 11: τὸν ἐν Ἰλλυριοῖς ταγμάτων ἡγούμενον.

[8] F. W o z n i a k, *East Rome, Ravenna and Illyricum 454–536 AD*, Hi 30, p. 359; P. M a c-G e o r g e, *Late Roman Warlords*, New York 2002, p. 40–41; J.B. B u r y, *History of the Later Roman Empire from the Death of Theodosius I. to the Death of Justinian*, vol. I, London 1958, p. 333.

[9] M. K u l i k o w s k i, *Marcellinus 'of Dalmatia' and the Dissolution of the Fifth-Century Empire*, B 72, 2002, p. 177–191.

period[10]. It is quite probable that the Illyrian army was disbanded when that territory was given to the Western Roman Empire, and as opposed to the Thracian army, it was never permanently reinstated[11].

The arguments presented above demonstrate that the system of the Eastern Roman high command recorded in *Notitia Dignitatum* cannot be extended over the whole period of the fifth century. In fact, it appears that for the majority of the discussed period there were four permanent territorial offices of *magistri militum* with corresponding field armies.

Tenures of *Magistri Militum*

When one considers the nature of the military elites in the Eastern Roman Empire it is paramount to establish whether military service in the highest ranks was limited in duration, or whether the emperor could nominate and fire his generals freely. First of all, this question determines the power dynamic between the ruler and the generals. Secondly, it is an important piece of evidence in establishing chronology. Unfortunately not much has not much was written about it in the particular period under consideration[12]. There is no legal source which would prove that tenures existed. Modern scholarship also rarely weighs in on that topic. In fact, I have managed to find just a few remarks originating from Arnold H.M. Jones, admittedly an undisputed authority in the realm of late antique offices and administration. His claims, however, do not seem to be supported by any sources or even by much in terms of argumentation. When speaking about the Roman tradition of tenures, the historian asserts that the high military offices were held for approximately a period of three to five years and any exception to that rule would indicate some sort of anomaly in the administrative

---

[10] Alexander D e m a n d t (*Magister*..., p. 737) observes the relative silence and lack of information concerning the Illyrian mastery; however, he supposes that it was due to the difficulty of keeping records in such uncertain times.

[11] There is the possibility that Leo tried to reinstate the office at some point in the 460s, to appoint Marcellinus as one of the *magistri militum*, cf. p. 154 of the present work.

[12] David A. P a r n e l l (*Justinian's Men. Careers and Relationships of Byzantine Army Officers 518–610*, London 2017, p. 83–84) has taken the problem of tenures under consideration, however, his observation that the generals did not serve for a fixed tenure, while probably correct for the period of his interest, namely the reign of Justinian, cannot be applied to the fifth century. One could not reasonably establish continuity between those periods because of all what happened during the very chaotic reigns of Zeno and Anastasius, which certainly affected the workings of the military system.

process[13]. This claim must have resonated with Glushanin, who referred to Jones in his own work on the military elites[14]. Unfortunately neither author sufficiently justified his opinion, so it is difficult to understand why exactly they made to such an assumption. It is the my understanding that they must have at least been following their scholarly instincts, which admittedly is not something very tangible, but considering the authority of afore-mentioned writers, it should not be discounted either.

On the other hand, there have been attempts at argue the opposite. In his doctoral thesis, unfortunately as yet unpublished, Łukasz Jarosz, argues that the terms of Eastern Roman military commanders were highly irregular[15]. It is admirable that the author attempted to gather all the available data and present an extensive analysis of the problem, however, his arguments do not hold up to scrutiny. He tries to present a statistical overview, yet the data set is not sufficient to do so[16]. Even if it were, I managed to detect several misinterpretations, which indicates that the data itself is faulty[17]. Despite these criticisms, the other parts of

---

[13] A.H.M. J o n e s, *The Decline of the Ancient World*, London 1966, p. 145–146.

[14] Е.П. Г л у ш а н и н, *Военная...*, p. 24.

[15] Ł. J a r o s z, *Wschodniorzymscy magistrowie militum w latach 395–527. Studium prosopograficzne*, Kraków 2017, p. 431 [unpublished Ph.D. thesis].

[16] The reality of the situation is that we know of only a small selection of the total number commanders in that period. Ł. Jarosz claims that it still gives him a data set of about 100 individuals, but then admits that for 43% the length of service cannot be established. Such a small data set creates problems, but it could still be useful if the selection were somehow representative of the whole group. However, one cannot agree with that. If a general happened to be recorded by the sources it was usually so because he left some mark on history, as opposed to the unknown number of those who did not. This means that most of the data points are in fact extraordinarily irregular and they cannot be used to draw generalized conclusions. Such an approach can be likened to conducting a survey of the public opinion at a rally of a political party and trying to pass the result as representative of what the society as a whole thinks.

[17] For example, the service of Varanes as *magister militum praesentalis* is claimed to have lasted one year, from 409 to 410. This is then a data point which Ł. Jarosz includes in his statistical overview. However, there is no evidence whatsoever that Varanes was nominated for the post in 409 and was dismissed the next year. The only information we possess is that he was a general in 409 and received the consulate in 410. He could still have remained in service in 410 and afterwards. He could have begun his service in that position well before 409. He could have been nominated as early as 405 and left service in 415, since there are no known *magistri militum praesentales* over that whole period aside of his colleague Arsakes, who is attested only in 409. If the range of results is between one and ten years, and the data set is so meagre, this example alone can affect the end-result immensely. And that is not the only problem of this sort. As another example, Theodulus is said to have ended service as *magister militum per Thracias* in 449, but there is no other general in that post until the 460s. So it is possible that he could have served for two years, as Ł. Jarosz claims, just as well as a dozen.

the dissertation are very interesting and valuable, and it is overall an impressive achievement.

When such is the state of evidence and discussion about the problem of tenures, it would be the safest to assume that it is not possible to make an unambiguous determination one way or the other. However, this question affects the understanding of so many problems which the present work tackles that, in my view, some manner of an informed assumption needs to be made. First of all, the lack of direct evidence for the existence of tenures is not evidence of their non-existence. It had been a long-standing Roman tradition for public offices to have time-limited terms. While it was usually a period of one year, it would make sense to extend that practice for military offices[18]. In order to provide security to the borders of the Empire the armies needed stable leadership by professional commanders, and exchanging them too often would certainly impact the readiness and effectiveness of the military. The result would be much greater than merely changing a single individual, since *magistri militum* managed extensive bureaucratic apparatus, as well as designated commanders of lower rank.

Finally, in the whole period under analysis there can be observed no evidence of the emperors being able to replace commanders of the armies at liberty, even if they seemed to really want to do that. In fact there are strong indications of the contrary. In 441, emperor Theodosius II issued a law clarifying the position of the special rank of *vacantes* in the hierarchy of offices. The law specifically mentioned a *magister militum vacans* named Germanus in the context of his nomination for the campaign against the Vandals on Sicily. It poses two questions: if the emperor was free to nominate and dismiss regular *magistri militum*, why would such category even exist and why would Theodosius feel the need to clarify its status?

Given all of the above considerations, it is my position that in the period of 408–474 there existed some form of time-limited tenure for the highest military offices. It is not possible to determine if this was regulated by an unknown law which did not survive to our day or if it was simply a matter of custom. For the purpose of the present analysis such a major difference matters less than if administration or prosopography were its subject. If it was commonly understood and expected that a military commander was to serve a fixed term, then it constituted a political reality irrespective of the legal basis, and going forward, it is my opinion and assumption that this was the case.

---

[18] It seems that the general tendency for military officers was to serve longer terms than their civilian equivalent, cf. A.H.M. J o n e s, *The Later...*, p. 380–381.

Appendix 2

As I indicated in the introduction, the overviews of the fifth-century Eastern Roman military history are not abundant, and the select ones that exist often focus on pointing out the multitude of problems that the Roman army was dealing with, rather than appreciating its qualities. In the more popular or general overviews, where the remnants of the 'decline' narrative often still live on, the image of the Roman Empire's military being but a shade of its former self is even more common.

It is thus understandable that for some readers, especially those who are primarily interested in military history, and could be classified as enthusiast, rather than researchers of late antiquity, the viewpoint that I presented on the pages of the present book could appear surprising. On the surface, the period of the fifth century does not seem glamorous in the context of the Roman military history, and the major political events of the period, most importantly the fall of the Roman Empire in the West, are undoubtedly, at least in part, caused by the failure of the army to protect the state from its multitude of enemies.

That being said, many of those claims originate from insufficiently thorough overviews of the military history of that period. An important factor was the fact that the various enemies of the Empire in the fifth century were much better organized and posed considerably greater threat to the integrity of its borders than before. The struggle to overcome them should not be blamed on the deterioration of the Imperial army and supposed ineptitude its leaders, but instead it behoves to appreciate and factor in the achievements of the Vandals, the Goths, the Persians, and the Huns, and the political and military accomplishments of their great leaders, such as Geiseric or Attila.

Furthermore, it is incorrect to apply the same lens when evaluating the conduct of the Roman military in the East. A detailed analysis of how the Eastern army fared against various enemies of the Empire shows that it was, more often than not, successful. While each of the conflicts has been described in the main body of the present work, I have decided to include an over-all overview of the military history of the years 408-474 in this appendix, in order to better illustrate my points and for readers' convenience.

The attached chart lists all of the conflicts in which the Eastern army was involved in the period of interest. I tried to keep the naming consistent throughout the overview, and to differentiate raids, under which I understand relatively minor, regional conflicts, when Roman forces had to contain the enemy raiding parties, and expeditions, to indicate Eastern Roman military interventions outside its borders.

Some of the events were omitted, if a case could be made that they should have, for example the growing tensions with the Huns around the time of the end of king Rua's reign, because there is little indication of any hostilities taking place, and it seems the issues were resolved diplomatically. The intervention in the conflict between Goth and Sciri also was not included, because it is most likely that the forces involved in it on behalf of emperor Leo were the soldiers of Marcellinus of Dalmatia and not the regular Eastern Roman armies.

Another important consideration is what actually constitutes a success. Every military operation must have had a set of objectives it was meant to accomplish. In some cases we can be relatively certain what those were, e.g. the aim of the expedition against the usurper John was clearly the overthrowing of the usurper and re-instating the members of the Theodosian dynasty back on the Western throne. In others, we cannot determine exact objectives, but as in the case of the expedition of Basiliscus from 468, it is obvious that whatever were its goals, they were not accomplished due to the whole force getting destroyed. Oftentimes, however, the situation is not as simple. For example, the Aspar's expedition to Africa in 431 suffered set-backs and failed to defeat the Vandals, but managed to protect the core of the province from the barbarians until a peace treaty was established. Only with the benefit of hindsight and knowledge of Geiseric's breaking of the agreement in 439 do we get the context for understanding why failing to completely defeat and subjugate the Vandals had such terrible consequences. Thus, I have tried my best to account for all discernible variables that could affect the contemporary evaluation of the conflicts in which the Eastern Roman military participated.

Some additional notes were also included to comment on any surrounding circumstances that could have affected our evaluation or make the distinction between success and failure not entirely clear. In some cases overall victory was won despite initial set-backs on tactical or operational level, e.g. in case of the expedition against usurper John; or the whole campaign ended in a fiasco due to other circumstances, despite the fact that the involved Roman forces remained intact, as was in case of the expedition of 441 that was bogged down in Sicily and had to retreat due to the Balkan provinces being threatened by the Huns.

	Conflict	Commanders	Outcome	Additional Notes
408	War with the Huns	(?)	Partial success	The Roman army was likely defeated in battle, but the Huns were stopped through subterfuge
421–422	War with Persia	Ardaburious the Elder Procopius Vitianus Anatolius (?)	Success	
422	Hun raids	Plintha (?)	Success	The Huns were likely stopped by a tribe of Goths allied to the Romans
424–425	Expedition against the usurper John	Ardaburious the Elder Aspar Candidianus	Success	The initial naval invasion ended up in disaster due to storm, it is also possible (but unlikely) that Aspar fought a pitched, bloody battle against Aetius and his Hunnic allies
427	War with the Huns	Plintha (?)	Success	
431–435	Expedition against the Vandals	Aspar	Partial success	The Romans lost a battle against the Vandals, but managed to hold Carthage until a peace was secured
441	Expedition against the Vandals	Areobindus Germanus Ansila Arintheos Innobindos	Failure	The expedition was probably meant to attack Africa, but was delayed on Sicily and had to be recalled due to the Hunnic threat
441	War with Persia	Anatolius	Failure	The war was very brief and peace treaty was quickly concluded by the Romans who could not have spared forces, having them occupied on Sicily and dealing with the incursions of Isaurians and Tzani

	Conflict	Commanders	Outcome	Additional Notes
441–442	War with the Huns	Aspar Areobindus	Failure	It is likely that the Roman forces could not engage the Huns, because main armies were away on Sicily. When they returned in 442 the Huns were repelled, yet, the damage had already been done
447	War with the Huns	Arnegisclus Apollonius Aspar Theodulus Fl. Zeno Areobindus (?)	Failure	After the failure of Roman defences and the disastrous defeat at Utus, it seems that the Huns were stopped and forced to retreat after the battle on Chersonesus, however, the following peace treaty was very unfavorable to the Roman side
451	Hun raids	Marcian Ardaburious Apollonius (?) Aspar (?)	Success	The raids were likely quite limited and did not involve the main forces of Attila
452	Expedition against the Huns	Apollonius Aetius (?) Ardaburious (?) Aspar (?)	Success	The expedition probably did not face much resistance, since Attila was involved in Italy
452–453	Arab raids	Ardaburious	Success	Very little is known about those events and the course of the conflict is impossible to ascertain
453	War with the Blemmyes and Nobades	Maximinus Florus	Success	The Blemmyes and Nobades invaded twice, but they were defeated each time
454	Expeditions to Lazica	(?)	Partial success	The first expedition was likely unsuccessful, and the Romans were forced to retreat, but the threat of Roman intervention seems to have convinced the Lazi to seek a diplomatic compromise
461	Ostrogoth raids	Anthemius	Success	
467–469	War with the Huns	Aspar Anagastes Basiliscus Ostrys Anthemius	Success	The Romans managed to win a victory early, however, it took nearly two years to finally defeat the Hun leader, Dengizich.
468	Expedition against the Vandals	Basiliscus	Failure	
470	Expedition against the Vandals	Heraclius Marsus	Failure	Was initially successful, but had to be recalled to deal with Aspar

An interesting observation based on the data collected in the above chart is that only 6 of 19 total conflicts ended in failure for the Romans, which constitutes about 32%. Even if we exclude minor raids and campaigns that were resolved mostly through diplomatic arrangements, it leaves us with 11 conflicts, 5 of which ended unfavourably, which raises the ratio of failures to 45%.

However, if we consider only the expeditions, there were 7 campaigns which could be classified as such, and out of them 4 were successful, but only 2 indisputably so. Even then, in one of those instances, the expedition against the usurper John, the Eastern Roman forces suffered severe casualties due to the naval contingent getting destroyed in a storm. It means that in this whole period, there was only one offensive military campaign which achieved all of its goals and did not take a serious toll on the forces involved; the expedition against the Huns in 452 which targeted largely undefended settlements.

The overall record of operations against the Vandals is quite poor, as 3 out of 4 expeditions resulted in failure, and the only one that could be called a partial success, was the one led by Aspar in 430s, which suffered a defeat in the field on its very onset. In 2 instances the failure, however, was a result of the Roman forces needing to retreat due to having to respond to other threats.

The conclusion from the above data is quite clear. The Roman army was adept in dealing with minor incursions and generally was able to succeed even in larger conflicts, but its ability to intervene outside of its borders was limited and potentially very risky. That being said, many of the set-backs suffered by the Roman army were caused by other circumstances, unrelated to the outcomes on the field of battle.

Thus, the above overview proves that the Roman army could be a capable military force, when used correctly; however, another interesting inference could also be made. The same conclusion that I arrived at in this evaluation could have been reached by those in the past; especially the generals who are the subject matter of the present work, and who had even better idea of all of those problems than a modern historian does, who is sadly limited by the scarcity of his sources.

List of Abbreviations

AAC	Acta Archeologica Carpathica
AB	Analecta Bollandiana
ACUSD	Acta Classica Universitatis Scientiarum Debreceniensis
АДСВ	Античная древность и средние века
AJAH	American Journal of Ancient History
B	Byzantion. Revue internationale des études byzantines
BP	Balcanica Posnaniensia. Acta et studia
Bsl	Byzantinoslavica. Revue internationale des études byzantines
ByzS	Byzantine Studies/Études byzantines
BZ	Byzantinische Zeitschrift
CAH	*Cambridge Ancient History*
Chi	Chiron. Mitteilungen der Kommission für alte Geschichte und Epigraphik des Deutschen Archäologischen Instituts
ChrA	Christianitas Antiqua
CJ	*Codex Justinianus*
CLRE	*Consuls of the Later Roman Empire*, ed. R.S. Bagnall, A. Cameron, S.R. Schwartz, K.A. Worp, Atlanta 1987
CP	Classical Philology
CQ	The Classical Quarterly
CTh	*Codex Theodosianus*
EHR	English Historical Review

GRBS   Greek, Roman and Byzantine Studies
Her   Hermathena. A Dublin University Review
Hi   Historia. Zeitschrift für alte Geschichte
HOJ   Histos. The On-line Journal of Ancient Historiography
IHR   International Historical Review
JLA   Journal of Late Antiquity
K   Klio. Beiträge zur alten Geschichte
Kok   Kokalos
L   Latomus
M   Meander. Miesięcznik poświęcony kulturze świata starożytnego
MGH.AA   *Monumenta Germaniae historica, Auctores antiquissimi*
Mil   Millennium. Jahrbuch zu Kultur und Geschichte des ersten Jahrtausends
                  n. Chr
ODB   *The Oxford Dictionary of Byzantium*, vol. I–III, ed. A. K a z h d a n,
                  Oxford 1991
PH   Przegląd Historyczny
Phoe   Phoenix. Journal of the Classical Association of Canada / Revue de la
                  Société canadienne des études classiques
PK   Prawo Kanoniczne
PL   *Patrologiae cursus completus, Series latina*, ed. J.P. M i g n e, Paris 1844–1880
PLRE, vol. II   M a r t i n d a l e J.R., *The Prosopography of the Later Roman Empire*,
                  vol. II, A.D. 395–527, Cambridge 1980
Porph   Porphyra. La prima rivista online su Bisanzio
PP   Past and Present: A Journal of Historical Studies
RE   *Paulys Real-Encyclopädie der classischen Altertumswissenschaft*, ed. G. W i s-
                  s o w a, W. K r o l l, Stuttgart 1894–1978.
ReG   Res Gestae
SCer   Studia Ceranea
Sem   Seminare
SF   Südost-Forschungen
SKA   Studia nad kulturą antyczną
Ty   Tyche. Beiträge zur Alten Geschichte, Papyrologie und Epigraphik
TAPhS   Transactions of the American Philosophical Society
USS   U Schyłku Starożytności. Studia Źródłoznawcze
VP   Vox Patrum. Antyk Chrześcijański
ZPE   Zeitschrift für Papyrologie und Epigraphik

Bibliography

Primary Sources

Acta synodorum habitarum Romae
Acta synodorum habitarum Romae, [in:] *MGH.AA*, t. XII, ed. T. M o m m s e n, Berolini 1894.

Agathias
Agathiae Myrinaei Historiarum libri quinque, ed. R. K e y d e l l, Berolini 1967.

Candidus
C a n d i d u s, *Fragmenta*, [in:] *Fragmentary Classicising Historians of the Later Roman Empire: Eunapius, Olympiodorus, Priscus and Malchus*, ed. R.C. B l o c k l e y, t. II, *Text, Translation and Historiographical Notes*, Liverpool 1983, p. 464–473.

Cedrenus
G e o r g i u s C e d r e n u s, *Synopsis Historikon*, ed. A.I. B e k k e r, t. I–II, Bonnae 1838–1839.

CJ
The Codex of Justinian, ed. B.W. F r i e r, transl. F.H. B l u m e, vol. I–III, Cambridge 2016.

C l a u d i a n, *De sextu consulate Honorii*
Claudian, t. II, ed. M. P l a t n a u e r, London 1922.

Chronica Gallica a. 452
Gallische Chroniken, ed. J.M. K o t t e r, C. S c a r d i n o, Paderborn 2017.

Chronicon Paschale
Chronicon Paschale, ed. L. D i n d o r f, Bonnae 1832.

Constantine Porphyrogennetos
Constantine Porphyrogennetos, *The Book of Ceremonies*, transl. A. M o f f a t,
    M. T a l l *with the Greek edition of the Corpus Scriptorum Historiae Byzantinae (Bonn, 1829)*,
    vol. I–II, Canberra 2012.

Continuatio Codicis Reichenaviensis
Continuatio Codicis Reichenaviensis, [in:] *MGH.AA*, t. IX, ed. T. M o m m s e n, Berolini 1892.

CTh
Theodosiani libri XVI cum constitutionibus Sirmondianis et leges Novellae ad Theodosianum perti-
    nentes, ed. T. M o m m s e n, P. M e y e r, Berolini 1905.

Cyril of Scythopolis, *Vita Euthymii*
Kyrillos von Scythopolis, *Leben des Euthymios*, [in:] *Vitae monachorum Palestinen-*
    sium, ed. E. S c h w a r t z, Leipzig 1939, p. 3–85.

Damascius
D a m a s c i u s, *Philosophical History*, ed. and transl. P. A t h a n a s s i a d i, Athens 1999.

Evagrius
The Ecclesiastical History of Evagrius, ed. J. B i d e z, L. P a r m e n t i e r, London 1898.

Ghazar P'arpec'i
Ghazar P'arpec'i's History of the Armenians, ed. R. B e d r o s i a n, New York 1985.

Gregory of Tours
Gregori Episcopi Turonensis Libri Historiarum X, [in:] *MGH.SM rer. Merov.*, t. I, ed. B. K r u s c h,
    W. L e v i s o n, Hannoverae 1951.

Hydatius
Hydatii Limici Chronica Subdita, [in:] R.W. B u r g e s s, *The Chronicle of Hydatius and Consula-*
    ria Constantinopolitana, Oxford 1993, p. 61–172.

John Lydus
J e a n l e L y d i e n, *Des magistratures de l'État romain*, trad. M. D u b u i s s o n, J. S c h a m p,
    t. I–II, Paris 2006.

Jordanes, *Getica*
Iordanis Romana and Getica, [in:] *MGH.AA*, t. V, ed. T. M o m m s e n, Beriolini 1882, p. 53–138.

Jordanes, *Romana*
Iordanis Romana et Getica, [in:] *MGH.AA*, t. V, ed. T. M o m m s e n, Beriolini 1882, p. 1–52.

Leo, *Epistulae*
Sancti Leonis Magni Romani Pontificis Epistolae, [in:] *PL,* t. 54, Paris 1846, p. 581–1218.

Malalas
Ioannis Malalae Chronographia, rec. J. T h u r n, Berolini et Novi Eboraci 2000.

Malchus
M a l c h o s, *Fragmenta*, [in:] R.C. B l o c k l e y, *Fragmentary Classicising Historians of the Later Roman Empire: Eunapius, Olympiodorus, Priscus and Malchus,* ed. R.C. B l o c k l e y, t. II, *Text, Translation and Historiographical Notes*, t. II, Liverpool 1983, p. 402–462.

Marcellinus Comes
The Chronicle of Marcellinus, ed. B. C r o k e, Sydney 1995.

Mauricius, *Strategikon*
Das Strategikon des Maurikios, ed. G. D e n n i s, E. G a m i l l s c h e g, Wien 1981.

Merobaudes
Flavius Merobaudes: A Translation and a Historical Commentary, ed. and transl. F.L. C l o v e r, TAPhS 61, 1971, p. 1–78.

Moses of Khoren
M o i s e d e K h o r e n e, *Histoire d'Armenie*, [in:] *Collection des historiens anciens et moderne de l'Armenie*, ed. V. L a n g l o i s, Paris 1869.

Novellae Valentiniani
Theodosiani libri XVI cum constitutionibus Sirmondianis et leges Novellae ad Theodosianum pertinentes, ed. T. M o m m s e n, P. M e y e r, Berolini 1905.

Notitia Dignitatum
Notitia Dignitatum, ed. O. S e e c k, Berolini 1876.

Olympiodorus
O l y m p i o d o r u s, *Fragmenta*, [in:] *Fragmentary Classicising Historians of the Later Roman Empire: Eunapius, Olympiodorus, Priscus and Malchus*, ed. R.C. B l o c k l e y, t. II, *Text, Translation and Historiographical Notes*, Liverpool 1983, p. 152–221.

Peri strategias
The Anonymous Byzantine Treatise on Strategy, [in:] *Three Byzantine Military Treatises*, ed. and transl. G. D e n n i s, Washington 1985, p. 9–135.

Philostorgius
P h i l o s t o r g i o s, *Kirchengeschichte*, ed. B. B l e c k m a n n, M. S t e i n, Paderborn 2015.

Pseudo-Zachariah
Z a c h a r i a h o f M i t y l e n e, *Syriac Chronicle*, ed., transl. F.J. H a m i l t o n, E.W. B r o o k s, London 1899.

Procopius, *History of the Wars*
Procopius, *History of the Wars*, ed. H.B. Dewing, vol. I–V, New York 1914–1928.

Prosper
Prosper Tiro, *Chronik. Laterculus Regnum Vandalorum et Alanorum*, ed. J.M. Kotter, M. Becker, Paderborn 2016.

Priscus
Priscus, *Fragmenta*, [in:] *Fragmentary Classicising Historians of the Later Roman Empire: Eunapius, Olympiodorus. Priscus and Malchus*, ed. R.C. Blockley, t. II, *Text, Translation and Historiographical Notes*, Liverpool 1983, p. 222–401.

Sidonius, *Epistolae*
Sidonius, *Poems and Letters*, ed. W.B. Anderson, London 1956, p. 329–483.

Sidonius, *Carmina*
Sidonius, *Poems and Letters*, ed. W.B. Anderson, London 1956, p. 1–327.

Sozomen
Sozomène, *Histoire ecclésiastique*, ed. J. Bidez, trad. A-J. Festugière, B. Grillet, t. I–IV, Paris 1983–2008.

Socrates
Socrate de Constantinople, *Histoire ecclésiastique*, ed. G. Hansen, trad. P. Périchon, P. Maraval, t. I–IV, Paris 2004–2007.

Suda
Suidae Lexicon, ed. A. Adler, t. I–V, Stutgaridiae 1967–1989.

Theodor Lector
Theodoros Anagnostes, *Kirchengeschichte*, hrsg. G.C. Hansen, Berlin 1995.
The Church Histories of Theodore Lector and John Diakrinomenos, ed. R. Kosiński, K. Twardowska, transl. A. Zabrocka, A. Szopa, Berlin 2021.

Theodoret, *Ep.*
Theodoret de Cyr, *Correspondance*, ed. Y. Azéma, t. I–IV, Paris 1955–1998.

Theodoret, *HE*
Theodoretus, *Kirchengeschichte,* ed. P. Parmentier, Leipzig 1911.

Theophanes
Theophanis Chronographia, rec. C. de Boor, t. I, Lipsiae 1883.

Vegetius
Publii Flavii Vegetii Renati Epitoma rei militaris, ed. F.L. Müller, Stuttgart 1997.

Victor of Vita
Victor von Vita, *Kirchenkampf und Verfolgung unter den Vandalen in Africa*, ed. K. Vössing, Darmstadt 2011.

Yeghishe

E l i s h e, *Histoire d'Armenie*, [in:] *Collection des historiens anciens et moderne de l'Armenie*, ed. V. L a n g l o i s, Paris 1869.

Zonaras

Ioannis Zonarae Epitome Historiarum, ed. L. D i n d o r f, t. I–III, Lipsiae 1868–1875.

Zosimus

Z o s i m e, *Histoire nouvelle*, ed., trad. F. P a s c h o u d, t. I–III, Paris 1979–2000.

Vita St. Danielis Stylitae

Vita St. Danielis Stylitae, ed. H. D e l e h a y e, AB 32, 1913, p. 121–229.

Vita Marcelli

La vie ancienne de saint Marcel l'Acémetes, ed. G. D a g r o n, AB 85, 1968, p. 271–321.

Secondary Literature

A l b e r t G., *Goten in Konstantinopel*, Wien 1984.

A l b e r t G., *Stilicho und der Hunnenfeldzug des Eutropius*, Chi 9, 1979, p. 621–645.

A l l e n P., *Evagrius Scholasticus the Church Historian*, Leuven 1981.

A n d e r s F., *Flavius Ricimer. Macht und Ohnmacht des weströmischen Heermeisters in der zweiten Hälfte des 5. Jahrhunderts*, Berlin 2010.

A u s b ü t t e l F., *Theoderich der Große*, Darmstadt 2003.

B a b c o c k M., *The Night that Attila died. Solving the Murder of Attila the Hun*, Berkeley 2005.

B a c h r a c h B., *A History of the Alans in the West. From Their First Appearance in the Sources of Classical Antiquity through the Early Middle Ages*, Minneapolis 1973.

B a l d w i n B., *Priscus of Panium*, B 50, 1980, p. 18–61.

B l e e k e r R.A., *Aspar and Attila: The Role of Flavius Ardaburius Aspar in the Hun Wars of the 440s*, AWo 3, 1980, p. 23–27.

B l e e k e r R.A., *Aspar and the Struggle for the Eastern Roman Empire, AD 421–71*, London 2022.

B l o c k l e y R.C., *East Roman Foreign Policy. Formation and Conduct from Diocletian to Anastasius*, Cairns 1992.

B l o c k l e y R.C., *Fragmentary Classicising Historians of the Later Roman Empire*, t. I, Liverpool 1981.

B l o c k l e y R.C., *The developement of Greek Historiography. Priscus, Malchus and Candidus*, [in:] *Greek and Roman Historiography in Late Antiquity. Fourth to Sixth Century A.D.*, ed. G. M a r a s c o, Boston 2003, p. 289–315.

B l o c k l e y R.C., *The Dynasty of Theodosius*, [in:] *CAH*, vol. XIII, *The Late Empire A.D. 337–425*, ed. A. C a m e r o n, P. G a r n s e y, Cambridge 1998, p. 111–137.

B o a k A.E.R., *The Roman Magistri in the Civil and Military Service of the Empire*, CP 26, 1915, p. 73–164.

B o h e c Y., *L'Armee Romaine sous le Bas-Empire*, Paris 2006.

B ó n a I., *Das Hunnenreich*, Stuttgart 1991.

B ö r m H., *Hydatius von Aquae Flaviae und die Einheit des Römiches Reiches im 5. Jahrhundert*, [in:] *Griechische Profanhistoriker des fünften nachristlichen Jahrhundert*, ed. T. S t i c k l e r, B. B l e c k m a n n, Stuttgart 2014, p. 195–214.

B r a n d t H., *Zur historiographischen konzeption des Izaurers Candidus*, [in:] *Griechische Profanhistoriker des fünften nachristlichen Jahrhundert*, ed. T. S t i c k l e r, B. B l e c k m a n n, Stuttgart 2014, p. 161–170.

B r o d k a D., *Die Geschichtsphilosophie in der spätantiken Historiographie. Studien zu Prokopios von Kaisareia, Agathias von Myrina und Theophylaktos Simokattes*, Frankfurt am Main 2004.

B r o d k a D., *Priskos und der Feldzug des Basiliskos gegen Geiserich (468)*, [in:] *Griechische Profanhistoriker des fünften nachristlichen Jahrhundert*, ed. T. S t i c k l e r, B. B l e c k m a n n, Stuttgart 2014, p. 103–120.

B r o d k a D., *Priskos von Panion und Kaiser Marcian. Eine Quellenuntersuchung zu Procop. 3,4,1–11, Evagr. HE 2,1, Theoph. AM 5943 und Nic. Kall. HE 15,1*, Mil 9, 2012, p. 145–162.

B r o o k s E.W., *The Emperor Zenon and the Isaurians*, Her 8, 1893, p. 209–238.

B u r g e s s R.W., *A New Reading for Hydatius „Chronicle" 177 and the Defeat of the Huns in Italy*, Phoe 42, 1988, p. 357–363.

B u r g e s s R.W., *Isaurian Factions in the Reign of Zeno the Isaurian*, L 51, 1992, p. 874–881.

B u r g e s s R.W., *The Accession of Marcian in the Light of Chalcedonian Apologetic and Monophysite Polemic*, BZ 86/87, 1994, p. 27–68.

B u r g e s s R.W., *The Chronicle of Hydatius and Consularia Constantinopolitana*, Oxford 1993.

B u r n s T., *A History of the Ostrogoths*, Bloomington 1984.

B u r y J.B., *History of the Later Roman Empire from the Death of Theodosius I. to the Death of Justinian*, vol. I, London 1958.

C a m e r o n A., L o n g J., *Barbarians and Politics at the Court of Arcadius*, Berkeley 1993.

C a m e r o n A., *Procopius and the Sixth Century*, London 1996.

C a m e r o n A., *The Mediterranean World in Late Antiquity AD 393–600*, New York 1993.

C a r d e l l e d e H a r t m a n C., *Philologische Studien zur Chronik des Hydatius von Chaves*, Stuttgart 1994.

C a s t r i t i u s H., *Die Vandalen. Etappen einer Spurensuche*, Berlin 2006.

C h e s n u t G., *The First Christian Histories. Eusebius, Socrates, Sozomen, Theodoret and Evagrius*, Paris 1986.

C l a u s s M., *Der magister officiorum in der Spätantike. Das Amt und sein Einfluss auf die kaiserliche Politik*, München 1980.

C l o v e r F.M., *The Family and Early Career of Anicius Olybrius*, Hi 27, 1978, p. 169–196.

Consuls of the Later Roman Empire, ed. R.S. B a g n a l l, A. C a m e r o n, S.R. S c h w a r t z, K.A. W o r p, Atlanta 1987.

C r a w f o r d P., *Roman Emperor Zeno. The Perils of Politics in Fifth-century Constantinople*, Barnsley 2019.

C r o k e B., *Anatolius and Nomus: Envoys to Attila*, Bsl 42, 1981, p. 159–170.

C r o k e B., *Count Marcellinus and his Chronicle*, New York 2001.

C r o k e B., *Dating Theodoret's Church History and Commentary on the Psalms*, B 54, 1989, p. 59–74.

Croke B., *Dynasty and Ethnicity. Emperor Leo I and the Eclipse of Aspar*, Chi 35, 2005, p. 147–203.

Croke B., *Evidence for the Hun invasion of Thrace in 422*, GRBS 18, 1977, p. 347–367.

Croke B., *Introduction*, [in:] *The Chronicle of John Malalas*, ed. E. Jeffreys, M. Jeffreys, R. Scott, Sydney 1986, p. XI–XLII.

Croke B., *Latin Historiography and the Barbarian Kingdoms*, [in:] *Greek and Roman Historiography in Late Antiquity. Fourth to Sixth Century A.D.*, ed. G. Marasco, Boston 2003, p. 349–389.

Croke B., *The Chronicle of Marcellinus*, Sydney 1995.

Croke B., *The Context and Date of Priscus Fragment 6*, CP 78, 1983, p. 297–308.

Croke B., *The Date and Circumstances of Marcian's Decease, A.D. 457*, B 48, 1978, p. 5–9.

Croke B., *The Imperial Reigns of Leo II*, BZ 92, 2003, p. 559–575.

Croke B., *Two Early Byzantine Earthquakes and their Liturgical Commemoration*, B 51, 1981.

Curtois Ch., *Les Vandales et l'Afrique*, Paris 1955.

Delmaire R., *Les Dignitaires Laics au Concile de Chalcedoine: Notes sur la Hierarchie et les Preseances au Milieu du Ve siecle*, B 54, 1984, p. 141–175.

Demandt A., *Der spätrömische Militäradel*, Chi 10, 1980, p. 609–636.

Demandt A., *Geschichte der Spätantike*, München 2008.

Demandt A., *Magister militum*, [in:] *RE*, t. XII suppl., 1970, p. 553–790.

Dennis G., *Einführung*, [in:] *Das Strategikon des Maurikios*, ed. G. Dennis, E. Gamillscheg, Wien 1981, p. 11–42.

Diesner H.J., *Die Bucellariertum von Stilicho und Sarus bis auf Aetius (454/455)*, K 54, 1972, p. 321–350.

Diesner H.J., *Das Vandalenreich. Aufstieg und Untergang*, Stuttgart 1966.

Dignas B., Winter E., *Rome and Persia in Late Antiquity. Neighbours and Rivals*, Cambridge 2007.

Elton H., *Illus and the Isaurian Aristocracy under Zeno*, B 70, 2000, p. 393–407.

Elton H., *Military Developments in the Fifth Century*, [in:] *Companion to the Age of Attila*, ed. M. Maas, Cambridge 2015, p. 125–139.

Elton H., *Military Forces*, [in:] *The Cambridge History of Greek and Roman Warfare*, vol. II, ed. P. Sabin, H. van Wees, M. Whitby, Cambridge 2008, p. 270–309.

Elton H., *Warfare in Roman Europe, AD 350–425*, New York 1996.

Feld K., *Barbarische Bürger: Die Isaurier und das Römische Reich*, Berlin 2005.

Garsoian N., *The Marzapanate (428–652)*, [in:] *The Armenian People from Ancient to Modern Times*, vol. I, ed. R.G. Hovannisian, New York 1997, p. 95–116.

Gautier E.F., *Genséric. Roi des Vandales*, Paris 1935.

Gillett A., *Envoys and Political Communication in Late Antique West 411–533*, Cambridge 2003.

Ginter K., *Wizerunek władców bizantyńskich w Historii Kościelnej Ewagriusza Scholastyka*, Łódź 2018.

Goffart W., *The Narrators of Barbarian History (A.D. 550–800). Jordanes, Gregory of Tours, Bede, and Paul the Deacon*, New Jersey 1988.

Goltz A., *Sizillien und die Germanen in der Spätantike*, Kok 53/54, 1997/98, p. 215–217.

Gordon C.D., *The Age of Attila. Fifth-Century Byzantium and the Barbarians*, Michigan 1961.

Gračanin H., Škrgulja J., *The Ostrogoths in the Late Antique South Pannonia*, AAC 49, 2014, p. 165–205.

Gračanin H., *The Huns and the South Pannonia*, Bsl 64, 2006, p. 29–76.

Greatrex G., *Perceptions of Procopius in Recent Scholarship*, HOJ 8, 2014, p. 76–121.

Halsall G., *Barbarian Migrations and the Roman West, 376–568*, New York 2007.

Harries J., *Sidonius Apollinaris and the Fall of Rome AD 407–485*, Oxford 1994.

Heather P., *Goths and Romans 332–489*, Oxford 1991.

Heather P., *The Huns and the End of the Roman Empire in Western Europe*, EHR 60, 1995, p. 4–41.

Heather P., *The Fall of the Roman Empire. A New History of Rome and the Barbarians*, Oxford 2006.

Hohlfelder R.L., *Marcian's Gamble. A Reassessment of Eastern Imperial Policy toward Attila AD 450–453*, AJAH 9, 1984, p. 54–69.

Holum K.G., *Pulcheria's Crusade A.D. 421–22 and the Ideology of Imperial Victory*, GRBS 18, 1977, p. 153–172.

Holum K.G., *Theodosian Empresses: Women and Imperial Dominion in Late Antiquity*, Berkeley–Los Angeles–London 1982.

Horvath A., *The Education of Sidonius Apollinaris in the Light of his Citations*, ACUSD 36, 2000, p. 151–162.

Hughes I., *Stilicho. The Vandal Who Saved Rome*, Barnsley 2010.

Humphries M., *International Relations*, [in:] *The Cambridge History of Greek and Roman Warfare*, vol. II, ed. P. Sabin, H. van Wees, M. Whitby, Cambridge 2008, p. 235–269.

Janiszewski P., *Historiografia późnego antyku*, [in:] *Vademecum historyka starożytnej Grecji i Rzymu*, t. III: *Źródłoznawstwo czasów późnego antyku*, red. E. Wipszycka, Warszawa 1999, p. 7–220.

Jankowiak M., *Bizancjum a kryzysy sukcesyjne w Cesarstwie Zachodniorzymskim w ostatnich latach jego istnienia (465–474)*, [in:] *Chrześcijaństwo u schyłku starożytności. Studia źródłoznawcze*, t. III, red. T. Derda, E. Wipszycka, Warszawa 2000, p. 193–244.

Janβen T., *Stilicho. Das weströmische Reich vom Tode des Theodosius bis zur Ermordung Stilichos (395–408)*, Marburg 2004.

Jarosz Ł., *Kariera Flawiusza Anatoliusza*, [in:] *Florilegium. Studia ofiarowane profesorowi Aleksandrowi Krawczukowi z okazji dziewięćdziesiątej piątej rocznicy urodzin*, red. E. Dąbrowa, T. Grabowski, M. Piegdoń, Kraków 2017, p. 429–444.

Jarosz Ł., *Wschodniorzymscy magistrowie militum w latach 395–527. Studium prosopograficzne*, Kraków 2017 [unpublished Ph.D. thesis].

Jimenez D.A., *Sidonius Apollinaris and the Fourth Punic War*, [in:] *New Perspectives on Late Antiquity*, ed. D.H. de la Fuente, Cambridge 2011, p. 158–172.

Jones A.H.M, *The Later Roman Empire 284–602. A Social, Economic and Administrative Survey*, vol. I–III, Oxford 1964.

Jones A.H.M., *The Career of Flavius Philippus*, Hi 4, 1955, p. 229–233.

Jones A.H.M., *The Decline of the Ancient World*, London 1966.

Jurewicz O., *Historia literatury bizantyńskiej*, Wrocław 1984.

Kaegi W.E., *Byzantine Military Unrest, 471–843: An Interpretation*, Amsterdam 1981.

Kaegi W.E., *Some Thoughts on Byzantine Military Strategy*, Brookline 1983.

K a l d e l l i s A., *Procopius of Caesarea: Tyranny, History and Philosophy at the End of Antiquity*, Philadelphia 2004.

K a r a y a n n o p u l o s J., *Byzantinische Miszellen*, [in:] *Studia in honorem Veselini Besevliev*, ed. V. G e o r g i e v, Sofia 1978.

K a s p e r s k i R., *Teodoryk Wielki i Kasjodor. Studia nad tworzeniem „tradycji dynastycznej Amalów"*, Kraków 2013.

K a z h d a n A., *A History of Byzantine Literature (650–850)*, Athens 1998.

K e l l y Ch., *The End of Empire. Attila the Hun and the Fall of Rome*, New York 2009.

K i m H.J., *The Huns, Romans and the Birth of Europe*, Cambridge 2013.

K i s l i n g e r E., *Sizilien zwischen Vandalen und Römischem Reich im 5. Jahrhundert: Eine Insel in zentraler Randlage*, Mil 11, 2014, p. 237–260.

K o e h n C., *Justinian und die Armee des frühen Byzanz*, Berlin 2018.

K o k o s z k o M., *Descriptions of personal appearance in John Malalas' Chronicle*, Łódź 1998.

K o m p a A., *In search of Syncellus' and Theophanes' own words: the authorship of the Chronographia revisited*, TM 19, 2015, p. 73–92.

K o s i ń s k i R., *Holiness and Power. Constantinopolitan Holy Men and Authority in the 5th Century*, Berlin 2016.

K o s i ń s k i R., *Początki kariery Tarasikodissy-Zenona*, [in:] *Byzantina Europaea. Księga jubileuszowa ofiarowana Profesorowi Waldemarowi Ceranowi*, red. M. K o k o s z k o, M.J. L e s z k a, Łódź 2007, p. 289–304.

K o s i ń s k i R., *The Emperor Zeno: Religion and Politics*, transl. M. F i j a k, Cracow 2010.

K o t t e r J.M., B e c k e r M., *Einleitung*, [in:] P r o s p e r T i r o, *Chronik. Laterculus Regnum Vandalorum et Alanorum*, ed. J.M. K o t t e r, M. B e c k e r, Paderborn 2016, p. 3–60.

K r u p c z y ń s k i P., *Trudności zachodnich wypraw Belizariusza*, Łódź 1984.

K u l i k o w s k i M., *Marcellinus 'of Dalmatia' and the Dissolution of the Fifth-Century Empire*, B 72, 2002, p. 177–191.

K u l i k o w s k i M., *Notitia Dignitatum as a Historical Source*, Hi 49, 2000, p. 358–377.

K u l i k o w s k i M., *The Tragedy of Empire. From Constantine to the Destruction of Roman Italy*, Cambridge 2019.

L a n i a d o A., *Aspar and his Phoideratoi: John Malalas on a Special Relationship*, [in:] *Governare e riformare l'Impero al momento della sua divisione. Oriente, Occidente, Illirico*, ed. U. R o b e r t o, L. M e c e l l a, Roma 2016, p. 325–344.

L e e A.D., *Abduction and Assassination: The Clandestine Face of Roman Diplomacy in Late Antiquity*, IHR 31, 2009, p. 1–23.

L e e A.D., *Information and Frontiers: Roman Foreign Relations in Late Antiquity*, Cambridge 1997.

L e e A.D., *The eastern empire: Theodosius to Anastasius*, [in:] *CAH*, t. XIV, ed. A. C a m e r o n, B. W a r d - P e r k i n s, M. W h i t b y, Cambridge 2008, p. 33–62.

L e e A.D., *Theodosius and his Generals*, [in:] *Theodosius II. Rethinking the Roman Empire in Late Antiquity*, ed. Ch. K e l l y, Cambridge 2013, p. 90–108.

L e e A.D., *War in Late Antiquity*, Oxford 2007.

L e n s k y N., *Captivity among the Barbarians and Its Impact on the Fate of the Roman Empire*, [in:] *The Cambridge Companion to the Age of Attila*, ed. M. M a a s, Cambridge 2015, p. 235–238.

L e s z k a M.B., L e s z k a M.J., *Zarys dziejów Konstantynopola w latach 337–602*, [in:] *Konstantynopol – Nowy Rzym. Miasto i ludzie w okresie wczesnobizantyńskim*, red. M.J. L e s z k a, T. W o l i ń s k a, Warszawa 2011, p. 42–101.

Leszka M.J., *Empress-Widow Verina's Political Activity during the Reign of Emperor Zeno*, [in:] *Mélanges d'histoire byzantine offerts à Oktawiusz Jurewicz à l'occasion de son soixante-dixième anniversaire*, red. W. Ceran, Łódź 1998, p. 128–136.

Leszka M.J., *Kilka uwag na temat losów Illusa Izauryjczyka w latach 479–484*, M 62, 2007, p. 99–107.

Leszka M.J., *The role of Empress Verina in the events of 475/476 – revisited*, Bsl 75, 2017, p. 30–42.

Leszka M.J., Wierzbiński Sz., *Komes Marcellin vir clarissimus. Historyk i jego dzieło*, Łódź 2022.

Letki P., *The state factories (fabricae) during the time of tetrarchy*, SKA 5, 2009, p. 49–64.

Liebeschuetz J.H.W.G., *Barbarians and Bishops. Army, Church, and State in the Age of Arcadius and Chrysostom*, Oxford 1991.

Lindner R.P., *Nomadism, Horses and Huns*, PP 92, 1981, p. 3–19.

Lotter F., *Völkerverschiebungen im Ostalpen–Mitteldonau–Raum zwischen Antike und Mittelalter*, Berlin 2003.

Luttwak E., *The Grand Strategy of the Byzantine Empire*, Cambridge 2009.

MacGeorge P., *Late Roman Warlords*, New York 2002.

Maenchen-Helfen O., *The World of Huns. Studies in Their History and Culture*, London 1973.

Mathisen R.W., *Avitus, Italy and the East in A.D. 455–456*, B 51, 1981, p. 232–247.

Mathisen R.W., *Patricians as Diplomats in Late Antiquity*, BZ 79, 1986, p. 35–49.

Mathisen R.W., *Sigisvult the Patrician, Maximinus the Arian, and political strategems in the Western Roman Empire c. 425–40*, EME 8, 1999, p. 173–196.

Max G.E., *Political Intrigue during the Reigns of the Western Roman Emperors Avitus and Majorian*, Hi 28, 1979, p. 225–237.

McEvoy M., *Becoming Roman? The Not-So-Curious Case of Aspar and the Ardaburii*, JLA 9, 2016, p. 483–511.

Meier M., *Candidus: um die Geschichte der Isauriers*, [in:] *Griechische Profanhistoriker des fünften nachristlichen Jahrhundert*, ed. T. Stickler, B. Bleckmann, Stuttgart 2014, p. 171–193.

Meier M., Drohisn C., Priwitzer S., *Einleitung*, [in:] Johannes Malalas, *Weltchronik*, ed. J. Thurn, M. Meier, Stuttgart 2009, p. 1–37.

Meier M., *Geschichte der Völkerwanderung. Europa, Asien und Afrika vom 3. bis zum 8. Jahrhundert n.Chr*, München 2019.

Merrills A., Miles R., *The Vandals*, Oxford 2010.

Mielczarek M., *Cataphracti and Clibanarii: Studies on the Heavy Armoured Cavalry of the Ancient World*, Łódź 1993.

Millar F., *A Greek Roman Empire. Power and Belief under Theodosius II 408–450*, Berkeley 2007.

Milner N.P., *Introduction*, [in:] *Vegetius: Epitome of Military Science*, ed. N.P. Milner, Liverpool 1996, p. XIII–XLIII.

Modéran Y., *Les Vandales et l'Empire Romain*, Arles 2014.

Müller F.L., *Einleitung*, [in:] *Publii Flavii Vegetii Renati, Epitoma rei militaris*, ed. F.L. Müller, Stuttgart 1997, p. 11–26.

Nikoronov V., *Cataphracti, Catafractarii and Clibanarii: Another Look at the Old Problem of their Identifications*, [in:] *Military Archeology. Weaponry and Warfare in the Historical and Social Perspective*, ed. G.V. Vilinbakhov, V.M. Masson, St. Petersburg 1998, p. 131–138.

O' F l y n n J.M., *A Greek on the Roman Throne: The Fate of Anthemius*, Hi 40, 1991, p. 122–128.

O o s t S., *Aetius and Majorian*, CPh 59, 1964, p. 23–29.

P a r n e l l D.A., *Justinian's Men. Careers and Relationships of Byzantine Army Officers 518–610*, London 2017.

P a w l a k M., *Walka o władzę w Rzymie w latach 425–435*, Toruń 2004.

P i g o ń s k i Ł., *Berichus and the Evidence for Aspar's Political Power and Aims in the Last Years of Theodosius II's Reign*, SCer 8, 2018, p. 237–251.

P i g o ń s k i Ł., *Kilka uwag na temat kariery magistra militum Flawiusza Plinty i jego wpływów na dworze Teodozjusza II*, BP 28, 2021, p. 23–30.

P i g o ń s k i Ł., *Polityka zachodnia cesarzy Marcjana (450–457) i Leona I (457–474)*, Łódź 2019.

P i g o ń s k i Ł., *Wpływ czynników religijnych na relacje rzymsko–wandalskie w latach 429–474*, ChrA 8, 2016, p. 98–113.

P i k u l s k a-R o b a s z k i e w i c z A., *Funkcjonariusze służb specjalnych w późnym Cesarstwie – „agentes in rebus"*, PK 37, 1994, p. 147–157.

P o p o v i ć V., *Die süddanubische Provinzen in der Spätantike vom Ende des 4. Bis zur Mitte des 5. Jahrhunderts*, [in:] *Die Völker Südosteuropas im 6. bis 8. Jahrhundert*, hrsg. B. H ä n s e l, Berlin 1987, p. 95–140.

P r o s t k o-P r o s t y ń s k i J., *Attila and Novae*, [in:] *Novae. Legionary Fortress and Late Antique Town*, vol. I, ed. T. D e r d a, P. D y c z e k, J. K o l e n d o, Warsaw 2008, p. 133–140.

P r o s t k o-P r o s t y ń s k i J., *Basiliskos: Ein in Rom anerkannter Usurpator*, ZPE 133, 2000, p. 259–265.

P r o s t k o-P r o s t y ń s k i J., *Roma– solium imperii. Elekcja, koronacja i uznanie cesarza w Rzymie w IV–VIII wieku*, Poznań 2014.

P r y o r J.H., J e f f r e y s E.M., *The Age of Dromon. The Byzantine Navy ca. 500–1204*, Leiden 2006.

R a n c e Ph., *A Roman–Lazi War in the "Suda": A Fragment of Priscus?*, CQ 65, 2015, p. 852–867.

R e d d e M., *Mare Nostrum. Les infrastructures, le dispositif et l'histoire de la marine militaire sous l'empire romain*, Roma 1986.

R o h r b a c h e r D., *Historians of Late Antiquity*, London 2002.

R o s e n K., *Attila. Der Schrecken der Welt*, München 2016.

R o u c h e M., *Attila. La violence nomade*, Paris 2009.

S a l a m o n M., *Basiliscus cum romanis suis*, [in:] *Studia Moesiaca*, red. L. M r o z e w i c z, K. Il-s k i, Poznań 1994, p. 179–196.

S a l z m a n n M.R., *Emperors and Elites in Rome after the Vandal Sack of 455*, AnTard 25, 2017, p. 243–262.

S c h a r f R., *Foederati. Von der völkerrechtlichen Kategorie zur byzantinischen Truppengattung*, Wien 2001.

S c h m i d t L., *Geschichte der Wandalen*, Leipzig 1901.

S c h m i t t O., *Die Bucellari. Eine Studie zum militärischen Gefolgschaftwesen in der Spätantike*, Ty 9, 1994, p. 147–174.

S c o t t L., *Aspar and the Burden of Barbarian Heritage*, ByzS 3, 1976, p. 59–69.

S e s t o n W., *Dioclétien et la Tétrarchie*, Paris 1946.

S h a h i d I., *Byzantium and the Arabs in the Fifth Century*, Dumbarton Oaks 2006.

S i e b i g s G., *Kaiser Leo I. Das oströmische Reich in den ersten drei Jahren seiner Regierung (457–460 n. Chr.)*, Berlin 2010.

S o u t h e r n P., D i x o n K., *Late Roman Army*, London 2014.

S t e i n E., *Histoire du Bas-Empire*, t. I, *De L'état romain à l'état byzantin (284–476)*, Paris 1959.

S t e i n a c h e r R., *Die Vandalen. Aufstieg und Fall eines Barbarenreichs*, Stuttgart 2016.

S t e w a r t M.E., *The First Byzantine Emperor? Leo I, Aspar and Challenges of Power and Romanitas in Fifth-century Byzantium*, Porph 22, 2014, p. 4–17.

S t i c k l e r T., *Aëtius. Gestaltungsspielräume eines Heermeisters im ausgehenden. Weströmischen Reich*, München 2002.

S t i c k l e r T., *Die Hunnen*, München 2007.

S t i c k l e r T., *Foederati*, [in:] *A Companion to the Roman Army*, ed. P. E r d k a m p, Oxford 2007, p. 495–514.

Studies in John Malalas, ed. E. J e f f r e y s, B. C r o k e, R. S c o t t, Sydney 1990.

S t y k a J., *Sydoniusz Apollinaris i kultura literacka w Galii V wieku*, Kraków 2008.

S z o p a A., *Notitia Dignitatum – „najbardziej rzymski z dokumentów"?*, ReG 8, 2015, p. 183–191.

The Acts of the Council of Chalcedon, ed. R. P r i c e, M. G a d d i s, Liverpool 2005.

The Oxford Dictionary of Byzantium, ed. A. K a z h d a n, Oxford 1991.

T h o m p s o n E.A., *A History of Attila and the Huns*, Oxford 1948.

T h o m p s o n E.A., *The Foreign Policies of Theodosius II and Marcian*, Her 76, 1950, p. 58–75.

T h o m p s o n E.A., *The Isaurians under Theodosius II*, Her 68, 1948, p. 18–31.

T r e a d g o l d W., *Byzantium and its Army 284–1081*, Stanford 1995.

T r e a d g o l d W., *History of Byzantine State and Society*, Stanford 1997.

U r b a i n c z y k Th., *Socrates of Constantinople. Historian of Church and State*, Ann Arbor 1997.

U r b a n i e c A., *Wpływ patrycjusza Aspara na cesarską elekcję Leona*, USS 11, 2011, p. 173–201.

V e r n a d s k y G., *Flavius Ardabur Aspar*, SF 6, 1941, p. 38–73.

V ö s s i n g K., *Das Königreich der Vandalen. Geiserichs Herrschaft und das Imperium Romanum*, Darmstadt 2014.

W h i t b y M., *Army and Society in the Late Roman World: A Context for Decline?*, [in:] *A Companion to the Roman Army*, ed. P. E r d k a m p, Oxford 2007, p. 515–531.

W h i t b y M., *Introduction*, [in:] *The Ecclesiastical History of Evagrius Scholasticus*, ed. M. W h i t b y, Liverpool 2000, p. XIII–XLIII.

W h i t b y M., *Siege Warfare and Counter-Siege Tactics (ca.250–640)*, [in:] *War and Warfare in Late Antiquity*, ed. A. S a r a n t i s, N. C h r i s t i e, Leiden 2013, p. 433–459.

W h i t b y M., *The Army c. 420–602*, [in:] *CAH*, t. XIV, *Late Antiquity: Empire and Successors, AD 425–600*, ed. A. C a m e r o n, B. W a r d - P e r k i n s, M. W h i t b y, Cambridge 2008, p. 288–314.

W i e m e r H.U., *Malchos von Philadelphia. Die Vandalen und das Ende des Kaisertums im Westen*, [in:] *Griechische Profanhistoriker des fünften nachristlichen Jahrhundert*, ed. T. S t i c k l e r, B. B l e c k m a n n, Stuttgart 2014, p. 121–159.

W i e m e r H.U., *Theoderich der Große. König der Goten – Herrscher der Römer*, München 2018.

W i j n e n d a l e J., *The early career of Aëthius and the murder of Felix (c. 425–430 CE)*, Hi 66, 2017, p. 468–482.

W i j n e n d a l e J., *'Warlordism' and the Disintegration of the Western Roman Army*, [in:] *Circum Mare: Themes in Ancient Warfare*, ed. J. A r m s t r o n g, Leiden 2016, p. 185–203.

W i l c z y ń s k i M., *Gejzeryk i „czwarta wojna punicka"*, Oświęcim 2016.

W i l c z y ń s k i M., *Germanie w służbie zachodniorzymskiej w V w. n.e.*, Oświęcim 2018.

W i l c z y ń s k i M., *Królestwo Swebów – Regnum in extremitate mundi*, Kraków 2011.

Wilkes J.J., *Dalmatia*, London 1969.

Wirth G., *Attila. Das Hunnenreich und Europa*, Stuttgart 1999.

Wolfram H., *Die Goten. Von den Anfängen bis zur Mitte des schsten Jahrhunderts*, München 2001.

Wolińska T., *Arabs, (H)agarenes, Ishmaelites, Saracens – a Few Remarks about Naming*, [in:] *Byzantium and the Arabs. The Encounter of Civilizations from Sixth to Mid-Eight Century*, ed. T. Wolińska, P. Filipczak, Łódź 2015, p. 22–37.

Wolińska T., *Rola Sycylii w wojnach wandalskich i gockich Justyniana*, PH 41, 2000, p. 321–340.

Wozniak F., *East Rome, Ravenna and Illyricum 454–536 AD*, Hi 30, p. 351–382.

Zecchini G., *Latin Historiography: Jerome, Orosius and the Western Chroniclers*, [in:] *Greek and Roman Historiography in Late Antiquity. Fourth to Sixth Century A.D.*, ed. G. Marasco, Boston 2003, p. 317–345.

Zołoteńki D., *Galia u schyłku panowania rzymskiego*, Kraków 2011.

Zuckermann C., *L'Empire d'Orient et les Huns. Notes sur Priscus*, TM 12, 1994, p. 159–182.

***

Глушанин Е.П., *Военная знать ранней Византии*, Барнаул 1991.

Козлов А.С., *Народные массы в конфликте Аспара и Льва*, АДСВ 10, 1973, p. 263–265.

Index of People

Index of Ethnic
and Geographic Names

Abstract

The subject of interest of this monograph are the Eastern Roman military elites and their influence on the functioning of the Empire during the reigns of the emperors Theodosius II, Marcian and Leo I (408–471).

The author explores the process of the re-establishment of the military elites after the revolt of Gainas, their growing importance thanks to the wars of the early reign of Theodosius II, and the dissatisfaction of the generals with the emperor's foreign policy towards the end of his rule. The resulting opposition brought together such different characters as Flavius Zeno, Aspar or Apollonius consolidating the group. It is argued that the following reign of Marcian was in many ways the realization of the political goals of the military elite. Over its course, Aspar, who outlived other commanders, became the most powerful man in the Empire, being able to single-handedly choose the next emperor – Leo. The author explores how the power of Aspar and his family manifested throughout Leo's reign, and how the general and the emperor ended up quarrelling, and how their conflict escalated.

The monograph challenges many preconceptions established in the scholarship, especially, the common in the older literature, framing of the conflicts between the emperors and the generals as driven by ethnic factors, but also re-evaluates more modern ideas that seek to explain the dynamic of those events in terms of dynastic or religious struggles.

The author claims that the primary motivation of the military elites was political in nature, and it was to protect the Empire, however, the conflicts between the generals and the emperors were due to differences in how it needs to be done. The military elites were generally opposed to engaging limited military resources in risky expeditionary campaigns, and it seems they did not perceive the attempts to help the Western Roman Empire as their duty, only feeling responsible for the security of the part centred around Constantinople.

Keywords: Eastern Roman Empire, military elite, Aspar, Theodosius II, Marcian, Leo I

Maps

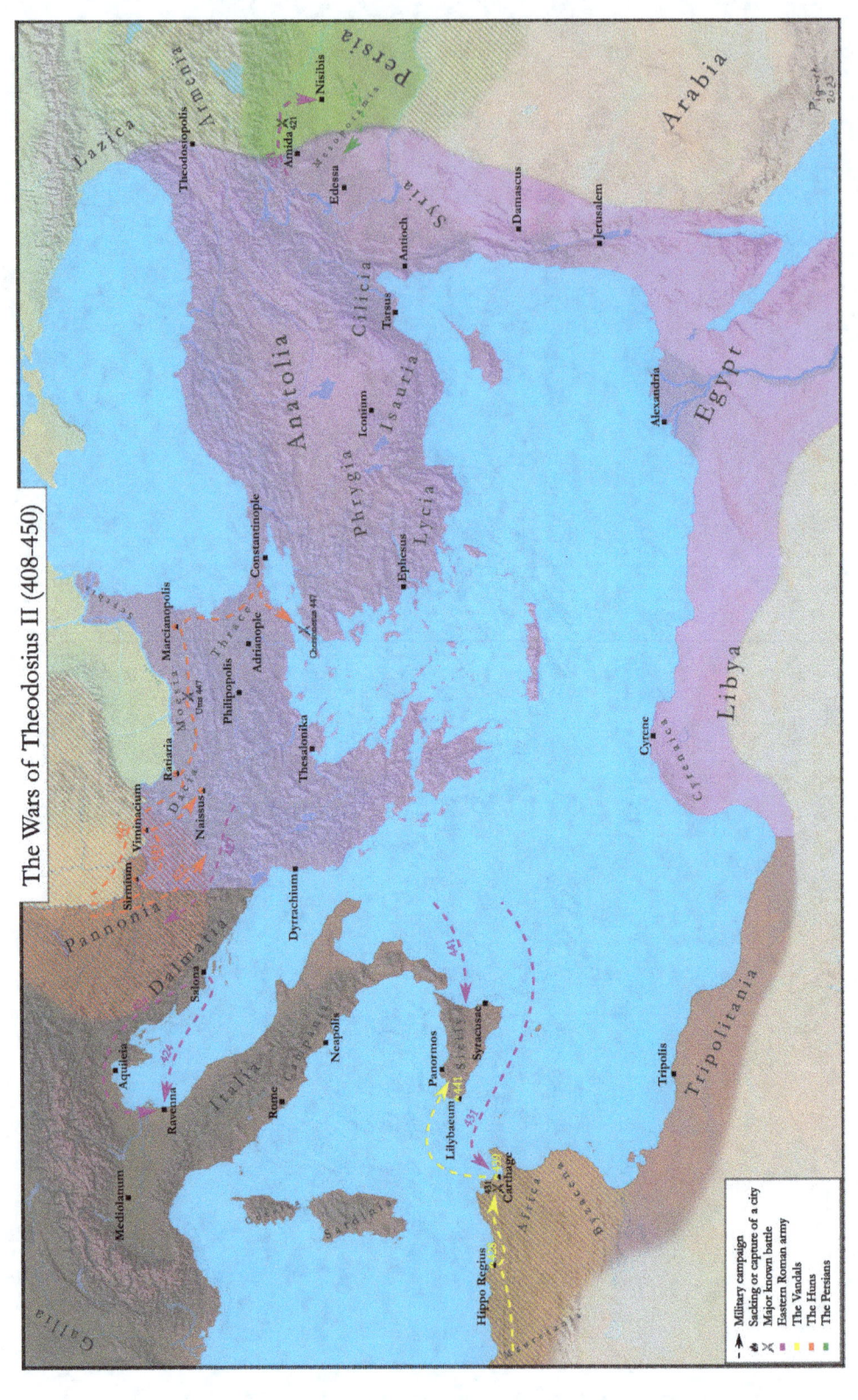

The Wars of Theodosius II (408–450)

Legend:
- Military campaign
- Sacking or capture of a city
- Major known battle
- Eastern Roman army
- The Vandals
- The Huns
- The Persians

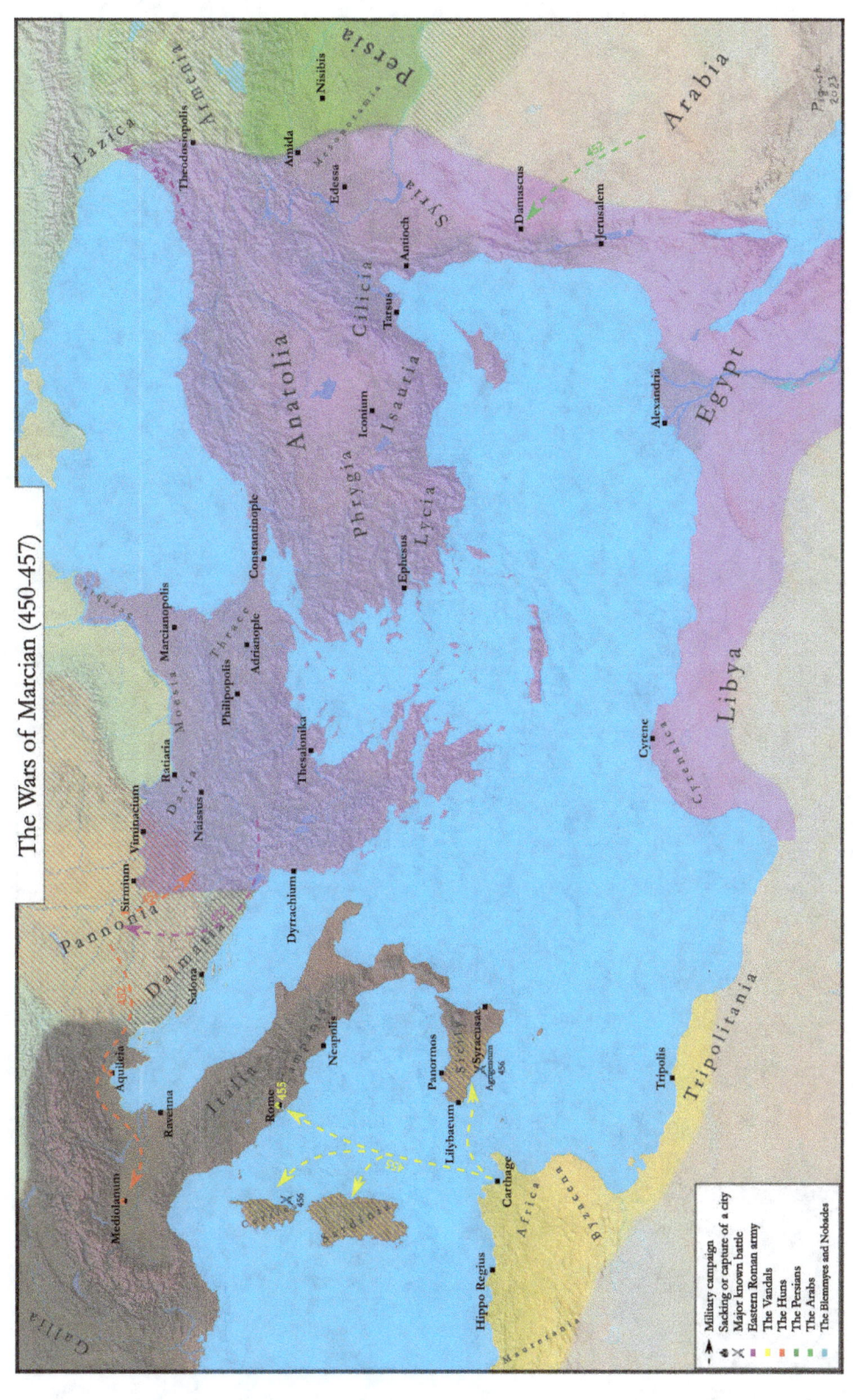

The Wars of Marcian (450-457)

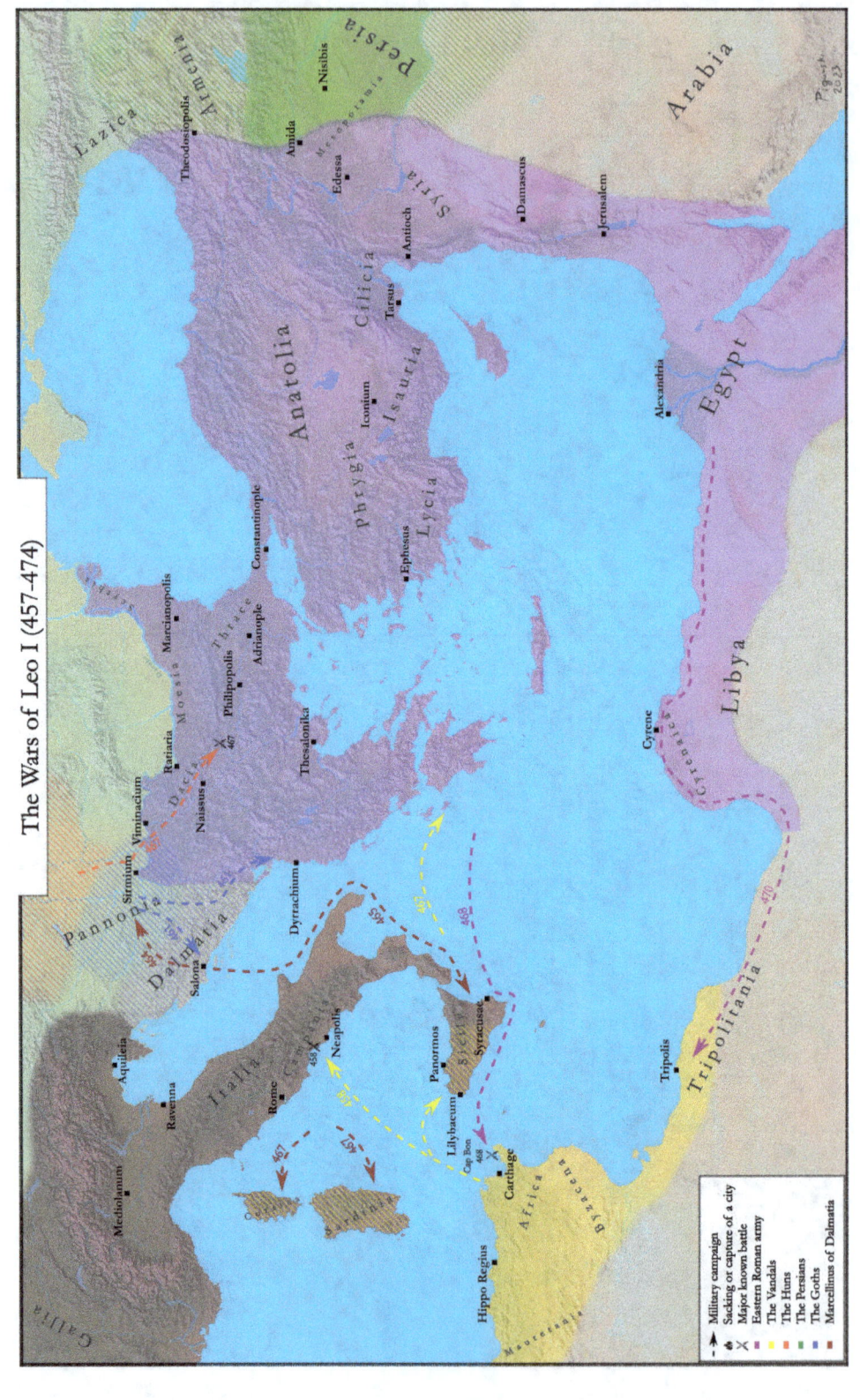

The Wars of Leo I (457-474)

Legend:
- Military campaign
- Sacking or capture of a city
- Major known battle
- Eastern Roman army
- The Vandals
- The Huns
- The Persians
- The Goths
- Marcellinus of Dalmatia

Byzantina Lodziensia
1997–2023

VI.

Waldemar Ceran, *Historia i bibliografia rozumowana bizantynologii polskiej (1800–1998)*, vol. I–II, Łódź 2001, pp. 786.
[*History and bibliography raisonné of Polish Byzantine studies (1800–1998)*]

VII.

Mirosław J. Leszka, *Wizerunek władców pierwszego państwa bułgarskiego w bizantyńskich źródłach pisanych (VIII – pierwsza połowa XII wieku)*,
Łódź 2003, pp. 169.
[*The Image of the First Bulgarian State Rulers Shown in the Byzantine Literary Sources of the Period from the 8th to the First Half of the 12th Centuries*]

VIII.

Teresa Wolińska, *Sycylia w polityce cesarstwa bizantyńskiego w VI–IX wieku*,
Łódź 2005, pp. 379.
[*Sicily in Byzantine Policy, 6th–9th Century*]

IX.

Maciej Kokoszko, *Ryby i ich znaczenie w życiu codziennym ludzi późnego antyku i wczesnego Bizancjum (III–VII w.)*, Łódź 2005, pp. 445.
[*The Role of Fish In Everyday Life of the People of Late Antiquity and Early Byzantium (3rd–7th c.)*]

X.

Sławomir Bralewski, *Obraz papiestwa w historiografii kościelnej wczesnego Bizancjum*, Łódź 2006, pp. 334.
[*L'image de la papauté dans l'historiographie ecclésiastique du haut Empire Byzantin*]

XI.

Byzantina Europaea. Księga jubileuszowa ofiarowana Profesorowi Waldemarowi Ceranowi, ed. **Maciej Kokoszko, Mirosław J. Leszka**, Łódź 2007, pp. 573.
[*Byzantina Europaea. Studies Offered to Professor Waldemar Ceran*]

XII.

Paweł Filipczak, *Bunty i niepokoje w miastach wczesnego Bizancjum
(IV wiek n.e.),* Łódź 2009, pp. 236.
[*The Riots and Social Unrest in Byzantine Cities in the 4th Century A.D.*]

XIV.

Jolanta Dybała, *Ideał kobiety w pismach kapadockich Ojców Kościoła
i Jana Chryzostoma,* Łódź 2012, pp. 480.
[*The Ideal of Woman in the Writings of the Cappadocian Fathers of the Church
and John Chrysostom*]

XV.

Mirosław J. Leszka, *Symeon I Wielki a Bizancjum. Z dziejów stosunków
bułgarsko-bizantyńskich w latach 893-927,* Łódź 2013, pp. 368.
[*Symeon I the Great and Byzantium: Bulgarian-Byzantine Relations, 893–927*]

XVI.

Maciej Kokoszko, Krzysztof Jagusiak, Zofia Rzeźnicka, *Dietetyka i sztuka
kulinarna antyku i wczesnego Bizancjum (II–VII w.),* part I, *Zboża i produkty
zbożowe w źródłach medycznych antyku i Bizancjum (II–VII w.),*
Łódź 2014, pp. 671.
[*Dietetics and Culinary Art of Antiquity and Early Byzantium (2nd–7th c.), part I,
Cereals and Cereal Products in Medical Sources of Antiquity
and Early Byzantium (2nd–7th c.)*]

XVII.

Andrzej Kompa, Mirosław J. Leszka, Teresa Wolińska, *Mieszkańcy stolicy
świata. Konstantynopolitańczycy między starożytnością a średniowieczem,*
Łódź 2014, pp. 490.
[*Inhabitants of the Capital of the World:
The Constantinopolitans between Antiquity and the Middle Ages*]

XVIII.

Waldemar Ceran, *Artisans et commerçants à Antioche et leur rang social
(seconde moitié du siècle de notre ère),* Łódź 2013, pp. 236.

XIX.

Dietetyka i sztuka kulinarna antyku i wczesnego Bizancjum (II–VII w.), part II, *Pokarm dla ciała i ducha*, ed. **Maciej Kokoszko**, Łódź 2014, pp. 607. [*Dietetics and Culinary Art of Antiquity and Early Byzantium (2ⁿᵈ–7ᵗʰ c.)*, part II, *Nourishment for the Body and Soul*]

XX.

Maciej Kokoszko, Krzysztof Jagusiak, Zofia Rzeźnicka, *Cereals of Antiquity and Early Byzantine Times: Wheat and Barley in Medical Sources (Second to Seventh Centuries AD)*, Łódź 2014, pp. 516.

XXI.

Błażej Cecota, *Arabskie oblężenia Konstantynopola w VII–VIII wieku. Rzeczywistość i mit*, Łódź 2015, pp. 213. [*The Arab Sieges of Constantinople in the 7ᵗʰ and 8ᵗʰ Centuries: Myth and Reality*]

XXII.

Byzantium and the Arabs: the Encounter of Civilizations from Sixth to Mid-Eighth Century, ed. **Teresa Wolińska, Paweł Filipczak**, Łódź 2015, pp. 614.

XXIII

Miasto na styku mórz i kontynentów. Wczesno- i średniobizantyński Konstantynopol jako miasto portowe, red. **Mirosław J. Leszka, Kirił Marinow**, Łódź 2016, pp. 348. [*Metropolis between the Seas and Continents: Early and Middle Byzantinine Constantinople as the Port City*]

XXIV.

Zofia A. Brzozowska, *Sofia – upersonifikowana Mądrość Boża. Dzieje wyobrażeń w kręgu kultury bizantyńsko-słowiańskiej*, Łódź 2015, pp. 478. [*Sophia – the Personification of Divine Wisdom: the History of the Notion in the Byzantine-Slavonic Culture*]

XXV.

Błażej Szefliński, *Trzy oblicza Sawy Nemanjicia. Postać historyczna –
autokreacja – postać literacka*, Łódź 2016, pp. 342.
[*Three Faces of Sava Nemanjić: Historical Figure, Self-Creation
and Literary Character*]

XXVI.

Paweł Filipczak, *An Introduction to the Byzantine Administration
in Syro-Palestine on the Eve of the Arab Conquest*, Łódź 2015, pp. 127.

XXVII.

Sławomir Bralewski, *Symmachia cesarstwa rzymskiego z Bogiem chrześcijan
(IV–VI wiek)*
t. I: *„Niezwykła przemiana" – narodziny nowej epoki*, Łódź 2018, pp. 312.
[*The Symmachy of the Roman Empire with the God of Christians
(IV–VI centuries), vol. I:
„Remarkable transformation"- the birth of a new age*]

XXVIII.

Zofia Rzeźnicka, Maciej Kokoszko, *Dietetyka i sztuka kulinarna antyku
i wczesnego Bizancjum (II–VII w.)*, part III, *Ab ovo ad γάλα. Jajka, mleko i produkty
mleczne w medycynie i w sztuce kulinarnej (I–VII w.)*, Łódź 2016, pp. 263.
[*Dietetics and Culinary Art of Antiquity and Early Byzantium (2nd–7th c.),
part III, Ab ovo ad γάλα: Eggs, Milk and Dairy Products in Medicine
and Culinary Art (1st–7th c. A.D.)*]

XXIX.

Łukasz Pigoński, *Polityka zachodnia cesarzy Marcjana (450–457)
i Leona I (457–474)*, Łódź 2019, pp. 223.
[*Western Policy of Emperors Marcian (450–457) and Leo I (457–474)*]

XXX.

Jan Mikołaj Wolski, *Kultura monastyczna w późnośredniowiecznej Bułgarii*,
Łódź 2018, ss. 225.
[*Monastic Culture in Late Medieval Bulgaria*]

XXXII.

Sławomir Bralewski, *Symmachia cesarstwa rzymskiego z Bogiem chrześcijan (IV–VI wiek)*
t. II: *Jedna religia w jednym cesarstwie Rzymscy imperatorzy sprzymierzeni z Bogiem na straży jedności Kościoła od Konstantyna I do Justyniana I*,
Łódź 2018, pp. 333.
[*The Symmachy of the Roman Empire with the God of Christians (IV–VI centuries)*, vol. II: *The Roman Emperors allied with God on guard of the unity of the Church from Constantine I to Justinian I*]

XXXIV.

The Bulgarian State in 927–969: The Epoch of Tsar Peter I,
ed. **Mirosław J. Leszka, Kirił Marinow**, Łódź–Kraków 2018, pp. 686.

XXXV.

Kazimierz Ginter, *Wizerunek władców bizantyńskich w Historii kościelnej Ewagriusza Scholastyka*, Łódź 2018, pp. 337.
[*The Image of Byzantine Emperors in Evagrius Scholasticus's Ecclesiastical History*]

XXXVI.

Zofia A Brzozowska, Mirosław J. Leszka, *Maria Lekapene, Empress of the Bulgarians*:
Neither a Saint nor a Malefactress, Łódź 2017, pp. 228.

XXXVII.

Szymon Wierzbiński, *U boku bazyleusa. Frankowie i Waregowie w cesarstwie bizantyńskim w XI w.*, Łódź 2018, pp. 422.
[*By the Side of Basileus: The Varangians and the Franks in Eleventh-century Byzantium*]

XXXVIII.

Zofia Rzeźnicka, Maciej Kokoszko, *Milk and Dairy Products in the Medicine and Culinary Art of Antiquity and Early Byzantium (1st–7th Centuries AD)*,
Łódź 2020, pp. 229.

XXXIX.

Widmo Mahometa, cień Samuela. Cesarstwo bizantyńskie w relacji z przedstawicielami innych religii i kultur (VII–XV w.), red. **Zofia A. Brzozowska, Mirosław J. Leszka, Kirił Marinow, Teresa Wolińska**, Łódź 2020, pp. 379.
[*Phantom of Muhammad, Shade of Samuel: Byzantine Empire in Relation to Members of Other Cultures and Religions (7th–15th c.)*]

XL.

Paweł Filipczak, *Namiestnicy rzymskiej Syrii w czasach przełomu (324–361 n.e.)*, Łódź 2020, pp. 286.
[*The governors of Roman Syria in the years of change (AD 324–361)*]

XLI.

Zofia A. Brzozowska, Mirosław J. Leszka, Teresa Wolińska, *Muhamad and the Origin of Islam in the Byzantine-Slavic Context: A Bibliographical History*, Łódź 2020, pp. 386.

XLII.

Teresa Wolińska, *Jastrzębie, onagry pustyni, wilki Arabii. Sąsiedzi cesarstwa wschodniorzymskiego z Półwyspu Arabskiego i ich wizerunek w źródłach. Okres przedislamski*, Łódź 2022, pp. 777.
[*Hawks, Desert Onagers, Arabian Wolves. Neighbours of the Eastern Roman Empire from the Arabian Peninsulaand Their Image in Sources. Pre-islamic Period*]

XLIII.

Błażej Cecota, *Islam, Arabowie i wizerunek kalifów w przekazach Chronografii Teofanesa Wyznawcy*, Łódź 2022, pp. 549.
[*Islam, the Arabs, and the image of the Caliphs in the accounts of the Chronography of Theophanes the Confessor*]

XLIV.

Zofia A. Brzozowska, *Chadidża i jej czarnookie siostry. Obraz kobiet bliskowschodnich z epoki narodzin islamu w średniowiecznej literaturze kręgu bizantyńsko-słowiańskiego*, Łódź 2021, pp. 298.
[*Khadijah and Her Black-Eyed Sisters: The Image of Middle Eastern Women from the Era of the Birth of Islam in the Medieval Literature of the Byzantine-Slavic Circle*]

XLV.

Mirosław J. Leszka, Szymon Wierzbiński, *Komes Marcellin, vir clarissimus. Historyk i jego dzieło*, Łódź 2022, pp. 280.
[*Comes Marcellinus, vir clarissimus. The Historian and his Work*]

BYZANTINA LODZIENSIA

Series of Department of Byzantine History of University of Łódź

№ XLVII

EDITORIAL BOARD

Mirosław J. Leszka – editor in-chief
Andrzej Kompa – secretary
Sławomir Bralewski
Paweł Filipczak
Maciej Kokoszko
Kirił Marinow
Teresa Wolińska

REVIEWERS

Dr hab. Rafał Kosiński, prof. UwB
Prof dr hab. Marek Wilczyński, UP w Krakowie

COVER DESIGN AND LAYOUT
Sebastian Buzar

TYPESETTING
Munda – Maciej Torz

DRAWINGS
Łukasz Pigoński

ADDRESS OF THE EDITORIAL BOARD
Katedra Historii Bizancjum UŁ
ul. A. Kamińskiego 27a
90–219 Łódź, Poland

The research project financed by the National Science Centre. Decision number: DEC-2018/31/B/HS3/03038
(*Eastern Roman Military Elites from Theodosius II to Anastasius I (408–518). A Socio-Political Study*)

Publisher's sheets 14.2; printing sheets 15.125

1st English edition • Printed on Stella Press 65 g by Paperlin X Sp. z o.o. • Printed in Poland
Łódź University Press / Wydawnictwo Uniwersytetu Łódzkiego • 90–237 Łódź, ul. J. Matejki 34A
www.wydawnictwo.uni.lodz.pl • ksiegarnia@uni.lodz.pl • phone 42 635 55 77

GPSR Authorized Representative: Easy Access System Europe, Mustamäe tee
50, 10621 Tallinn, Estonia, gpsr.requests@easproject.com

www.ingramcontent.com/pod-product-compliance
Lightning Source LLC
Chambersburg PA
CBHW080129150626
46550CB00018B/2908